PRESIDENTIAL DECISION MAKING
The Economic Policy Board

Presidential

CAMBRIDGE UNIVERSITY PRESS

decision making

The Economic Policy Board

Roger B. Porter
Harvard University

CAMBRIDGE
NEW YORK   NEW ROCHELLE   MELBOURNE   SYDNEY

Published by the Press Syndicate of the University of Cambridge
The Pitt Building, Trumpington Street, Cambridge CB2 1RP
32 East 57th Street, New York, NY 10022, USA
10 Stamford Road, Oakleigh, Melbourne 3166, Australia

First published 1980
First paperback edition 1982
Reprinted 1987, 1988

Printed in the United States of America

Library of Congress Cataloging in Publication Data
Porter, Roger B
Presidential decision making.
Bibliography: p.
Includes index.
1. United States. President's Economic Policy Board. 2. United States –
Economic Policy – 1971–
1. Title.
HC106.7.P67   353.0082   80-10165
ISBN 0 521 23337 2 hard covers
ISBN 0 521 27112 6 paperback

FOR ANN

Contents

Preface

This book is about organizing and managing decision making. Its focus is the President of the United States and the problem he faces in making decisions on a host of issues in such a way that he can intelligently shape the pattern of his administration's policies. The President every day in many ways relies on others for information, analysis, and advice. How he organizes this advice and makes decisions is the subject of this book. It is concerned with how decisions are made rather than with their content. It recognizes the significant relationship between the process by which decisions are made, the quality of those decisions, and the likelihood that such decisions will be implemented.

This volume is intended for scholars; government officials; students taking courses on the Presidency, executive decision making, and public management; and general readers interested in how the President makes decisions and in what the process of advising him looks like from inside the White House. It is not concerned with what our policy purposes should be. The lessons of this study do not depend on one's holding particular policy preferences. They can be applied equally well by executives of different persuasions.

This book had its beginnings in 1974 in Washington, D.C., where I, as a White House Fellow, served on Gerald Ford's White House staff as Executive Secretary of the Economic Policy Board and later as Special Assistant to the President. This study benefitted from the reflections and observations shared with me in over a hundred interviews with cabinet secretaries, subcabinet officials, and career civil servants. All of the principal economic policy figures in the Ford administration as well as subcabinet and staff-level officials in more than a score of departments and agencies generously spent hours responding to my questions. Virtually all of the interviews were taped with the understanding that I would maintain the anonymity of those interviewed.

In writing this volume I received much help from many quarters. My work was aided by financial support from the Meyer Kestnbaum Fund. I am grateful to Harvard University, where most of this book has been written, for those most precious commodities: freedom and time for writing. I am also grateful to the Brookings Institution where this work was begun while I was there as a Guest Scholar. Many thoughtful and gracious people helped in the preparation of this study. I am most appreciative for the encouragement and assistance of Professors John T. Dunlop and Richard E. Neustadt. I have had the benefit of the advice of several friends and colleagues who read parts or all of this manuscript. Among them are: Graham Allison, Francis M. Bator, Richard G. Darman, I. M. Destler, Alexander L. George, Hugh Heclo, Mark H. Moore, Joseph L. Nye, Paul H. O'Neill, P. Michael Pitfield, Don K. Price, L. William Seidman, and James Q. Wilson. Had I had the wit to take into account all their criticisms, this would have been a better book. For remaining errors of judgment, interpretation, and fact I alone am responsible.

Roger B. Porter

Cambridge, Massachusetts
December 1979

Introduction and overview

$\mathcal{J}$his study is at once theoretical, historical, and prescriptive. It examines how the President makes policy decisions, specifically, economic policy decisions. One underlying premise is that the President makes decisions on a multitude of issues about which he is not an expert. He must depend on others for information, analysis, and expert opinion. How he organizes this pattern of advice and the process by which he makes his decisions is important and sometimes crucial.

Without denying the impact of advice from other sources, this study concentrates primarily on the executive branch's institutional arrangements for advising the President. As I. M. Destler has noted:

> It is such inside advice that any President gets the most of, and that responds most directly to particular problems as he must deal with them. It is, by all evidence, what influences Presidents most, most of the time, when they make particular . . . decisions. . . . As Joseph Kraft noted ten years ago, the size and complexity of modern government have sharply limited the advisory influence of outsiders compared to the "trained intellectual bureaucrat" who is there, inside the government, to push his objective hour by hour, day by day.[1]

A "good" decision-making process cannot guarantee "good" or wise decisions. It can, however, provide the means for the President to make his decisions intelligently and not ignorantly. It can present the trade-offs, the costs and benefits between competing values and objectives, but it cannot weigh those trade-offs for him from his perspective.

[1] I. M. Destler, "National Security Advice to U.S. Presidents: Some Lessons from Thirty Years," *World Politics* 29 (January 1977), 144–145. Joseph Kraft, *Profiles in Power* (New York: New American Library, 1966), pp. 63–68.

I

This challenge is not unique to the President of the United States. It is the almost universal problem of those called upon to make executive decisions. An executive may listen to those who think themselves expert, but when they differ, as they often do, he must be decisive amidst the uncertainties. Thus, the study of how the President makes economic policy decisions can prove useful as well as interesting to other public and private executives.

A central objective of this study, then, is to show how an executive can organize advice and structure a decision-making process. Chapter 1 describes two major organizational challenges that the President faces – the interrelatedness of the issues he is expected to address and the fragmented, virtually feudal structure of the executive branch he presides over.

Interrelatedness between issues has always existed. But the complexity of government and the awareness of interrelatedness among issues has increased dramatically in recent years. One consequence of interrelatedness for the way the President makes decisions is that, for many issues, what he does on problem *A* will affect the range of choices and the relative attractiveness of those choices for dealing with problems *B*, *C*, and *D*. How he organizes to make his decisions – compartmentally or comprehensively – will influence how much integration occurs between individual policy decisions and how much of that integration he must do himself.

Moreover, every president makes decisions through a variety of channels, some formal and some informal. Established parts of the institutional presidency, such as the Office of Management and Budget and the National Security Council, sit astride regular flows of information and decisions. A second consequence of the interrelatedness of issues is that problems do not fit neatly into a single action channel, raising another organizational question for the President. How do the various pieces of his decision-making machinery fit together and relate to one another?

The answer to this question lies in the structure of the executive branch, the nature and extent of departmentalism, the position of the cabinet secretary at the crossroads of conflicting pressures, and White House–departmental relations as viewed by the President. Every president implicitly or explicitly determines what staff resources he wants and needs, and how he and his personal staff relate to line department and agency heads and their organizations. Viewing life in the executive branch from the respective vantage points of the career bureaucracy, the cabinet secretary (and other top level political appointees), and the President, is an essential first step in considering alternative ways of organizing policy advice and the pattern of White House–departmental relations.

Organizational arrangements *cannot* alter certain challenges a president faces – rising inflation, persistently high unemployment, or intractable adversaries abroad. Organizational arrangements *can* prove decisive in whether a president can fashion a coherent set of policies on related issues and in how well he can mobilize and unify the disparate elements of the executive branch. Thus, Chapter 1, in discussing organizational challenges, raises several organizational issues. How many channels of advice should the President rely on? Who, if anyone, should have operational control of these channels? What are the roles of the President's immediate staff and of executive branch departments and agencies?

The following six chapters examine the President's Economic Policy Board (EPB), created by Gerald Ford in September 1974. Three factors make the Economic Policy Board a useful subject for investigation. First, it is possible to construct a relatively full and accurate account of what the Board did and how it functioned. While serving as executive secretary of the EPB during the two and a half years of the Ford administration, I attended virtually all of the meetings of the Board and its Executive Committee and the EPB's meetings with the President. During this time I kept extensive notes as well as a detailed diary of events, impressions, and observations. My impressions and observations have been supplemented by over a hundred interviews with nearly all of the major participants. Since the interviews were conducted during the first year and a half after the Ford administration ended, their memories of events and their experiences on the Board were reasonably fresh and intact.

Second, examining the Economic Policy Board can provide useful insights into presidential decision making because it was an active part of the presidential decision-making machinery. The President used it regularly throughout his entire administration. As his days in the White House drew to a close, Gerald Ford observed that the Economic Policy Board was "the most important institutional innovation of my administration."

Third, unlike many cabinet-level committees and councils, the Economic Policy Board met regularly and frequently – over 500 times during the two and one-quarter years of its existence. Furthermore, the scope of issues that it considered ranged broadly over domestic and foreign economic policy. Thus, it represents one of the most comprehensive and systematic attempts to advise the President across a broad policy area in recent decades.

Chapter 2 describes the origins and historical evolution of the EPB, reviewing the organizational arrangements inherited by Gerald Ford in August 1974, the recommendations of his transition team regarding economic policy organization, the events culminating in establishing the Board, and the stages of the EPB's institutional development.

Chapter 3 describes the organization, operation, and functions of the

EPB. What precisely did the EPB do? How did it organize to perform its functions? What roles did the executive director perform? Surprisingly, few accounts are available, in part because of the inaccessibility of necessary information, on how cabinet-level committees and councils have actually operated. Chapter 3 helps fill this gap. The chapter concludes with an analysis of such factors as frequency of meetings, the scope and range of issues considered, and which agencies were the most active in preparing papers and bringing issues to the Board for consideration. In short, the chapter is designed to provide a succinct but comprehensive description of how the Economic Policy Board actually operated.

Chapters 4, 5, and 6 present case studies of how the EPB handled three issues: the 1975 State of the Union tax proposals, the U.S.–U.S.S.R. Grain Agreement, and the 1976 footwear import escape clause case. These three cases are spread over the period of the EPB's existence. The 1975 State of the Union tax proposals were developed during the first months the Board was in operation. The suspension on grain sales to the Soviet Union and the negotiation of the U.S.–U.S.S.R. Grain Agreement of 1975 occurred during the late summer and fall of that year at about the midpoint of the EPB's history. The footwear decision occurred in April 1976. The case studies also illustrate a mix of issues involving major foreign and domestic concerns, macroeconomic and microeconomic questions, tax policy, trade policy, and agricultural policy.

Chapter 7 evaluates the Economic Policy Board by assessing how well it performed certain basic advisory functions and what additional strengths and limitations it exhibited.

The final chapter, drawing from the EPB experience, delineates a set of organizational principles for structuring multiple advocacy entities and outlines a proposal for organizing the White House for presidential decision making.

1

Organizational challenges

*T*he expanding role of governmental activity in American society, the continuing proliferation of government entities and federal agencies, and the pervasive impact of the post–World War II technological and communications revolutions have left unchanged a central fact of American life – that the presidency continues as the focus of political leadership and administrative authority in the federal government. The communications revolution has focused increased attention on the President as the single most powerful figure in an age in which television places a premium on individuals instead of institutions. Even scandal and a resignation in disgrace did not result in major institutional changes, although several were proposed and enthusiastically supported for a time.

This national attention on the office of the President is accompanied by high expectations for performance. The demands on a president and his time range from guiding the conduct of the nation's foreign policy to establishing the country's domestic agenda, from maintaining a healthy economy to formulating policies to address a host of social ills. A president's capacity to meet these expectations is directly related to how he is organized to make decisions.

Presidents can and do make decisions in a number of ways. The machinery, the participants, and the substance varies for decisions about national security, the budget, economic policy, and social policy. Each president's decision-making pattern is unique and involves a mix of methods and approaches.

The purpose of this study is to illuminate our understanding of presidential decision making by focusing on economic policy issues. Economic policy, both foreign and domestic, has assumed increasing importance in the period since Franklin Roosevelt and now consumes large amounts of a president's time. Moreover, in contrast with national se-

5

curity policy-making machinery, presidential economic policy-making machinery has received relatively little attention from scholars.

THE INTERRELATEDNESS OF ISSUES

Two features of modern government present the President with a major organizational challenge. The first is the interrelatedness of the substantive problems that government is expected to address. Interrelatedness between issues has always existed. But the complexity of government and the awareness of interrelatedness among issues has increased dramatically in recent years.

One driving force behind the growing complexity is the expansion of governmental activity. In 1929, federal, state, and local governments spent 9 percent of the gross national product for purposes other than national defense and foreign affairs. Three decades later, spending on the domestic programs of government accounted for 17.5 percent of national income. By 1976, the proportion of national income devoted to domestic government programs had risen to 28 percent.

Growing cash transfers for direct income support to individuals and interest on the national debt now consume one-third of domestic spending. The remainder consists either of subsidies or direct provision of various goods and services. The proportion of national income spent for these purposes by the federal government was less than 1 percent of national income in 1929, but grew to 2.8 percent by 1960, and reached 6.5 percent by 1976.[1]

An explosion of federal regulatory activity has accompanied the increase in the number and size of federal programs. During the two decades following 1955 the number of pages published annually in the *Federal Register* increased from slightly over ten thousand to more than sixty thousand. This growth has accelerated in recent years and is concentrated in the period since 1970. Between 1970 and 1975, the average annual rate of growth was nearly 25 percent – up from just under 5 percent between 1955 and 1970.[2]

Charles L. Schultze has aptly described the changing environment of government:

> Until perhaps fifteen or twenty years ago, most federal activities in the domestic sphere were confined to a few broad areas: providing

[1] See Charles L. Schultze, *The Public Use of Private Interest* (Washington, D.C.: Brookings Institution, 1977), p. 7.

[2] Testimony of William Lilley III and James C. Miller III before the Subcommittee on Economic Stabilization, Committee on Banking, Currency and Housing, U.S. House of Representatives, December 17, 1976. See also William Lilley III and James C. Miller III, "The New 'Social Regulation,'" *Public Interest* 47 (Spring 1977):50.

cash income under social security programs for which eligibility was fairly easily determined; investing in the infrastructure in a few sectors of the economy, principally highways, water resources, and high-rise public housing; regulating selected industries allegedly to control monopoly or prevent certain abuses; and operating various housekeeping activities such as the Post Office, the national parks, the merchant seamen's hospitals, and the air navigation system. But in the short space of twenty years the very nature of federal activity has changed radically. Addressed to much more intricate and difficult objectives, the newer programs are different; and the older ones have taken on more ambitious goals.[3]

The expansion of federal concerns and the enlarged scope of federal programs have increased the demands on the President. The new demands arise not simply from the assumption of additional responsibilities, but also from the complexity that results from the inevitable overlap. Elliot Richardson describes the impact of interrelatedness on individual departments and agencies:

> Any increase in the number and scope of federal programs leads to a proportionally greater increase in the potential for conflict among them. As the range of federal concerns expands, program areas tend increasingly to converge and overlap. Fewer and fewer major problems still fall within the exclusive province of a single department or agency.[4]

Thus, the President is not merely responsible for administering these arithmetically expanding programs; he is also responsible for resolving the geometrically expanding conflicts between their objectives and priorities. Doing so is the first, but not the last, step in presidential leadership of the executive branch.

A second factor contributing to the complexity of policy making is the growing number of considerations that must be taken into account. Environmental considerations have acquired a new prominence in the last decade. The end of the cheap energy era has added another dimension. Consumer interests are now much better organized and more visible than a decade ago.[5]

A third factor is the blurring of the traditional distinction between domestic and foreign economic policy during the past quarter century.

---

[3] Schultze, p. 9.

[4] Elliot Richardson, *The Creative Balance* (New York: Holt, Rinehart and Winston, 1976), pp. 66–67.

[5] The Ford administration, which consistently opposed the creation of a consumer protection agency, nonetheless made explicit provision for consumer representation in a single office in each major department and agency and encouraged careful consideration of consumer interests in developing departmental positions on major issues.

With the rise of the multinational corporation, business is increasingly global in its outlook. A significant reduction in the natural, artificial, and psychological barriers to foreign trade and international capital movements has occurred. National economies have become more open and more sensitive to developments in the economies of their trading partners.[6]

A variety of developments reveal the increased openness of the U.S. economy. One key measure of increasing international economic interdependence is the marked increase in trade-to-GNP ratios.[7] The export share of the U.S. gross national product has doubled in the past fifteen years, and the import share has doubled in just seven years.[8] The U.S. exports approximately 20 percent of its industrial production and over one-third of its farm output. About one-third of U.S. corporate profits come from overseas activities, primarily direct foreign investment.

Consumers also feel the impact of increasing interdependence. External factors accounted for an estimated one-quarter to one-half of the steep rise in the rate of inflation during the 1972 to 1974 period. Finally, the U.S. presently imports more than 50 percent of its needs for nine of the thirteen key industrial raw materials.[9] The American economy, in short, is becoming increasingly dependent on foreign markets and on foreign products.

This new vulnerability has become crucially important for U.S. economic policy. The International Economic Summit Conferences at Rambouillet in 1975, Puerto Rico in 1976, London in 1977, Bonn in 1978, and Tokyo in 1979 struggled with how sensitive the economies of the major industrial democracies have become to each other. The impact of international developments on the health of the U.S. domestic economy and the expanding role of economics in international diplomacy suggest that domestic and international economic policy objectives are increasingly intertwined.[10]

Food policy making similarly illustrates the changing environment of

[6] Richard N. Cooper, *The Economics of Interdependence: Economic Policy in the Atlantic Community* (New York: McGraw Hill, 1968).

[7] See Peter J. Katzenstein, "International Interdependence: Some Long-Term Trends and Recent Changes," *International Organization* 29 (Autumn 1975): 1021–1034.

[8] These ratios are rapidly approaching those in Japan and the European Common Market as a group. C. Fred Bergsten and William R. Cline, "Increasing International Economic Interdependence: The Implications for Research," *American Economic Review* 66 (May 1976):155.

[9] *Ibid.*

[10] Richard N. Cooper has argued that the rule of law in international trade is now increasingly threatened and that this trend "will lead to much greater intrusion of domestic economic interests, through trade policy, into general foreign policy." Richard N. Cooper, "Trade Policy is Foreign Policy," *Foreign Policy* 9 (Winter 1972–73):29

government. Before 1972, commodity surpluses and depressed prices resulted in an agricultural policy that sought to strengthen farm income. Not surprisingly, the Department of Agriculture dominated decision making.

Crop shortfalls in several major agricultural countries and the pervasive effects of worldwide inflation helped change the environment for policy making, one in which farm interests must be considered in light of overall economic policy and foreign policy objectives.

Today a wide variety of groups and interests can legitimately claim that they deserve a voice in formulating agricultural and food policy.[11] Agricultural policy has become increasingly important to the health of the domestic economy. Food now comprises nearly 25 percent of the consumer price index. Furthermore, the importance of agricultural trade to the balance of payments has become critical in recent years. In 1978 U.S. agricultural exports were valued at $29.4 billion (American) compared with $7.2 billion in 1970. Crucial to the U.S. balance of payments position in 1976 was a $14.6 billion agricultural trade surplus.

Food is also an important factor in U.S. foreign policy. Agricultural policy has been a primary area of friction with Japan and Western Europe. Agricultural exports have constituted the major component in the expansion of American trade with the U.S.S.R and the People's Republic of China. PL-480 food aid has played a major role in our relations with such countries as Indonesia, South Korea, and Egypt.

The temporary suspension of grain sales to the Soviet Union in 1975 and the negotiation of a long-term U.S.–U.S.S.R. grain agreement illustrate the multitude of factors that a president must weigh and balance. The commitment to an agricultural policy of full production without export controls, the effect on domestic food prices of additional grain sales to the Soviet Union, the disruptive impact of the wide fluctuations in Soviet grain purchases in recent years, the relationship to general foreign policy objectives and to Soviet behavior on other issues, the potential leverage in securing shipping arrangements benefitting the depressed U.S. merchant marine, the usefulness of a temporary sales suspension as a lever in obtaining a long-term agreement requiring regular Soviet purchases of American grain – all were considered.

Government officials increasingly recognize this new environment of more complex policy making. Secretary of Agriculture Earl Butz, in congressional testimony in January 1976, acknowledged that food is an issue "you can't treat in isolation. It is one that cuts across departmental

[11] See Kenneth Farrell, "Public Policy, the Public Interest, and·Agricultural Economics," *American Journal of Agricultural Economics* 58 (December 1976): 786. See also Thorald Warley, "Agriculture in International Economic Relations," *American Journal of Agricultural Economics* 58 (December 1976):826.

lines . . . I have got to say that when food and international politics become so important, decision making has to be elevated to an interdepartmental level."[12]

The interrelatedness phenomenon also characterizes other policy areas. The thicket of welfare programs is the subject of much discussion and debate. Henry Aaron, Assistant Secretary of Health, Education, and Welfare and chairman of the Carter administration's study group on welfare reform, described one of their principal findings as follows:

> I think the main surprise was the degree of interrelatedness among the various programs, the diverse objectives of the various programs, a recognition that each of these programs when enacted piecemeal over the past years has had a good and sufficient justification. The surprise came that each of these programs, that makes so much sense taken individually, when fitted together produces a system of very serious complexity, one that creates perverse incentives that affect the recipients and that badly does need reform.[13]

The prospect seems strong that the interrelatedness of policy issues is not a passing phenomenon.[14]

Issue interrelatedness has important organizational implications for the President. It is unlikely that any individual department or agency will be aware of and sensitive to all the interlocking elements of a complex problem. This has resulted in a large role for the Office of Management and Budget and the White House staff in identifying interrelationships between issues and interests. Since fewer problems remain within the purview of a single department or agency, the pressure grows to have either the President or White House officials resolve issues. As one cabinet veteran of three administrations acknowledged, a president "can reckon with the implications of interrelatedness only at the cost of creating a requirement for coordination and integration where no such requirement was previously recognized."[15] Responses to interrelatedness

---

[12] *Who's Making Foreign Agricultural Policy?*, Hearings before the Subcommittee on Foreign Agricultural Policy, Committee on Agriculture and Forestry, United States Senate, January 22–23, 1976 (Washington, D.C.: GPO, 1976), pp. 11, 24. Butz reiterated this view in an interview the following December. See "New USDA Chief Faces Battles Within: Butz," *Journal of Commerce* (December 9, 1976).

[13] MacNeil/Lehrer Report, May 3, 1977.

[14] The complexity of government has also been enhanced by at least two other factors in addition to those outlined. First, demographic trends and medical advances have contributed to a new awareness of the problems and needs of the elderly who are now an increasingly important constituency. Second, social value regulation to enhance the health and safety of workers, to protect consumers from the products they purchase, and to contribute to the quality of the physical environment have added to the complexity of the government's role in the economic life of the nation.

[15] Richardson, p. 68.

have varied from administration to administration, but inevitably, in one form or another, they have included enlarging staff functions.[16]

Donald H. Rumsfeld, Chief of Staff in the Ford White House, after little more than a year in that position, observed:

> The problems of today don't fit the compartments [of government, but rather spill over several areas]. It is therefore important that the White House serve the President by trying to bring the threads of a given problem toward him in a reasonably coherent way. The Domestic Council, the National Security Council, the Economic Policy Board, and the Energy Resources Council – these are attempts to take those different domestic or foreign forums, departments, and agencies and their views and bring them in toward the President in a way that is digestible and workable, so that he can make judgments in a timely fashion . . . [The President must serve as] the connection between those different spokes as they come in because the decisions don't fit on any one spoke.[17]

Thus, the President needs to know how his organization addresses or fails to recognize the relevant connections between problems. To what extent are broad policy areas such as national security, economic policy, and social policy considered as a whole? To what extent are policy issues addressed separately or compartmentally as independent parts?[18]

A FRAGMENTED EXECUTIVE BRANCH

The fragmented structure of the executive branch presents a second major organizational problem for the President. The federal government's executive branch mirrors the American political system in its wide distribution of power and authority – in Stephen Bailey's apt phrase, it is "a many splintered thing."[19] This fragmentation has grown in recent decades: officials are organized into more layers in the upper reaches of departments and divided into more specialized divisions – with more

[16]   *Ibid.*, p. 80.
[17]   James T. Barron, "Advising the President," *Princeton Alumni Weekly* (November 24, 1975), p. 10.
[18]   For an interesting short discussion of "interconnections" see George P. Shultz and Kenneth W. Dam, *Economic Policy Beyond the Headlines* (Stanford: Stanford Alumni Association, 1978), pp. 6–8.
[19]   Stephen Bailey, "The President and His Political Executives," *Annals of the American Academy of Political and Social Science* 307 (September 1956):24. Shultz and Dam use the equally apt phrase the "balkanization of the executive branch." *Economic Policy Beyond the Headlines*, p. 6.

staff – in each layer.[20] This contributes to the organizational challenges facing the President that Hugh Heclo has described:

> Externally, government presents a less united front to the larger number of groups making claims on it. Internally, different parts of the government machinery are less able to take realistic account of each other's intentions and actions. People who do not know each other across the fragmented top layers are less likely to be able to coordinate operations (who does what), information (who knows what), planning (who foresees what), or any of the other working relations in government. Even with goodwill on all sides, it can become vastly more difficult to arrive at mutual understandings and to agree on courses of action for the executive branch as a whole – which is also to say, for purposes with a presidential perspective.[21]

Departmentalism

More specifically, and particularly important for the President, executive departments and agencies are organized around specific constituencies and special interests.[22] Each department properly has specialized capabilities, perspectives, and interests. Francis Bator has argued that:

> If the Government is to avoid immobility, a good deal of decentralization is essential. Each department must carry on its business in its area of primary responsibility. . . .Its actions will be informed by a general conception of presidential policy. But inevitably it will be influenced by the perspectives and tasks that are more narrowly its own, and by the concerns of its particular constituency.[23]

[20] See Hugh Heclo, *A Government of Strangers* (Washington, D.C.: Brookings Institution, 1976), pp. 56–59.

[21] *Ibid.*, p. 64.

[22] John Gardner, former Secretary of Health, Education, and Welfare, made this point in perhaps its most extreme form when he wrote that "a large part of what is called The Federal Government is not a coherent entity at all, but a collection of fragments under the virtual control of highly organized special interests in the private sector. In the Special Interest State that we have forged, every well-organized interest 'owns a piece of the rock.' . . . Instead of the United States being run by a well-knit behind-the-scenes power group (as the conspiracy theorists would have it), it is whipsawed by a great multiplicity of special interests." *Wall Street Journal*, November 30, 1976.

[23] *U.S. Foreign Economic Policy: Implications for the Organization of the Executive Branch*, Hearings before the Subcommittee on Foreign Economic Policy, Committee on Foreign Affairs, United States House of Representatives, Ninety-Second Congress, Second Session (Washington, D.C.: GPO, 1972), p. 111. Hereafter Bator Hearings.

Inevitably, a department or agency's viewpoint is more parochial than the President's. Most executives and officials tend to think and act in terms of their specific responsibilities.[24] Furthermore, close ties develop between departments and their constituencies.[25] The beneficiaries of departmental programs want to maintain those benefits. And an agency will lose its health, reputation, and autonomy if it can't marshal sufficient continuing political support.[26] Moreover, the relationships between interest groups and agencies or bureaus extend beyond a single presidency.

The sharp rise in the influence of professionalism in government has also sustained departmentalism. Frederick Mosher dates the rise of "the Professional State" from the mid-1950s when "government by administrators," characteristic of the New Deal, made way for "government by professionals." The growth of specialized sciences and their application to public policy gave "professional specialisms" a major role in policy making.[27] Samuel H. Beer has termed this development the "professional bureaucratic complex," a general phenomenon including the "military industrial complex," the "educational establishment," the "health syndicate," and the "welfare establishment," among others. Beer explains:

> The main element in such a complex of political power is a core of officials with scientific and professional training. This bureaucratic core also normally works in close cooperation with two other com-

---

[24] I. M. Destler, *Presidents, Bureaucrats, and Foreign Policy* (Princeton: Princeton University Press, 1972), pp. 56–57.

[25] Recent public attention on the relationship between departments and agencies and special interest groups may have weakened many traditionally close ties, or they may have simply become invisible. The dramatic growth of congressional staffs, in fact, may have actually encouraged the growth of these ties.

One cabinet officer described the department's relationship with interest groups in terms of both openness, exhibited in a willingness to genuinely listen, and independence:

It may be too strong a statement to say that they regarded us as their advocate. They regarded us as their door into, and we certainly could say, Mr. President the homebuilders really want this. . . . We often were their nemesis too. They would be pushing something that we knew we couldn't sell or didn't want to sell and we would try and stop the argument there. I would say we were more the doorway in rather than the real advocate; if persuaded we would be the advocate. And we certainly impacted them with all of our policies so that they were a part of the process.

[26] Richard F. Fenno, Jr., *The President's Cabinet* (Cambridge: Harvard University Press, 1959), p. 229. See also Norton Long, "Power and Administration," *Public Administration Review* 9 (Autumn 1949):258.

[27] Frederick C. Mosher, *Democracy and the Public Service* (New York: Oxford University Press, 1968), p. 105.

ponents: certain interested legislators, especially the chairmen of the relevant specialized subcommittees, and the spokesmen for the group that benefits from the program initially brought into existence by bureaucrats and politicians. Such a tripartite complex or subsystem is, of course, Seidman's "iron triangle."[28]

Mutual dependence encourages mutual support. Constituency groups consider departments and agencies their advocates in the executive branch. Departments and agencies expect support from constituency groups as they work to maintain and enhance their authority and prestige in the executive branch and Congress.

The perception of departments as constituency oriented is shared both within and outside the government. One former official recently observed:

> There is an apparently ineradicable perception – for which there is some recurring evidence – that every Department, including State, is representative of a specialized constituency rather than a holistic concept of American interests. In the Executive Branch (and in much of the Congress and probably the electorate), State is, rightly or wrongly, regarded as the representative of the interests of foreign countries, of placidity in international affairs without regard to the cost in commercial or military advantage, and, sometimes, of interests reflecting concern for the President's personal standing as statesman rather than any broader conception of foreign policy.[29]

The farm community views the Department of Agriculture as representing farm interests within the executive branch and is anxious for the USDA to have maximum authority over agricultural policy decisions. As one farm community executive explained:

> I am disturbed, of course, not only by the fact that there is increased Government involvement in grain sales, but that the involvement comes more and more from agencies other than the USDA. I feel the USDA alone within the framework of the executive branch has enough sensitivity to agriculture and the agricultural marketing to deal with these subjects. I am disturbed when I

---

[28]   Samuel H. Beer, "Political Overload and Federalism," *Polity* 10 (Fall 1977): 9–10. See also Harold Seidman, *Politics, Position and Power* (New York: Oxford University Press, 1970), p. 37.

[29]   Edward K. Hamilton, "Summary Report: Principal Lessons of the Past Decade and Thoughts on the Next," in U.S. Commission on the Organization of the Government for the Conduct of Foreign Policy, *Appendices* (Washington, D.C.: GPO, June 1975), Vol. 3, p. 9.

hear of involvement by Cabinet agencies which have really no responsibility to the farmer. It bothers the farmers quite a bit.[30]

One member of the Senate Agriculture and Forestry Committee voiced the feelings of many of his colleagues when he told the Secretary of Agriculture: "We feel more power should be vested in the Secretary of Agriculture. We believe you speak more for the farmer."[31]

Departmental representatives naturally view themselves as responsible, to some extent, for defending and advancing the interests of their constituency. A State Department official commenting on agricultural policy making noted that "obviously, the USDA is there to protect the interests of the U.S. agricultural sector."[32] He might have added that the State Department was present to advance and protect certain foreign policy interests.[33]

The structure of the career bureaucracy also contributes to departmentalism. In the British civil service, generalists are cultivated by service in a variety of departments; most U.S. career civil servants, however, typically remain with a single department or agency.[34] The U.S. pattern can produce invaluable specialized expertise; it can also produce a narrow view of the government and its problems.[35] There are few vested interests as powerful as the vested interests of the mind.

[30] *Who's Making Foreign Agricultural Policy?*, p. 133. Testimony of Joseph Halow, Executive Vice President, Great Plains Wheat, Inc.

[31] *Ibid.*, p. 15. Statement of Senator Robert Dole.

[32] *Ibid.*, p. 44. Testimony of Deputy Secretary of State Charles W. Robinson.

[33] Theodore Sorensen concluded that "bureaucratic parochialism and rivalry are usually associated in Washington with the armed services, but they in fact affect the outlook of nearly every agency." Theodore Sorensen, *Decision Making in the White House* (New York: Columbia University Press, 1963), p. 69.

[34] Eugene B. McGregor, Jr., in his study of the career mobility of federal bureaucrats, found that "only a rare 'successful' higher civil servant makes more than one interdepartmental or interagency move in a lifetime of public service and that this move is most likely to occur early in a man's career." He concluded that "as 'successful' civil servants rise to their highest levels of power and influence they become more anchored in a single agency or department." Eugene B. McGregor, Jr., "Politics and the Career Mobility of Bureaucrats," *American Political Science Review* 68 (March 1974):22, 24.

[35] Robert C. Wood has claimed that "the chief criticism leveled at the American civil service has been its parochial professional bias. . . . Lacking the British tradition of the generalist administrative class, and building its first positive programs around scientific and engineering activities, the United States government recruits by profession – lawyers, accountants, architects, engineers, appraisers. Such specialized education and occupation encourage bureau and program parochialism, and many career men become insensitive and even resistant to broad policy activity." Robert C. Wood, "When Government Works," *Public Interest* 18 (Winter 1970):47–48.

However, the Fulton Committee Report on the British Civil Service issued in June 1968, criticized the "cult of the generalist" or "all-rounder" as obsolete and noted that the com-

Staying in one department also means that a career civil servant's professional reputation, security, and advancement are closely tied to the health of particular programs. He acquires a personal stake in the outcome of bureaucratic battles. Not surprisingly, these professionals develop strong institutional ties that influence their outlook.

The desire for agency autonomy is another major contributor to departmentalism. Departments and agencies, like individuals, possess powerful survival instincts. The quest for security is a strong influence on the behavior of bureaucracies. Jurisdictional prerogatives central to the mission of a department or agency are jealously, often fervently, guarded. Defending and expanding one's bureaucratic domain can influence one's perspective on policy issues.

The tendency is strong for departments and agencies to approach problems with a view to protecting the interests of their constituency and, perhaps even more importantly, enhancing the agency's authority and jurisdictional prerogatives. Departmentalism helps policy development by providing representation of interests and by helping reflect constituencies' intensity of feeling on issues. But departmentalism inhibits policy development when it leads agencies to bias their information and analyses in favor of their policy preferences, when it limits their innovativeness and flexibility in problem-solving, and when it makes departments unwilling to see some issues considered in an interagency context.

Moreover, departmentalism inhibits developing a sense of common cause and identity among an administration's officials. Political appointees in top departmental and agency positions may not give first loyalty to the administration team since their incentives generally center within their own department, agency, or bureau. As one perceptive observer noted:

> The unstable teams within departments are positively collegial when compared with the attenuated relations of political appointees across departments. At least within departments there may be the shared need to protect and promote a common set of agency programs. Weighed against this territorial imperative, political appointees elsewhere can seem like alien tribes.
>
> ... The lines of mutual interdependence normally run vertically down the departments and their loosely related programs – not

mittee had been favorably influenced by "the role played by specialists in both the United States and France." Yet, the committee also observed that in the United States "there was not enough mobility between agencies on the part of civil servants, and it too often happened that a specialized agency was run by an expert who had never seen life outside his bureau." Cmnd. 3638. *The Civil Service* Vol. 1, Report of the Committee 1966–68, Lord Fulton, Chairman (London: Her Majesty's Stationary Office, 1968), pp. 9, 11, 13, 145.

horizontally across the layers of political leadership in various departments. Insofar as top political executives need each other (as opposed to needing the President's support or endorsement) the needs are temporary and issue specific, not enduring.[36]

In short, departmentalism is a way of life in the executive branch. Departments and agencies cultivate and are cultivated by special interests and specific constituencies. On many issues, particularly those that touch their interests and constituencies most closely, departments and agencies inevitably emphasize concerns that reflect a narrow and parochial view. They weigh and balance the trade-offs between competing alternatives differently than do those with different primary concerns or with broader viewpoints. Specialization and relative immobility between departments by career civil servants sustain departmentalism, as does the simple desire to survive and enhance, if possible, one's authority, autonomy, and prestige amidst the shifting tides of power in Washington.

The cabinet secretary at the crossroads

Cabinet secretaries, who head the major entities within the executive branch, are the President's chief line officers. Yet, while a cabinet secretary is selected by the President and dependent on his pleasure for continued tenure, he faces a number of cross-cutting pressures.[37]

A new cabinet secretary faces a career bureaucracy generally resistant to change. Its internal relationships are established; its external relationships with special interest groups are comfortable. Richard Fenno notes: "Most of [the cabinet secretary's] organization is staffed with career per-

---

[36] Heclo, pp. 106–107. Recent administrations have attempted from time to time to organize interdepartmental general purpose groups beyond the cabinet such as the Undersecretaries' Group begun at the end of the Johnson administration. But, as Heclo discovered, neither the White House nor the departments considered the effort a success. As one presidential aide put it: "I didn't get the feeling they were acting like prima donnas, [but] it's just generally hard to get their attention, even concerning the federal regional councils, if they don't feel it's important to their departmental operations. One undersecretary went to the heart of the matter:

> You can't build a governmentwide executive team through artificial structures like the Undersecretaries' Group. It's a group in search of a mission. You can't build an executive team by pressing issues that aren't particularly relevant to people just for the sake of having everybody in on them. You can't do it by bypassing people to get to another layer. (Insofar as there is going to be a team) it has to begin at the top and use the cabinet secretaries." [Ibid., pp. 108, 109.]

[37] See Fenno, p. 225. For an interesting short account of how one new cabinet officer defined his role, see Shultz and Dam, p. 5. Hugh Heclo aptly characterizes Washington's political executives as existing in "a twilight zone of political leadership." Heclo, ɔ. 88.

sonnel, relatively unaffected by changes in high-level policy. Power relationships among constituent elements of the department, or between departmental units and clusters of interests outside the department, tend to
be in an equilibrium which reflects an optimum adjustment for all concerned."[38]

The career bureaucracy sees him as a temporary fixture and with few
exceptions cabinet secretaries have relatively short tenure – from an average of forty months during 1933–1965 to eighteen months during the
Nixon administration.[39] The permanent bureaucracy generally knows, in
a technical sense, a great deal more about most issues than does the
cabinet secretary. A cabinet secretary who ignores the views of his permanent bureaucracy risks impairing their morale and efficiency. Thus, a
cabinet secretary who consistently seeks to view problems from a
broader perspective may discover that he has moved some distance from
his troops.

One of the most powerful pressures, then, on a cabinet secretary is to
respond to the institutional viewpoint of the department he heads. Elliot
Richardson, four times a cabinet secretary and in high positions in four
administrations, wrote that "cabinet members are forced by the very nature of their institutional responsibilities to be advocates of their departmental programs. This, essentially, was the point behind Vice President
Charles G. Dawe's famous remark that 'the members of the Cabinet are
a President's natural enemies.'"[40]

[38] Fenno, p. 226.
[39] See David T. Stanley, Dean E. Mann, and Jameson W. Doig, *Men Who Govern: A
Biographical Profile of Federal Political Executives* (Washington, D.C.: Brookings Institution, 1967), chapter 4; see also Heclo, pp. 103–105.
  This finding also holds for presidents and subcabinet officials. McGregor found that
"higher civil servants remain within one organization more than twice as long as do re-
elected presidents and at least eight times as long as most assistant secretaries." "Politics
and the Career Mobility of Bureaucrats," p. 24. See also Dean E. Mann and Jameson W.
Doig, *The Assistant Secretaries: Problems and Processes of Appointment* (Washington,
D.C.: Brookings Institution, 1965). About half the top political executives in the executive
branch can expect to stay in their jobs less than two years.
[40] Richardson, p. 76. David Truman concluded that the departmental pressures on
cabinet members are so strong that they "may make even a personal supporter act as the
President's 'natural enemy' when he heads a major department." David Truman, *The Governmental Process* (New York: Knopf, 1951), p. 406. See also John R. Steelman and H.
DeWayne Kreager, "The Executive Office as Administrative Coordinator," *Law and Contemporary Problems* 21 (Autumn 1956): 700–01; and McGeorge Bundy, *The Strength of
Government* (Cambridge: Harvard University Press, 1968), pp. 37–40.
  Graham K. Wilson, in a generally unpersuasive article, has argued that cabinet secretaries are essentially immune to constraints by departmental bureaucracies and interest
groups. Graham K. Wilson, "Are Department Secretaries Really a President's Natural Enemies?" *British Journal of Political Science* 7 (July 1977):273–299.

A second centrifugal force acting on a cabinet member is that his success is closely tied to his relationship with his constituency. A secretary of agriculture spurned by the farm community or a secretary of labor feuding with the major organized unions has small value to his department or the President. Cabinet secretaries must weigh carefully the often competing demands of their constituency and their loyalty to the Chief Executive.

Presidents implicitly acknowledge the value of a cabinet secretary's relationship with his constituency by selecting someone "acceptable" to the various interests served by that department. Of course, a multitude of considerations – geographical distribution, demographic balance, political debts, internal harmony within the party, demonstrated competence in previous government assignments, professional reputation, personal trust, friendship and respect – may influence, even decisively, the selection of a cabinet secretary. Moreover, few departments serve a cohesive and monolithic set of interests. But it is rare for the President to ignore the probable reaction of those interests closely affected by the department in selecting a cabinet secretary. Unacceptability is a price most presidents are reluctant to pay.[41]

A third centrifugal force contributing to a cabinet member's indepen-

---

Hugh Heclo notes the strong attraction of institutional advocacy for top departmental political executives:

> Thus the more adept a political appointee becomes in building his circles of confidence and in protecting his prerogatives, the more the value of his *advocacy* appreciates in the eyes of the bureaucrats below. In every department in every recent administration, one of the chief ways political executives gained support in the bureaucracy was by being, or at least appearing to be, their agency's vigorous spokesman. "Fighting your counterparts in other departments creates confidence and support beneath you," one acknowledged. In reference to a strong advocate in his department, a civil servant said: "He was well regarded on the Hill and dealt from strength with [the interest group]. A lot of White House people were afraid of him. You could get more of what was wanted approved and through Congress." [Heclo, p. 196.]

[41]   Robert C. Wood has argued against the tendency of many "Washington watchers" to overemphasize the role of constituency groups in the selection of cabinet officials. "Appointments made strictly because of ties with interest groups or for reasons of geography grow rarer, as these considerations become less important in presidential politics. The demand increases for effective program performance, and managerial skills are valued higher than partisan symbolism." Wood, p. 46.

For a more traditional view see Aaron B. Wildavsky, "Salvation by Staff: Reform of the Presidential Office," in Wildavsky, ed., *The Presidency* (Boston: Little, Brown, 1969), p. 696; and Norman C. Thomas, "Presidential Advice and Information: Policy and Program Formulation," *Law and Contemporary Problems* 35 (Summer 1970):547–548. Perhaps the most balanced description of the selection of federal political appointees is provided in Heclo, pp. 98–99.

dence is his relations with the Congress. Not only must the Congress confirm him, but it passes on the legislation he seeks, oversees his administrative performance, helps determine the level of appropriations his department will receive, and has endowed his office with independent statutory powers.

The cabinet secretary must also manage his large bureaucracy. In many executive departments, the deputy secretary or an under secretary handles day-to-day management, but a large number of management decisions inevitably reach the secretary's desk. Moreover, he must explain and promote departmental policies to the Congress, the public, and sometimes to his own department. In short, while he is appointed by and responsible to the President and may consider his role as a presidential adviser his most important function, a cabinet secretary lives "in a world which has many extra-presidential dimensions."[42]

The picture of the cabinet secretary faced by a permanent bureaucracy resistant to change, beset by special interests with persuasive pleas that he champion their cause, and beseiged by congressmen who consider cabinet departments the easiest place to exercise leverage, is incomplete and misleading. The theory underlying this view suggests that policy is made by "iron triangles" or subgovernments consisting of powerful interest groups, permanent departmental and agency bureaucracies, and congressional committees and their staffs. The major difficulty with this theory is that it oversimplifies. It identifies powerful forces and major participants and then attributes to them a decisiveness that ignores several other important influences on policy.

Most cabinet secretaries preside over a department that more nearly resembles a holding company than a monolithic and single-minded institution. In every cabinet department there are multiple and conflicting internal viewpoints. On most major issues, a cabinet secretary is not confronted with a single view from his permanent bureaucracy, but with competing interests and conflicting views that he must weigh and balance.

The Congress and interested outside parties mirror this pluralism. For every iron triangle or triple alliance on an issue there is usually a counter iron triangle or counter triple alliance. The interplay between these contending forces permits the cabinet secretary, as well as the President, considerable room to maneuver. As Robert C. Wood, former Secretary of Housing and Urban Development, observed: "The 'triple alliances' are, in fact, not intractable, but subject to redirection and even to neglect, as more massive forms of public appeal become available."[43]

[42] Fenno, p. 231.   [43] Wood, p. 46.

Most cabinet secretaries discover considerable independence at the crossroads of conflicting pressures. Richard Neustadt's observation of the Secretary of State's role applies equally well to most cabinet officers:

> The Secretary of State has work of his own, resources of his own, vistas of his own. He is in business under his own name and in his name powers are exercised, decisions taken. Therefore he can press his personal authority, his own opinion, his adviser's role, wherever he sees fit across the whole contemporary reach of foreign relations. . . . His status and the tasks of his Department give him every right to raise his voice where, when, and as he chooses.[44]

Finally, it is instructive to review how most cabinet members spend their time. Cabinet secretaries, like others, are in part products of their environment. The hours in a cabinet officer's typical week are consumed by internal staff meetings; scores of memorandums, documents, correspondence, and regulations that he must read and respond to; meetings with outside groups interested in matters under his direct jurisdiction; preparing for and delivering testimony before congressional committees; meetings with individual congressmen and senators; speech making and travel.

In most of the meetings he attends, he is the senior official. In his appearances, before the public, the press, or the Congress, he advocates or defends a position. He rarely has time for reflection. His day focuses primarily on the public policy problems that most directly affect his department. Seldom confronted by peers, he is most often with subordinates who desire his favor and support. He is normally not pressed to consider problems in a broad context. In short, the cabinet secretary lives in a world of cross-cutting forces; and while he has considerably more discretion than some have suggested, the pressures for a parochial outlook are strong, though not overwhelming.[45]

---

[44] Testimony of Richard E. Neustadt before the Senate Subcommittee on National Security Staffing and Operations, in Wildavsky, pp. 522–523.

[45] Alexander L. George argues that, placed at the crossroads of conflicting pressures, many cabinet-level and subcabinet officials lean one way or the other or behave erratically:

> Caught in the middle and subject to conflicting demands and pressures, cabinet-level and sub-cabinet officials may seek to avoid the ensuing dilemma by leaning heavily in one direction or the other, or by behaving erratically. There is no assurance, therefore, that his appointees will succeed in achieving what the chief executive often needs most from them — namely, their help in bridging presidential and departmental perspectives. However carefully a President attempts to select his appointees to these positions, some of them will resolve the role conflict their position places them in by becoming loyal "President's men," at the cost of weakening their ability to provide

The view from the White House

The President occupies a unique position in the American political system. With the exception of the Vice President, he is the only official elected by the entire national electorate. He has a genuinely national constituency and is the focus of national political attention. Not only is his constituency unique, but his range of responsibilities knows virtually no bounds. He must be concerned with what the diplomats are doing to the nation's military strategy, and vice versa, and what defense spending and foreign commitments will cost in taxes and inflation. His policy perspective, like his constituency, is broader than that of his individual cabinet officers.

It is the President from whom the Congress and the country expect initiative and direction. It is the President who is expected to coordinate coherent public policies. These expectations flow in part from the President's public status and national following, which give him resources for leadership, bargaining, and persuasion that no other political figure can match.

Because of the breadth of his responsibilities, perspective, and constituency, the President has two crucial interests that are affected by his organizational arrangements. First, as architect of the nation's foreign policy and, to a lesser extent, its domestic agenda, the President must seek to integrate policy. He wants the parts to bear some relationship to the whole since he is uniquely accountable for the comprehensiveness and coherence of his administration's policies.[46] As Allison and Szanton have observed, the integration of policy "is the overriding problem of policy making under conditions of diffused power."[47]

Second, the President has an interest in balancing the competing forces and interests in major areas of public policy. His decisions will be best informed if the objectives and considerations presented to him reasonably correspond to their real importance. Thus, he will want to have organizational arrangements that not only provide representation for all

leadership and representation for their own departments; others will come to identify largely with the specialized perspective of their own agencies. [Alexander L. George, "The Collegial Policymaking Group," in U.S. Commission on the Organization of the Government for the Conduct of Foreign Policy, *Appendices* (Washington, D.C.: GPO, June 1975), Vol. 2, p. 120.]

[46]   Conceivably, the President could approve and support conflicting policies as a compromise solution to a difficult set of problems. Naturally, it is in his interest that such inconsistencies represent conscious decisions rather than a failure to properly coordinate.

[47]   Graham Allison and Peter Szanton, "Organizing for the Decade Ahead," in Henry Owen and Charles L. Schultze, eds., *Setting National Priorities: The Next Ten Years* (Washington, D.C.: Brookings Institution, 1976), p. 253.

important interests, but that also do not significantly favor one perspective over another.[48]

Two general prescriptions are frequently urged on presidents for overcoming or transcending departmentalism. One perennial proposal is reorganizing departments into larger units on the ground that a broader constituency should produce a broader outlook. Lyndon Johnson urged consolidating the departments of Labor and Commerce; Richard Nixon, drawing on the proposals of the Ash Council, recommended consolidating the "outer" seven departments into four new departments; Jimmy Carter, during the 1976 presidential election campaign, pointed to his record of departmental consolidation as Governor of Georgia and vowed that, if elected, he would undertake a similar effort to reorganize the federal government.

Advocates of more comprehensive executive departments believe that consolidation will undermine narrow departmental perspectives. Yet, few would argue that the size and scope of the Department of Defense or the Department of Health, Education, and Welfare have eliminated, or even significantly reduced, the power of special interests and specific constituencies. Consolidation may simply transfer certain decisions from the White House to the departmental secretaries, while preserving competing narrow interests. Furthermore, there is no guarantee that the President's interests will prevail in decisions made at the departmental level. Even large consolidated departments will have a different outlook, perspective, and constituency from the President.

A second prescription is cabinet government. Almost every president, usually early in his administration, talks of reviving the cabinet as an institution and indicates that he intends to hold regular and frequent cabinet meetings. Yet, most presidents come to regard the full cabinet as an unsatisfactory forum for considering major policy issues.[49] Few prob-

---

[48] As Shultz and Dam put it, the President "must have some way of balancing competing interest groups against one another while at the same time building a policy structure that can take account of broader considerations." *Economic Policy Beyond the Headlines*, p. 5.

[49] Abe Fortas expressed a widely held view of the cabinet when he said:

With regard to the Cabinet as an institution, as differentiated from the individuals who compose it, as I have seen it operate under three Presidents, it is a joke. As a collegium, it doesn't exist. Its members, serving as a Cabinet, neither advise the President nor engage in any meaningful consideration of serious problems or issues. I remember Harold Ickes describing Cabinet meetings as 'dormitory sessions.' Of the sessions that I took part in under Roosevelt and Truman, I am sure that nothing of importance, beyond mere reporting was ever said. [Quoted in Emmet John Hughes, *The Living Presidency* (New York: Coward, McCann and Geoghegan, 1972), p. 335.]

lems engage either the interest or the expertise of all members of the cabinet. The sheer work volume and time demands on top-level federal executives suggest the wisdom of focusing their expertise in broad areas of public policy – national security, economic policy, social policy – rather than using the entire cabinet to seriously deliberate policy issues.

Full cabinet meetings nevertheless continue to be held, although in greater frequency by some presidents than others. John F. Kennedy, who considered cabinet meetings of limited value, held them for symbolic purposes, in part because "public confidence [is] inspired by order and regularity."[50]

Regular participants in cabinet meetings held by the last five presidents uniformly describe them as mainly exercises in exchanging information and getting direction from the President. Reports on how the administration's program is faring in the Congress, an account of the latest foreign mission of the Secretary of State or the prospects for successfully concluding current negotiations with foreign countries, a description of the current state of the economy and the principles underlying the administration's economic policy are representative of the agenda items that are standard fare at cabinet meetings.

Since major policy discussions rarely occur in full cabinet meetings, cabinet secretaries, anxious to secure presidential support for new or expanded programs, seek other avenues. Most cabinet secretaries prefer a private meeting with the President to the scrutiny of a group of senior officials who may oppose or raise serious problems with their recommendation. Many presidents, including Franklin D. Roosevelt, John F. Kennedy, and Lyndon B. Johnson, have held extensive bilateral sessions with individual cabinet officers.

Recognizing that eventually some White House assistants will advise the President on their issue, cabinet officers often seek support for their proposal from the President's circle of White House advisers. Since jurisdictional responsibilities on the White House staff are fluid and sometimes overlapping, cabinet secretaries may test several alternatives in building support for their proposal in the West Wing.

Presidents soon recognize that their cabinet secretaries, although loyal and committed to the administration's success, have a more narrow, departmentally based view and are advocates for a particular constituency or set of objectives. The objective may be broad – a successful foreign policy or a strong domestic economy – or narrow – strengthening farm income or increasing low-income urban housing. But invariably a cabinet member's overriding objectives do not match the full range of political, economic, social, and foreign policy concerns of the President.

[50] Sorensen, p. 58.

If reliance either on departmental consolidation or on the entire cabinet as a decision-making forum are of limited value in helping the President, what other arrangements can he establish to organize the advice he receives and to structure the relations between himself, his staff, his cabinet and subcabinet officials, and the permanent government?

ORGANIZATIONAL ALTERNATIVES

The President has numerous organizational options ranging from institutionalizing a devil's advocate to an essentially unregulated pluralistic system such as partisan mutual adjustment.[51] Since 1939, with the establishment of the Executive Office of the President and an enlarged White House staff, presidents have generally pursued one of three basic strategies to organize the pattern of advice they receive from their immediate staff and from executive departments and agencies.

One approach is adhocracy, which minimizes regularized and systematic patterns of providing advice and instead relies heavily on the President distributing assignments and selecting whom he listens to and when. It frequently typifies the early weeks and months of an administration when the President and his appointees are learning about each other and are first grappling with the problems of governing as opposed to the challenges of campaigning. Adhocracy may involve giving different advisers competing assignments to develop an initiative. Whether explicitly competitive or not, adhocracy involves few regularized channels. A different group examines virtually every major problem. Moreover, the random distribution of assignments and responsibilities frequently results in jurisdictional battles. The adhocracy of Franklin D. Roosevelt resulted in almost interminable chaos. Roosevelt dispensed conflicting assignments in almost random fashion. There was little institutional machinery to pick up the pieces. Today, over three decades later, adhocracy is still a possible approach to presidential decision making, but is less random and less chaotic than in Roosevelt's time. Relatively entrenched pieces of presidential machinery – the Office of Management and Budget, the White House Staff Secretary's office, the National Security Council staff, and the Domestic Policy staff – often act like safety nets assuming re-

[51] See Alexander L. George, "The Case for Multiple Advocacy in Making Foreign Policy," *American Political Science Review* 66 (September 1972): 751; and "The Devil's Advocate: Uses and Limitations," in U.S. Commission on the Organization of the Government for the Conduct of Foreign Policy, *Appendices* (Washington, D.C.: GPO, June 1975), Vol. 2, pp. 83–85. See also Joseph de Rivera, *The Psychological Dimension of Foreign Policy* (Columbus: Merrill, 1968), pp. 61–64, 209–211; Irving L. Janis, *Victims of Groupthink* (Boston: Houghton Mifflin, 1972), pp. 215–216.

sponsibility for making a decision or organizing advice for a presidential decision unless the President intervenes. In short, adhocracy no longer operates in a vacuum.

Centralized management is a second organizational model emphasizing heavy reliance on the White House staff and entities within the Executive Office of the President. These staffs filter the ideas, proposals, and recommendations of departments and agencies before they go to the President. Reliance on staff entities within the Executive Office of the President and the White House is grounded in a desire for analysis and recommendations from individuals who share the President's perspective. Theoretically, these staffs not only manage the flow of day-to-day communications between departments and the President, but also provide neutral, objective analysis, and structure policy alternatives to transcend departmental parochialism.

Multiple advocacy is a third organizational model. It is an open system designed to expose the President systematically to competing arguments and viewpoints made by the advocates themselves. In contrast to partisan mutual adjustment, multiple advocacy is a managed process relying on an honest broker to insure that interested parties are represented and that the debate is structured and balanced. It emphasizes carefully weighing all views and considerations and is grounded in the concept that a competition of ideas and viewpoints is the best method of developing policy – not unregulated entrepreneurial advocacy but orderly, systematic, and balanced competition. The honest broker and his staff are not intermediaries between departmental advocates and the President, like a centralized management staff, but they do more than simply insure due process. They promote a genuine competition of ideas, identifying viewpoints not adequately represented or that require qualification, determining when the process is not producing a sufficiently broad range of options, and augmenting the resources of one side or the other so that a balanced presentation results. In short, they insure due process *and* quality control.

These three approaches or models may have many variations. Moreover, these three models clearly do not exhaust either the reasonable possibilities or the advisory systems that presidents have actually employed. For example, both Presidents Ford and Truman handled foreign and national security policy primarily through delegation to, and heavy reliance upon the Secretary of State. Likewise, Richard Nixon delegated much responsibility on economic policy issues to Treasury Secretary John Connally and later to his successor George Shultz.

Adhocracy, centralized management, and multiple advocacy each have certain theoretical advantages and limitations. An essay discussing the characteristics, strengths, and weaknesses of each model is found in the Appendix. Different circumstances require different organizational responses. No single model is invariably preferable. The wise executive will be versatile and adaptive in making intelligent use of all three from time to time.

This book is principally about multiple advocacy. There are two reasons for this emphasis. First, multiple advocacy has great promise in theory, but remains largely unexamined in practice. Examining its operation in detail can advance our understanding of its potential strengths and limitations. Second, successfully operating multiple advocacy presents considerable challenges. Through examining it we can learn much about the management of policy development.

As a general organizational strategy, multiple advocacy, properly managed, has several compelling theoretical advantages. It provides representation of all points of view and a full exploration of the arguments advanced in support of alternative courses of action. It helps bridge the gap between policy formulation and implementation. It creates a context for policy making that reflects the political forces it will later have to engage. And, it strengthens the President's influence throughout the executive branch. Multiple advocacy mobilizes the resources of the executive branch more systematically than does adhocracy and more completely than does centralized management.

Yet multiple advocacy depends on officials working together in groups. It benefits from continuity among those who advise the President. A stable core of senior advisers and principal advocates sharing responsibility for collectively advising the President over the entire range of issues in a broad policy area can provide him with breadth and depth in his decision making. Such a group can screen issues and sharpen debate. The call for such groups extends back at least to the first Hoover Commission Report.[52]

But such a strategy is difficult to implement and those who have analyzed attempts at organizing senior advisers at the highest levels have found the performance of such committees mixed at best. I. M. Destler, in his thoughtful analysis of national security advice to Presidents since the second world war, concluded that "Presidential use of the National Security Council as a regularized, major advisory forum is the exception rather than the rule."

A major reason is that the Council's main virtues to its proponents — formality and regularity of membership and meetings; preestablished, well-disseminated agendas — prove to be drawbacks in

---

[52] See *General Management of the Executive Branch: A Report to the Congress by the Commission on Organization of the Executive Branch of the Government* (Washington, D.C.: GPO, 1949), pp. 17–21.

tice. N.S.C. meetings tend to attract too many people for serious advice to be conveyed – senior advisers and Presidents are constrained to speak "for the record" notwithstanding the formal secrecy of the proceedings, since their remarks are likely to be passed on by word of mouth to a much wider audience inside the Government. Cabinet members consider themselves judged on how effectively they push their departmental briefs; Presidents must take care lest their tentative suggestions close off discussion or be disseminated after the meetings as clear Presidential preferences. These drawbacks can be reduced by limiting attendance, and all Administrations that took the Council at all seriously have made some efforts in that direction . . . But security and frankness can be achieved even more effectively through informal meetings or "one-on-one" sessions, and it is these on which Presidents ultimately tend to rely for serious advice.[53]

Similarly, Francis Bator has argued that there are at least five operational difficulties with a "fixed membership superstructure" or large formal standing committee:

> First, serious work just does not happen in a crowd. . . . Cabinet secretaries surrounded by a bevy of committed and watchful retainers . . . will tend to argue their bureaucratic brief. . . . Second, fixed committees have a fixed tendency to expand and almost no capacity for shrinkage. . . . Third, fixed committees tend to breed special staffs, divorced from on-going operations. . . . Fourth, fixed committees make the problem of reasonable press security impossible. Fifth, the result of all of the above is that when fixed committees exist – except when their limited functional role as a board of directors is absolutely clear, and numbers are kept rigidly limited – the real bargaining tends to take place outside of the committee framework.[54]

In short, the conventional wisdom suggests that high-level fixed membership committees do not work in several important senses. First, they fail to engage the commitment, measured either by time or resources, of their members. Subordinates soon replace their superiors at meetings. Endless discussions with the protagonists arguing from inflexible positions produce boredom rather than results. Second, they do not serve as

---

[53] Destler, "National Security Advice to U.S. Presidents: Some Lessons from Thirty Years," p. 150. See also I. M. Destler, *Presidents, Bureaucrats, and Foreign Policy: The Politics of Organizational Reform*, pp. 207–212; Henry A. Kissinger, *The Necessity for Choice* (New York: Harper & Row, 1960), pp. 344–347.

[54] Bator Hearings, pp. 115–116.

the actual channel for presidential decisions. Key administration officials, able through the weight of their office or personal relationship with
the President to get access to him, conduct their serious business with
him outside committee meetings. Smaller, informal sessions are more secure, candid, and productive. Similarly, bargaining among senior officials "tends to take place outside of the committee framework." Third,
such committees, to the extent they do meet and function, are often dominated by one or more members. They go through the motions of making
policy, but either by strength of personality, superior institutional resources, or the procedures under which they operate, they are effectively
controlled by one or more members.

The Economic Policy Board was a cabinet-level council created to advise the President on domestic and foreign economic policy issues. Although not consciously established to put multiple advocacy into practice, its operations and procedures were consistent with the principles on
which the concept of multiple advocacy is based. It thus provides students of the Presidency with an opportunity to examine in detail how
real are the theoretical advantages of multiple advocacy and how substantial are the criticisms of high-level formal committees.

2

The Economic Policy Board: creation and historical evolution

A NEW ADMINISTRATION MIDTERM

The early weeks and months of any new administration are inevitably a period of learning, clarifying working relationships, and establishing policy-making patterns. The Ford administration was unique for several reasons.

First, Gerald Ford assumed the presidency without having run for national office. Neither he nor his staff had been through the testing period of a national campaign.

Second, unlike other vice presidents who have assumed the remainder of their predecessor's term, Ford needed to put some distance between himself and his predecessor as quickly as possible. His capacity to lead the nation depended in part, he was repeatedly told, on putting a new and distinctive imprint on the presidency. Personal style and organization could help create a new image of openness and candor.

Third, the permanent government was dissatisfied with the pattern of White House–departmental relations; specifically, departments and agencies felt infrequently and inadequately included in the White House decision-making process. Moreover, Ford faced the inevitable task of a vice president succeeding to the presidency in mid-term – meshing his vice presidential staff and the White House staff. These factors encouraged organizational innovation and are important in understanding the context in which the Ford administration's economic policy-making apparatus evolved.

THE NIXON LEGACY

When Gerald Ford assumed the presidency on August 9, 1974, the White House economic policy organization was in its "post-Shultz" period. George Shultz, successively Secretary of Labor, Director of the Office of Management and Budget, and Secretary of the Treasury, was widely regarded as one of the most able organizers in the Nixon administration.

As Assistant to the President for Economic Affairs from January 1973 until his departure from government in May 1974, Shultz was the chief spokesman for the administration on economic policy issues and was clearly the dominant figure in formulating the administration's economic policy.

Shultz held a daily morning meeting of key senior economic advisers in his West Wing office in the White House. He also helped create and maintain numerous interdepartmental committees to address different policy issues. Richard Nixon had no compelling desire to manage economic policy in detail and delegated a great deal of decision-making authority on economic policy matters to Shultz. Thus, Shultz, as Secretary of the Treasury and Assistant to the President for Economic Affairs, simultaneously assumed the roles of organizer, advocate, broker, and magistrate.

When Shultz resigned in the spring of 1974, the administration reexamined its economic policy-making arrangements. The Cost of Living Council had played a role in formulating economic policy that went beyond its primary mandate to administer the system of wage and price controls first instituted in August 1971; its authorizing legislation would expire on June 30, 1974, and the Nixon administration had no interest in seeking its extension.[1] Moreover, there were two strong contenders for Shultz's powerful role – William Simon, Shultz's deputy at the Treasury and Nixon's choice to succeed Shultz as Secretary of the Treasury, and Roy Ash, Director of the Office of Management and Budget. Nixon decided against elevating one above the other and appointed Kenneth Rush, Deputy Secretary of State, as Counsellor to the President for Economic Affairs and as chairman of most of the major interdepartmental committees dealing with economic matters, including the Council on Economic Policy (CEP) and the Council on International Economic Policy (CIEP).[2] Rush was in the first months of his new job when the Nixon administration came to its abrupt end.[3]

[1] The Cost of Living Council was established by Executive Order 11615 on August 15, 1971, and continued by Executive Order 11627 on October 15, 1971, until it was terminated on June 30, 1974.

[2] The Council on International Economic Policy was originally created by presidential memorandum on January 19, 1971, and statutorily authorized by the International Economic Policy Act of 1972 (86 Stat. 646). The Council on Economic Policy was created by presidential memorandum on February 2, 1973, "to help ensure better coordination in the formulation and execution of economic policy and to perform such functions relating to economic policy as the President or the Chairman of the Council may from time to time specify." CIEP, which enjoyed its own appropriation, operated with a relatively large staff. The CEP was run by Shultz and a small staff attached to him in his capacity as Assistant to the President for Economic Affairs. Neither CIEP nor the CEP met frequently although Shultz held regular informal meetings with other senior economic officials.

[3] On March 15, 1974, Roy L. Ash had sent the President a memorandum on the organization of economic affairs. It recommended that in considering the structure of eco-

In understanding the White House economic policy apparatus Gerald Ford inherited, it is useful to review the major characteristics of the economic policy organization that existed while Rush was Counsellor to the President for Economic Affairs in the late spring and summer of 1974.

Rush retained Shultz's 8 A.M. meetings at the White House of the top economic policy advisers, known as the "Economic Group." Those attending typically included a representative from the Treasury, the Director of OMB, the Chairman of the CEA, the Executive Director of CIEP, the Administrator of the Federal Energy Administration, and one or more members of Rush's small staff. Thus, the group was largely composed of individuals in the Executive Office of the President.

A member of Rush's staff generally prepared an agenda for Rush, who chaired the meetings. It was not distributed to the attendees; Rush used it to raise certain issues or inform the group of other matters. Rush's executive assistant kept a summary of the meeting, but neither the summary nor minutes went to the participants.

There was no move at this time to consolidate the large number of ad hoc, often cabinet-level, interdepartmental committees dealing with various aspects of economic policy. As late as August 1, Rush was attempting to schedule a meeting with Secretary of the Treasury Simon and Federal Energy Administrator John Sawhill to discuss the mandate of a new energy committee. Moreover, the summaries of the morning meetings, as well as interviews with participants at the meetings, suggest that most serious discussion about substantive economic policy matters occurred outside the daily morning sessions.

The President himself did little aside from making a major economic

nomic policy organization, the President should fit the structure "to the particular capabilities of the new appointee(s)."

The memorandum outlined four options. First, the President could appoint an Assistant to the President for Economic Affairs and a separate Secretary of the Treasury rather than combining the two posts as he had in George Shultz. The Assistant to the President for Economic Affairs would have a professional staff similar to the National Security Council staff and would chair the Troika and the Quadriad.

A second option outlined for the President was to appoint as an Assistant to the President for Economic Affairs either the Secretary of the Treasury, the Chairman of the CEA, or the Director of OMB. The individual so designated would also serve as chairman of the Troika.

A third option was not to appoint anyone as Assistant to the President but simply to designate the Secretary of the Treasury, the Director of OMB, or the Chairman of the CEA as chairman of the Troika and the Quadriad, and for them to assume that function without any White House identification.

A fourth alternative was for the President not to appoint an Assistant for Economic Affairs but to designate a Troika chairman without aggregating "economic functions under him except narrow and routine policy coordination." Ash personally recommended that the President appoint an Assistant for Economic Affairs consistent with the first option.

policy speech on July 25, 1974, and meeting with the Quadriad and a group of businessmen earlier in the month. As Counsellor to the President for Economic Affairs, Rush made certain types of policy decisions on the President's behalf.[4]

Although Rush had previously served as Deputy Secretary of State, the State Department, at the highest levels, participated only marginally in the activities of the rest of the economic policy community. As one administration official acknowledged: "The Department of State was simply not plugged in very well." Frequently in the meeting summaries, statements like "no one knows what Kissinger has done on this" occur. The State Department was not represented at the Economic Group's morning meeting partly because the position of Under Secretary of State for Economic Affairs was vacant. Many at State did not view themselves as part of the economic policy community and suspected attempts to move issues inside the ambit of formal high-level interagency machinery outside State Department control.

In short, Gerald Ford inherited a White House economic policy organization with four characteristics. First, most of the principal economic advisers, particularly those in the Executive Office of the President, met and exchanged information regularly. Second, most interagency activity on economic policy was ad hoc; forming a new committee was the reflex response to a new problem. Third, the Economic Group's morning meetings were informal; advising the President was not a primary purpose, and he remained somewhat detached from the regular flow of economic decision making. Fourth, the Department of State was not integrated into the highest levels of the interagency economic policy machinery.

THE FORD TRANSITION

At 2:00 P.M. on August 9, the day he was sworn in as President, Gerald Ford met with his senior economic advisers and asked them to submit their views and possible alternatives on inflation, unemployment, and real output.[5] The timing – he would not meet with the National Security

---

[4]   For example, the day before President Nixon resigned, a memorandum from the Office of the Counsellor to the President for Economic Affairs informed "attendees of the 8:00 A.M. meeting" that "Mr. Rush has decided that the administration position on the basic deposit insurance will be to seek its increase from the present $20,000 to $35,000 per account."

[5]   These statements were ultimately submitted to the President on August 13. The August 9 meeting included the President, Secretary of the Treasury William E. Simon, Chairman of the Federal Reserve Arthur F. Burns, Counsellor to the President Kenneth Rush, Chairman of the Council of Economic Advisers Herbert Stein, Director of the Office of

Council or the Cabinet until the next day – suggested the importance he would give economic policy during his early administration.

The morning economic group continued their meetings in Kenneth Rush's West Wing office. A number of interdepartmental committees on food policy, utilities, airlines, and other issues also continued to meet. The first thinking about reorganization would come from the transition team advising Ford on how he should structure his staff and put his image on the presidency.

On August 8, 1974, the day Nixon announced he would resign as President, Ford had received a four-page memorandum on transition that requested a series of decisions on personnel and organization. The memo came from Philip Buchen, a long-time personal friend and former law partner of Ford's, a senior member of his vice presidential staff, and soon to become Counsel to the President. The following day the White House announced the formation of a four-member transition team: Ambassador Donald H. Rumsfeld, Secretary of the Interior Rogers C. B. Morton, John O. Marsh, Jr., and Governor William Scranton.[6] The President held his initial meeting with the transition team during the late afternoon and evening of August 9, assigning them to consider how he should organize the White House to address economic policy, domestic policy, press relations and public affairs, personnel matters, and legal issues. Commencing Monday, August 12, the transition team met daily at 7:15 A.M.

From the outset, the team worked on White House–departmental relations. Rogers Morton coordinated a canvass of current department and agency heads and on August 12, sent them letters asking for their views on White House–departmental relations and organization; the letter also asked for descriptions of their interaction with the Domestic Council, the Office of Management and Budget, and the National Security Council. Morton spent considerable time during the week of August 12 discussing organizational issues with cabinet officers and agency heads, reporting his findings to the transition team on Friday, August 16. Predictably, department and agency heads almost unanimously expressed concern; they felt that the Executive Office dominated them,

Management and Budget Roy L. Ash, Chairman-designate of the Council of Economic Advisers Alan Greenspan, Counsellor to the President Robert T. Hartmann, former Pennsylvania Governor William Scranton, and L. William Seidman.

    [6]   A reasonably full and accurate account of the origins of the transition team is found in James M. Naughton, "The Change in Presidents: Plans Began Months Ago," *New York Times* (August 26, 1974), pp. 1, 24. Other useful accounts of the transition team's work are David S. Broder, "Ford Team Seeks Small, Open Staff," *Washington Post* (August 17, 1974); and Godfrey Sperling, Jr., "Ford Method: Quiet Transition," *Christian Science Monitor* (August 16, 1974).

complained that their ideas did not receive a fair hearing at the White House, and often did not know in what form their proposals reached the President.

On Thursday, August 15, the transition team held its second meeting with the President. The themes articulated by transition team members harmonized with much of Ford's thinking – avoiding "isolation of the President by providing a flow of information, access to the President, and a span of control that can be handled while still allowing time for reflection, and an orderly but inclusive decision making process."[7]

They supported a strengthened cabinet departmental system, suggesting greater access to the President for cabinet officers and less White House and OMB involvement in the operational details of many programs. Ford approved the suggestion that he organize his White House around eight major functions with those responsible for the eight areas guaranteed direct access to him. Economic policy, one of the eight areas, was discussed at the August 15 meeting but no decisions about its organization were made.[8]

The following Monday morning, the transition team reviewed the first full draft of the final report to the President. Three themes relevant to economic policy organization emerged during the discussion. The first theme, strongly articulated by Rogers C. B. Morton, was the need to restore the role of cabinet members in the presidential decision-making process. Such a move, Morton argued, would reverse the Nixon pattern that centered power in the White House, with the executive staff serving as intermediaries between department and agency heads and the President. This proposal would require reducing the White House and Executive Office staff.

A second theme concerned the chairmanship and composition of the Troika, traditionally the most important and prestigious interagency group dealing with macroeconomic policy issues.[9] The team agreed that the chairmanship should be moved out of the White House to the Secretary of the Treasury.[10] They also agreed that the Domestic Council and

---

[7]   Transition team briefing document for the President, August 15, 1974.

[8]   The other seven major functions were personnel, congressional relations, public relations, legal advice, and coordination of the budget, domestic policy, and foreign policy.

[9]   Beginning in the Kennedy administration, a group known as the Troika – the Secretary of the Treasury, the Chairman of the Council of Economic Advisers, and the Director of the Bureau of the Budget – assumed responsibility for advising the President on macroeconomic policy issues. When the Troika group was expanded on occasion to include the Chairman of the Board of Governors of the Federal Reserve System, it was referred to as the Quadriad. See Arthur Okun, "The Formulation of National Economic Policy," *Perspectives in Defense Management* (December 1968): 9–12.

[10]   At the time, the Counsellor to the President for Economic Affairs was chairman of all the major cabinet-level interagency committees dealing with economic policy.

the National Security Council should attend Troika meetings as observers, for coordination purposes.

A third theme was a concern over the Nixon administration's capacity to implement policy effectively. The team agreed that any organizational structure adopted by the new administration should reflect a higher priority on insuring that the decisions made were effectively implemented.

The next day the report was completed and presented to the President at his third meeting with the full transition team. The discussion reported the historical background of the current arrangements, then centered on the transition team's recommendations. The Office of the Counsellor to the President for Economic Affairs, they reported, was established to ameliorate a conflict between the Secretary of the Treasury and the Director of OMB. CIEP was established to reduce conflict among the Departments of State and Treasury and the Special Representative for Trade Negotiations. The Council on Economic Policy was designed for George Shultz's special role. The transition team had also discussed the role of the Council of Economic Advisers with Alan Greenspan, the chairman–designate, and reported to the President that Greenspan saw the CEA as "a consulting operation for one client, not 'the spokesman' for economic policy."

The transition team's final report included four principal concepts about economic policy organization. First, the report identified economic policy as a major area on an equal standing with national security, domestic policy, and the budget. Yet, while each of these policy areas had a single coordinating mechanism – the National Security Council, the Domestic Council, and the Office of Management and Budget, respectively – the transition team did not propose a similar entity for coordinating economic policy. Their proposed organizational charts included the Council of Economic Advisers, the Council on Economic Policy, the Council on International Economic Policy, the Troika, and the Quadriad. There was no discussion or recommendation of abolishing any or all of the existing economic policy entities.

A second theme of the report was its recommendation to discontinue the Office of Counsellor to the President for Economic Affairs since nearly everyone contacted by the transition team questioned its effectiveness. Moreover, abolishing the office would help reduce the White House policy making profile and accentuate that of cabinet departments and agencies.

The report also presented the President with the question of whether to divide responsibility for coordinating domestic and international economic policy between individuals responsible for each, or whether to focus responsibility in a single individual, the Secretary of the Treasury. The transition team recommended giving responsibility to one person, primarily because domestic and international economic policy were so closely intertwined that separating them would inevitably produce greater conflict and place a heavier burden on the President.

Finally, the transition team recommended that the Troika and the Quadriad continue to meet (this was somewhat illusory since the Troika and the Quadriad were then meeting infrequently and were not the forums through which most major economic policy decisions were made), with the cabinet secretary and a National Security Council representative as observers. The transition team also suggested that the Quadriad, the cabinet secretary, and the NSC representative discuss and review major economic policy questions before submitting the issues to the President for decision.

Perhaps the most interesting thing about the transition team's report to the President is what it did not recommend. The report did not even raise as an alternative creating a single entity for coordinating all economic policy. Instead, the report debated whether to maintain or reorient existing entities. Moreover, the report was silent on any White House role in coordinating economic policy. It recommended eliminating the Office of the Counsellor to the President for Economic Affairs but not how to absorb its functions. Although the basic thrust of the transition team's advice was clear – rely much more heavily on cabinet department and agency heads and transfer the key chairmanships outside the White House – the details of how the various interagency councils should relate to each other and to the President remained fuzzy.

During the early weeks of his administration, Gerald Ford met frequently with his "senior economic advisers." From the outset, these were collective meetings. Clearly the demands on his time did not allow a large number of one-on-one sessions. Moreover, observing the interchange in group discussions between advisers was congenial to his style, honed during more than two decades as a congressional leader and committee participant.

Kenneth Rush, as Counsellor to the President for Economic Affairs, submitted a briefing paper to the President for each meeting with the senior economic advisers. For the most part, individual departments or agencies prepared the memorandums that accompanied the cover briefing paper. Initially, the group of senior economic advisers included William E. Simon, Secretary of the Treasury, Roy L. Ash, Director of the Office of Management and Budget, Alan Greenspan and/or Herbert Stein, representing the Council of Economic Advisers, Arthur F. Burns, Chairman of the Federal Reserve Board, Kenneth Rush, and L. William Seidman.[11]

---

[11] Seidman had served as Assistant to the Vice President for Administration and was in charge of closing down the Ford vice presidential office.

The frequency of the President's meetings with his senior economic advisers reflected the seriousness of the economic problems facing the country.[12] At the August 20 meeting, the President received the Council of Economic Adviser's outlook for the economy. The most recent consumer price index monthly indicator had increased 0.8 percent with food down 0.9 percent and nonfood items up 1.1 percent. The President was told that wage increases were averaging 10 percent annually, that unit labor costs were up 12 percent, and that the overall outlook was for continued double-digit inflation in the near future. Unemployment, then at 5.3 percent, was expected to break through the 6 percent level sometime early in 1975 and might go as high as 6.5 percent by midyear. Concerned over the deteriorating economy, the President requested a review of a public service employment program at the September 3 meeting of his economic advisers.

Preparation for the meeting reflected both the state of economic policy organization and the President's desire not to exclude major executive branch entities with an interest in the issue. Counsellor Rush's office, which coordinated materials for the meeting, invited all of the senior economic advisers to submit papers on their views. In addition, the Department of Labor was encouraged to provide its views and Under Secretary of Labor Richard Schubert was invited to attend the meeting. Ultimately, the President received five separate papers on the issue.[13] Thus,

During the weekend of August 10 and 11, the President accepted the recommendation made in a joint congressional resolution to hold a Summit Conference on Inflation to mobilize ideas and focus attention on the deteriorating economic situation. The Steering Group for the Conference on Inflation included four congressional representatives, two each from the House of Representatives and the Senate, and four administration representatives, the Secretary of the Treasury, the Director of OMB, the Chairman of the CEA, and Rush.

On August 19, the President asked William Seidman to serve as executive director of the Summit Conference and to organize the conference under the direction of the steering group. On September 4, the White House announced that Kenneth Rush would be the next U.S. Ambassador to France.

[12]   The President met with his senior economic advisers on August 9, 15, 20, 27 and September 3, 17, and 19. In addition the President met with the bipartisan leadership of the Congress on August 20, focusing most of the meeting on the state of the economy. Moreover, the August 26 cabinet meeting was devoted to economic policy including a discussion of budget restraint, the economic outlook, and the role of various cabinet departments and agencies in the Summit Conference on Inflation.

[13]   Herbert Stein submitted a short one and one-half page memorandum outlining his concerns with the basic proposals being made to the President. Arthur Burns submitted a tightly drafted five-page memorandum outlining both advantages and disadvantages of a public service jobs program. William Simon also submitted a five-page memorandum outlining advantages and disadvantages of a public service jobs program and providing the President with his recommendation. The Department of Labor submitted a twenty-six page single-spaced document reflecting the department's views on public service jobs programs in general and proposing a new and expanded public service employment program. Roy Ash submitted a memorandum commenting on some of the other proposals and making a

the system of advising the President provided him with a wide range of views from those in the executive branch most interested in the public service employment question. However, the papers were prepared at different times and varied in specificity. Some of the documents referred to other documents and some did not. Moreover, no single document summarized the different viewpoints and illuminated the trade-offs between competing ideas.

ESTABLISHING THE ECONOMIC POLICY BOARD

During these early weeks the President's thinking on economic policy organization began to take form. He met on at least three occasions (August 15 and 19, and September 13) with Seidman and Rush to discuss the upcoming Conference on Inflation and organizational matters. The President also met with Seidman individually on August 27 to discuss the organization of economic policy making in his administration. In these discussions, Seidman pointed out the problem caused by the large number of interdepartmental committees acting with little overall coordination and argued for an organization that would bring all existing committees under one entity. Rush, somewhat detached and dispassionate after his nomination as Ambassador to France, didn't disagree with the Seidman consolidation proposal. His principal contribution was to urge that the White House have operational responsibility – not a department. Rush recommended that the President appoint an assistant for economic affairs and put him in charge of the new entity.

Thus, during his first weeks in office, the President received two main strands of advice regarding economic policy organization. His transition team urged him to give more power to his cabinet officers; Seidman and Rush urged consolidating policy-making responsibility in a single entity operating out of the White House.

In mid-September, the President asked his White House Chief of Staff, Alexander Haig, to prepare a paper outlining the organizational alternatives for meeting the dual needs to bring cabinet officers to the fore and to coordinate economic policy decisions at the highest levels. Initially, Ford leaned toward dividing the responsibilities between Simon and Seidman, making Simon the spokesman and Seidman the operator of the coordinating mechanism. He specifically instructed Haig to develop a plan that would divide the "key duties" controlling "the formu-

proposal for extending unemployment insurance as an alternative to public service employment. Ash also recommended that, if the President were to approve public service employment, the program be limited to the long-term unemployed who had exhausted their unemployment insurance benefits.

lation and execution of economic policy" between Simon and Seidman. "Simon would be given those duties controlling policy development and Seidman would have coordinating responsibility for economic affairs as an Assistant to the President."[14]

Subsequently, Haig successfully persuaded the President that if it were to work, someone had to be in charge. They agreed that the one person should be Simon. Before formally sending the President the requested memorandum, Haig showed Seidman the paper and outlined the reasons for his recommendation. He explained that while Simon would be chairman, Seidman's White House assignment and access to the President would give him approximately equal power.

On September 19, Haig sent the President the memorandum stressing that it was "very difficult" to divide responsibility for policy development and policy coordination because frequently "the coordinating responsibility is the power lever that guides the formulation of the policy itself." He concluded that "both Seidman and Simon will have to exercise an unusual degree of cooperation to make the system work."[15] The memorandum contained little organizational philosophy or description of how a new entity might be structured. Instead, the memorandum dealt largely with personal relationships and the respective roles of the Secretary of the Treasury and the President's Assistant for Economic Affairs.

The President approved the organizational option tying "Simon and Seidman together as one unit where Simon is the key economic adviser and Seidman, under Simon's direction, provides the coordination of policy development and implementation." He further directed that Simon and Seidman should work with Haig in developing the implementing documents and public announcement.

On September 22, with the concluding meetings of the Summit Conference on Inflation less than a week away, Haig informed Simon and Seidman that the President had decided to create a new economic policy entity, that Simon would be its chairman, and that Seidman would be the President's assistant for economic affairs and executive director of the new entity to insure proper coordination among it, the White House, and cabinet departments and agencies.

That afternoon, Simon, Seidman, and their assistants met at the Treasury to discuss how best to implement the President's decisions. Seidman suggested, and the others quickly agreed, that the existing array of interdepartmental entities responsible for economic policy issues was both unnecessary and confusing, and that the new structure should rationalize the existing arrangements. The senior economic advisers had frequently

---

[14] Haig memorandum to the President, Economic Organization, September 19, 1974.
[15] *Ibid.*

discussed the need to consolidate the fragmented structure of economic committees; nearly everyone agreed on its desirability, including most subcabinet officials. On August 2, 1974, Jack Bennett, Under Secretary of the Treasury for Monetary Affairs, had sent Simon a memorandum noting that "the extent of overlaps in the existing committees – some required by law and some not – is now so great that a vast amount of time is spent in 'turfsmanship' arguments over where particular subjects will be discussed and considerable difficulty is encountered in scheduling the time of the senior officials who are simultaneously involved in many of the committees. I doubt there is any one who can recite from memory a complete list of such committees."[16] Simon and Seidman also agreed that if the new arrangement were to succeed, it would require a clear, unambiguous, and broad mandate from the President in the form of an executive order.[17]

The provisions in the executive order ultimately signed by the President on September 30, 1974, reveal much of the philosophy of the President and his advisers.

The new entity was given three broad responsibilities: (1) to "provide advice to the President concerning all aspects of national and international economic policy;" (2) to "oversee the formulation, coordination, and implementation of all economic policy of the United States;" and (3) to "serve as the focal point for economic policy decision-making."[18] This unusually broad and comprehensive mandate was designed to provide the basis for consolidating responsibility in a single entity. Moreover, for statutory bodies such as the Council on International Economic Policy (CIEP), the Council on Wage and Price Stability (CWPS), and for the National Advisory Council on International Monetary and Financial Policies (NAC), and the President's Committee on East–West Trade

[16] Memorandum from Jack Bennett, Under Secretary of the Treasury for Monetary Affairs, to William E. Simon, August 2, 1974.

At the September 22 meeting, Simon requested his staff to prepare a list of high-level interagency committees dealing with economic policy. The list he received the following day included eighteen committees. Those who prepared the list cautioned that there was no way of knowing if the list were comprehensive.

The Council of Economic Advisers' report to the President on their activities during 1973 noted that "the Council and its professional staff served on more than 35 interagency groups reviewing economic problems and coordinating policy." *Economic Report of the President 1974* (Washington, D.C.: GPO, 1974), p. 238.

[17] The Council on Economic Policy, established in February 1973 by Richard Nixon, was formally created by presidential memorandum, generally considered less prestigious than an executive order. The September 19 Haig memorandum to the President had referred to developing "the necessary implementing memorandum and public announcement" although there was no explicit discussion of whether the new arrangements should be established by executive order or by presidential memorandum.

[18] Executive Order 11808, Section 3.

Policy, the executive order stipulated that the Secretary of the Treasury would serve as chairman and the Assistant to the President for Economic Affairs as deputy chairman. Simon and Seidman also agreed that all non-statutory committees presently dealing with economic policy issues would be responsible to the new board. Seidman would serve as the liaison with the soon-to-be-established President's Labor–Management Committee and with the productivity commission.

The executive order also delineated the division of responsibilities between Simon and Seidman. Simon, as Secretary of the Treasury, would serve as chairman of the new entity and "act as the principal spokesman for the Executive Branch on matters of economic policy."[19] This "spokesman" designation was not included in the initial draft of the executive order but was added at Simon's request with Seidman's agreement. Seidman, as Assistant to the President for Economic Affairs, would "be the Executive Director of the Board and of the Executive Committee, and, as such, [would] be responsible for coordinating the implementation of economic policy and providing liaison with the Presidential staff and with other Government activities."[20]

Initially, drafts of the public announcement referred to the establishment of "an expanded Council on Economic Policy." By the end of the week, however, the President and his advisers, anxious to distinguish it from the past and emphasize its distinctive character, decided to name it the Economic Policy Board.

This executive order also clarified two structural issues – the composition of an executive committee and the relationship of the Federal Reserve to the new board. The full board, which included virtually the entire cabinet, was considered inappropriate as a forum for considering the great majority of economic policy issues.[21] An executive committee was created to provide a manageable forum and to avoid excessively large

[19] Executive Order 11808, Section 3.
[20] Executive Order 11808, Section 5.
[21] The executive order specified the following officials as members:
    Secretary of the Treasury, Chairman
    Assistant to the President for Economic Affairs, Executive Director
    Secretary of State
    Secretary of the Interior
    Secretary of Agriculture
    Secretary of Commerce
    Secretary of Labor
    Secretary of Health, Education, and Welfare
    Secretary of Housing and Urban Development
    Secretary of Transportation
    Director, Office of Management and Budget
    Chairman, Council of Economic Advisers
    Executive Director, Council on International Economic Policy
Certain departments and agencies, although not formally members of the EPB, participated

meetings. A primary criterion for membership on the Executive Committee was a legitimate interest in a broad range of economic policy issues. Equally important in selecting executive committee members was the roster of current personnel.

There was unanimous agreement that Treasury, OMB, and the CEA, along with the Assistant to the President for Economic Affairs, should form the core of the group. The desire to draw domestic and international economic policy closer together led to agreement that the Executive Committee should include a member of the international economic policy community. William Eberle, the Special Representative for Trade Negotiations (STR) and newly appointed Executive Director of CIEP, well respected by his colleagues and a regular attendee at the morning economic group meetings, was a logical appointment to the Executive Committee. Some, however, argued that including the Department of State on the Executive Committee would help solve the problem of inadequate coordination with State. The stumbling block was who would represent State. The heavy demands on Secretary Kissinger's time and his relative lack of interest in economic matters meant he was unlikely to attend executive committee meetings. The position of Under Secretary of State for Economic Affairs, the next most logical choice, was vacant. Thus, there was ultimately a consensus to include the Executive Director of CIEP on the five-member Executive Committee.

Simon, Seidman, and the other senior economic advisers were anxious to preserve the independence of the Federal Reserve while insuring that fiscal and monetary policies did not work at cross purposes due to an isolation of the Federal Reserve from the President's advisers in the executive branch. Initially, they decided to designate the Chairman of the Federal Reserve Board as an ex officio member of the EPB and its Executive Committee. Ultimately, to insure the Federal Reserve's independence, the executive order stipulated that "the Chairman of the Board of Governors of the Federal Reserve System is invited to attend meetings of the Board" and "to attend meetings of the Executive Committee."[22]

The beginning of a presidential administration is frequently marked

from time to time in its deliberations and were members of some EPB task forces. This was true of the Departments of Justice and Defense, the Environmental Protection Agency, and the Federal Energy Administration, among others.

In February 1976, the President designated three additional members of the Board: Rogers C. B. Morton, Counsellor to the President; the Administrator of the Small Business Administration; and the Special Representative for Trade Negotiations. Presidential Orders of February 3, 12, and 13, respectively. On February 2, 1976, the President signed Executive Order 11903, amending Executive Order 11808 to provide that: "The President may, from time to time, designate additional members to serve on the Board."

[22] Executive Order 11808, Sections 2 and 4. The executive order also established the position of Executive Director and specified that the Executive Committee should meet daily.

by institutional innovation. It is significant that the Economic Policy Board was created early when the policy process was fluid, and when the executive branch was prepared to adapt to a new president and a new style – for a new coordinating council inevitably meets resistance from those who do not want to be coordinated.[23]

Each new institutional innovation is in large part a product of its time and of a unique set of circumstances. The Economic Policy Board was no exception.[24] Three crucial factors helped establish the Economic Policy Board in September 1974. First, the creation of a new and visible cabinet-level institution to advise the President was a concrete response at a time of serious economic crisis. It demonstrated presidential interest and highlighted the importance he attached to economic policy.[25]

Second, the composition of the new board and the appointment of the Secretary of the Treasury as its chairman reflected the President's desire to return cabinet members to a greater role as presidential advisers. It demonstrated his commitment to incorporating departments and agen-

---

[23]   As one participant later reflected:

This was a period when things were changing so fast. There was a new president and that helped in making a major change. After all, this [creating the EPB] dumped a whole bunch of people out before they even woke up to the fact that it had happened. If you had tried this in the middle of an administration you would have had the damndest bureaucratic fight in history. It was really the equivalent of a major reorganization which took place so fast that the normal bureaucratic ability to react and start a fight didn't happen. This was particularly true because there was a new president and it seemed to come from his close advisers. So nobody stood up to fight. This was one of those rare times you could get that done.

Not only was there a change in the Oval Office, but there were also a number of other changes in the front ranks of economic policy advisers – Alan Greenspan was new as Chairman of the CEA, Seidman was new as Assistant to the President for Economic Affairs, and James Lynn would soon replace Roy Ash as Director of OMB. Within a matter of months there were also changes at Labor, Commerce, STR, CIEP, and two new members of the CEA.

[24]   It is interesting to contrast the factors motivating the creation of the Economic Policy Board with those prompting the creation of the National Security Council in 1947. Paul Y. Hammond has delineated three: (1) an interest in the British Committee of Imperial Defense and its apparent insulation from politics; (2) a desire to counterbalance a single strong department or personality; and (3) a desire to mold presidential behavior and provide more systematic consideration of policy than the disorderly pattern that characterized the Roosevelt administration. Paul Y. Hammond, "The National Security Council as a Device for Interdepartmental Coordination: An Interpretation and Appraisal," *American Political Science Review* 54 (December 1960):906.

[25]   The serious deterioration of the economy was reflected in the September 12 wholesale price index (WPI) report: Wholesale prices rose 3.9 percent in August, a pace exceeded only once during the post–World War II years. In July wholesale prices had risen 3.7 percent and during the most recent three-month period the WPI had risen at an annual rate of 37.3 percent.

cies more fully in presidential decision making. Creating the board redressed some of the morale problems of cabinet officers who felt that the Nixon administration had excluded them from much of the White House decision-making process.

Third, creating the Economic Policy Board represented an attempt to consolidate responsibility for all economic policy in one body. The widespread perception that the existing structure of economic policy committees was excessively fragmented contributed to the interest in and mandate of the new board.

THE OCTOBER 1974 ECONOMIC PROGRAM

The President included his announcement of the Economic Policy Board in his remarks at the conclusion of the Summit Conference on Inflation and simultaneously announced that the new board would work with him in formulating an economic program that he would present to the Congress within the next ten days.[26] Over the weekend, Seidman developed a schedule and assignments for the coming week. The Executive Committee met Monday morning, approved the schedule and assignments, scheduled the first meeting of the full board later in the week, scheduled another with the newly created Labor–Management Committee, discussed the issue of confidentiality in executive committee meetings, and considered follow-up activities after the President announced the program.

On Tuesday the Executive Committee reviewed options papers on budget alternatives, food, public service employment, and energy. The daily pattern for the remainder of the week was for the Executive Committee to hold two meetings of approximately two hours each followed by a two to three hour meeting with the President. The scope of the program, ranging from macroeconomic and tax policy to energy and food policy, involved the interests of most cabinet departments. The Executive Committee sessions, including the meetings with the President, were generally large and involved representatives from all departments and agencies with an interest in the issue under consideration. The meeting of the full board also provided an opportunity for input from virtually the entire cabinet.

The result of this intensive group effort was a ten-point program with thirty-one separate initiatives. Many within and outside the administration observed that it looked more like a laundry list than a well-devel-

---

[26] Gerald R. Ford, "Remarks Concluding the Summit Conference on Inflation," September 28, 1974, *Public Papers of the Presidents, 1974* (Washington, D.C.: GPO, 1975), pp. 205–210.

oped and philosophically coherent program.[27] Whatever the substantive merits or limitations of the proposals, the process used in developing the program had three important effects on the launching of the new board.

First, the President's commitment to give his program to Congress in ten days made board members work closely together from the outset, rapidly learning each other's strengths and weaknesses and the Executive Committee's procedures. Second, developing a large number of presidential proposals let the group become accustomed to the new President and observe his decision-making style. The process revealed that he was comfortable with a participatory system that operated on inclusion, not exclusion. Third, the President's exclusive use of Economic Policy Board meetings for making the decisions involved in his first major policy address to the Congress signaled the executive branch that the EPB was his economic policy-making body.

THE EARLY PERIOD

During the first months of the EPB's operation, executive committee meetings were generally restricted to principals with occasional attendance by subcabinet officials who had particular expertise in the subject matter under discussion. The agendas, distributed a day in advance, generally contained three or more items for discussion; meetings lasted approximately forty-five minutes.[28] Whether nonexecutive committee departments and agencies participated varied considerably. For example, Albert Rees, the director of the new Council on Wage and Price Stability, participated regularly because of frequent discussions on inflation. The State Department did not attend executive committee meetings frequently.[29]

The first weeks are a time of testing for any new entity. The Economic Policy Board was no exception. Departments and agencies looked for

[27] One observer concluded: "The speech showed that the new coordinating board could shuffle suggestions deftly but that it had not learned yet how to shape policy." Daniel J. Balz, "Juice and Coffee and the GNP – The Men Who Meet in the Morning," *National Journal* 8 (April 3, 1976):427.

[28] Compared to later periods, executive committee meetings during the first months took up more items per meeting. See Table 1, Chapter 3.

[29] The State Department, however, maintained an interest in the work of the EPB. Concerned that the Executive Committee would discuss issues of vital interest to the State Department without having notified the department that the issue was scheduled for consideration, Deputy Secretary of State Robert Ingersoll worked out an arrangement with William Eberle, Executive Director of CIEP and a member of the EPB Executive Committee, whereby Eberle's office would send a copy of the next day's executive committee agenda each afternoon to Ingersoll's office.

signs of its influence with the President. Political appointees and permanent civil servants assessed its ability to resolve disputes successfully, to maintain access to the President, and to get support from their own department's or agency's leading officials.

The EPB made a second major effort in policy formulation during this testing period: the economic proposals contained in the President's 1975 State of the Union Message. Their development is described in Chapter 4. Unlike President Ford's first economic policy program, developed under the pressure of a ten-day deadline, the Economic Policy Board formulated, discussed, and debated recommendations for stimulating the economy for several weeks. Again, the EPB's reputation benefitted from the prominent role the President gave economic policy and his reliance on the Board for developing his economic proposals.

A crucial factor in the EPB's viability during this formative period was the relationship between Simon and Seidman. Each was cautious, almost wary, of the other during the early weeks as organizational arrangements and roles were being sorted out. Seidman had known Gerald Ford for years as a constituent in his congressional district and had worked on Ford's vice presidential staff as his Assistant for Administration. The President had known Simon only in his official capacities at the Treasury during the previous two years. Simon's relationship with Ford and his White House staff had not yet stabilized. Likewise, Seidman, while more confident in his relationship with the President, faced some uncertainties regarding his roles on the White House staff and his relationships with other senior officials. Both Simon and Seidman were conscious of the speculation regarding who would emerge as the dominant force in the EPB. Three factors contributed to a close, noncompetitive relationship between them.

First, the objectives that both Simon and Seidman prized most were mutually compatible. Simon relished the role of advocate and public spokesman. Because of his persistence, the executive order creating the EPB included a sentence designating him as the "principal spokesman" for the administration on economic policy matters. Because Seidman agreed – and maintained a low public profile – he soon convinced Simon that he was not interested in challenging him for the role of the administration's "Mr. Outside." At the same time, Seidman quickly established operational control of the EPB apparatus. From the first meeting of the Executive Committee, it was Seidman's office that sent out the agendas, told people when and where the meetings would be held, kept and distributed the minutes and papers, and developed the Board's procedural rules. Had Simon wanted to contest his control, Seidman later reflected, "he would have had to order us not to do it. And he wasn't in a position to do that. After all it [the executive order] said that I was the Executive

Director and therefore I moved in and ran it. There was not much he could do about it unless he wanted to directly create a battle."

Just as Seidman was not interested in serving as the administration's chief economic spokesman, Simon was not interested in controlling the EPB's operations. During the early weeks Simon and Seidman were the only executive committee members accompanied to the meetings by an aide. Subsequently, satisfied that the process was fair, Simon agreed that he would be governed by the same rules that applied to other members and no longer brought an aide with him. And so a mutually satisfactory division of roles emerged, with Simon as chairman, advocate, principal spokesman, and "Mr. Outside," and Seidman as executive director, honest broker, process manager, and "Mr. Inside."

Second, trust was a necessity, not a luxury. After the EPB's creation, the press was filled with reports that Simon was out of favor at the White House and was one of the cabinet officers on the way out. Simon initially assumed that Seidman had started the rumors, but after extensive checking, confirmed that was not the case. Simon needed friends and allies in the White House; Seidman needed Simon's support and cooperation for the EPB's success. They agreed to have no secrets from each other, and over time, developed a genuine trust.

Finally, their relationship benefitted from the fact that they grew to like one another. Friendship replaced need as the bond that held them together.

Seidman, aware that the EPB could not succeed if Treasury or any other member agency dominated it, treated all members alike, including Simon, on procedural and substantive matters. Simon respected Seidman's position and shared his interest in seeing the system work. He did not attempt to control the agenda, either of the daily executive committee meetings or the weekly meetings with the President. Moreover, he insisted that the Treasury bring major policy issues to the Board, even when it previously would have settled them unilaterally or through a Treasury-dominated interagency group. The smooth working relationship between Simon and Seidman, coupled with the fact that, over time, member departments and agencies became convinced the EPB was not a Treasury-dominated body, helped the EPB solidify its role within the administration.

INCREASING INSTITUTIONALIZATION

During the early months of 1975, a number of procedural refinements and innovations increasingly institutionalized the EPB system.[30] A

---

[30] These procedural innovations are described more fully in Chapter 3.

weekly agenda sent to all board members replaced the daily agenda sent to executive committee members. Special sessions were instituted to address issues requiring more extended discussion than the daily morning meetings allowed.

The EPB expanded the briefing papers it sent the President in preparation for their meetings with him to include a weekly report on board activities and a weekly economic fact sheet. It developed six-month and three-month work plans to encourage more attention to longer-term studies and to provide a framework for anticipating problems and issues. It instituted formal Economic Policy Decision Memorandums (EPDMs) to augment and improve the implementation of presidential decisions. Finally, the decision memorandums submitted to the President were more tightly written, making the options more precise and identifying departments and agencies as supporting particular options.[31]

By arrangement, three other major White House coordinating bodies attended the daily executive committee meeting: the executive directors of the Domestic Council and the Energy Resources Council and a representative of the National Security Council.[32]

THE DEPARTMENT OF STATE AND THE EPB

Creating the Economic Policy Board did little initially to bridge the gap between the Department of State and the rest of the economic policy community. Appointing the Secretary of the Treasury chairman of the EPB confirmed a widespread feeling in the Department of State that the Economic Policy Board was a Treasury-dominated body, and not a forum where the State Department's viewpoint would receive a fair hearing. Moreover, the Secretary of State, unlike most of his cabinet colleagues, already had daily access to the President; the Economic Policy Board, then, was neither a necessary nor important means of making the State

---

[31] Most early memorandums defined options broadly and agencies revealed their positions only verbally in the meetings with the President.

[32] The daily EPB executive committee meeting served as the focal point for exchanging information and coordinating activities of the major White House policy bodies.

On January 28, 1975, Donald Rumsfeld, White House Chief of Staff, sent the following memorandum to the executive directors of the Domestic Council and the Energy Resources Council: "The President has decided that to achieve proper coordination, it would be desirable for you to attend the meetings of the Economic Policy Board's Executive Committee."

A similar memorandum, dated February 22, 1975, instructed Seidman that Secretary of Commerce Morton (Chairman of the Energy Resources Council) and Frank Zarb (Executive Director of the ERC) were to be regularly included in "the Economic/Energy Meetings with the President."

Department's views known to the President on major economic policy issues.[33]

Secretary Kissinger's address to the World Food Conference in November 1974 raised the first major difficulty between the State Department and the rest of the economic policy community since the EPB's creation. Substantively, agencies disagreed strongly over the level of U.S. food aid, the advisability of proposing new international committees and coordinating bodies, the establishment and structure of world grain reserves, the level of U.S. contributions to international cooperative agricultural research, multiyear planning, and tying oil funds and recycling to food purchases. Procedurally, economic and food policy makers objected to what they considered an attempt by the State Department to make policy in isolation.

It was not until October 31, 1974, that EPB executive committee members finally secured copies of the draft Kissinger keynote speech scheduled for delivery on November 2. The morning executive committee meeting, expanded to include representatives from State, Agriculture, STR, and the NSC, clarified several differences over the tone and content of the speech.[34] Ultimately, the principals met with the President in the Cabinet Room while a "Deputies" meeting in the Roosevelt Room discussed refinements in the speech's less controversial parts. The meeting with the President resolved many of the substantive differences but did not address the procedural concerns; they surfaced again in the follow-up to the Food Conference.

On November 6, Secretary Kissinger sent the President a memorandum recommending the establishment of a cabinet-level interdepartmental International Food Review Group (IFRG) to assume responsibility

---

[33] As one knowledgeable State Department official candidly explained:

My impression was that the Enders–Kissinger view, particularly Enders, was that the EPB was a bad forum for foreign policy. The best way to deal with it was to ignore it. This was relatively easy when Kissinger was wearing two hats. He could use the NSC channel to go directly to the President and virtually ignore the interdepartmental machinery. Chuck Robinson was of the view that the State Department should participate. Once Kissinger lost his other hat [Assistant to the President for National Security Affairs], then the option of going through the NSC was not available, or at least not so easy ... It was my impression that there was not really full cooperation until Enders left.

Thomas Enders was Assistant Secretary of State for Economic and Business Affairs. Charles Robinson was appointed Under Secretary of State for Economic Affairs in early 1975. Enders was appointed Ambassador to Canada in the fall of that year.

[34] They included Secretary Butz, Assistant Secretary Yuetter, and Deputy Assistant Secretary Bell from USDA; Deputy Secretary Ingersoll and Assistant Secretary Enders from State; Deputy STR Malmgren; and Deputy Assistant to the President Brent Scowcroft and Robert Hormats from the NSC.

for follow-up to the World Food Conference. The proposed IFRG would be chaired by the Secretary of State with the Secretary of Agriculture as vice chairman. The group would "coordinate its recommendations, as they relate to U.S. agriculture and trade policy with the EPB Executive Committee." Senior administration economic officials viewed the Kissinger proposal as diffusing the concentration of economic policy-making responsibility in a single entity. Moreover, they saw in the proposal evidence that the State Department was unwilling to cooperate fully with other executive departments and agencies in formulating overall international economic policies.

Half a dozen leading economic officials sent the President a joint memorandum two days later recommending that he *not* establish the proposed committee and arguing that the Economic Policy Board with full participation by the State Department should handle the follow-up to the World Food Conference. Ultimately, the President did approve the new committee. Its operation did little to reassure the economic policy community.[35]

During the first eight months of the EPB's operation, the State Department was invited to and attended EPB executive committee meetings as issues involving its interests were scheduled for consideration, but the overriding concern with domestic issues meant less attention for international economic issues until the spring of 1975.

That spring brought a major foreign and economic policy issue – the U.S. response to Third World demands for a new international economic order – virtually guaranteeing a clash within the executive branch. The catalyst came in the form of Secretary Kissinger's speech at Kansas City on May 13.

Over the weekend of May 10–11, 1975, with many key administration economic officials out of Washington, William Seidman received a draft of Secretary Kissinger's remarks for his comment. He distributed copies at the Monday morning executive committee meeting and asked members to comment as soon as possible so that he could transmit them to the State Department.

Reaction against the speech's tone and some of the substance was swift, particularly from Treasury and the CEA. Late that afternoon, Seidman convened a meeting of the major parties with Thomas Enders, Assistant Secretary of State for Economic and Business Affairs, who was responsible for the final preparations on the speech. The meeting, held in Seidman's White House office, lasted for almost two hours and suc-

---

[35] The cabinet-level IFRG met only twice during the following eight months, and ultimately a grain reserves policy emerged only after the EPB Executive Committee raised the issue in the spring of 1975.

ceeded in reaching agreement on language revisions satisfying the major parties on most of the issues.[36]

But resentment remained against the practice of developing policy outside "the system." At the conclusion of a meeting on a different subject, three executive committee members informed the President they were dissatisfied with the lack of adequate consultation on Kissinger's international economic policy speeches. The President requested a copy of the recommended changes the Executive Committee had sent to Kissinger and subsequently instructed his Chief of Staff, Donald Rumsfeld, to sort out any differences that remained unresolved. The major specific concerns had already been resolved by the revisions, but the main problem — resentment over procedure — remained. EPB members had three objections: (1) receiving draft copies so close to the delivery date of the speech; (2) requests for responses from individual departments, not from the group (Much of the discussion between Enders, who coordinated the preparation of the speeches for Kissinger, and his counterparts in other departments and agencies was bilateral, causing some to claim that they felt they were being played off against each other); and (3) little if any collective discussion of major themes or specific proposals, unlike the process for developing most domestic economic policy.

Less than two weeks later, it happened again. By Friday, May 23, several executive committee members had obtained various drafts of Kissinger's May 28 address to the Organization for Economic Cooperation and Development (OECD) in Paris and objected to announcements of new policy initiatives that had not been thoroughly discussed within the administration. A "principals only" session of the Executive Committee that morning decided to take the issue to the President and a meeting was scheduled for the following morning.

At noon, Seidman and Porter discussed the situation with Enders and Scowcroft. They agreed that Seidman would give Enders an outline of EPB objections to the speech. Seidman and Enders would handle minor differences with major differences covered at a meeting the following afternoon that would include Simon, Kissinger, Seidman, Enders, Scowcroft, Parsky, and Bennett. Any unresolved differences would go to the President. Seidman then postponed the meeting with the President.

On Saturday morning, May 24, Seidman convened a meeting in his White House office including Enders, Charles Cooper and Gerald Parsky from Treasury, Alan Greenspan, Labor Secretary John T. Dunlop, Don-

---

[36] The May 12 meeting included Seidman, Alan Greenspan, Assistant Secretary of the Treasury for International Affairs Gerald Parsky, Enders, and EPB Executive Secretary Roger Porter.

ald Ogilvie of OMB, Porter, and himself to review the speech and identify basic areas of disagreement. There were six areas of basic disagreement: Some concerned the tone and attitude conveyed by the speech's
language; some concerned specific proposals. During the afternoon, Kissinger, Simon, Seidman, Scowcroft, and their aides resolved most of the
differences and agreed to review the general thrust of the speech with the
President on Monday.

Following the meeting, Kissinger called Seidman and expressed distress at the way the whole process was working. Seidman suggested that
it might help if the Department of State attended EPB executive committee meetings regularly. Kissinger agreed that the State Department should
participate fully and become a member of the EPB Executive Committee.

A new draft of the speech was completed by early afternoon on Sun-
day, May 25, 1975, and Seidman sent a copy to the President at Camp
David. Simon, Seidman, Lynn, Parsky, Bennett, Cooper, Zarb, and Porter then met in Treasury Secretary Simon's office, reviewed the new draft
line by line, and prepared a memorandum outlining what relatively few
major differences remained.

The Monday morning meeting with the President lasted over an hour
and included the first full and candid discussion with the President and
his advisers on the administration's approach to the new economic order
and response to the less developed countries' demands. At the outset of
the meeting, Kissinger acknowledged some problems in the speech clearance process, adding that he had discussed these problems with Bill Seidman and that they had agreed on a better procedure for handling such
issues in the future.[37]

On June 3, 1975, Seidman sent the President a memorandum on
"Economic Policy Organization" recommending that the EPB Executive
Committee include the Department of State and the Department of Com-
merce.

> The need for more effective international economic policy devel-
> opment and coordination is recognized by all of the major partici-
> pants. I have met with the present Executive Committee mem-
> bers – Secretary Simon, Jim Lynn, Alan Greenspan, and Secretary
> Dunlop – to discuss ways of improving international economic
> policy development. I have also met with Secretary Kissinger to
> discuss procedural improvements.
>
> All parties agree that it is essential that the Department of State

[37] The meeting with the President included Secretaries Kissinger, Simon, Dunlop, and
Morton, James Lynn, Arthur Burns, Alan Greenspan, Frank Zarb, Robert Hartmann, Donald Rumsfeld, James Cannon, John Marsh, Ron Nessen, Max Friedersdorf, Richard Cheney, Brent Scowcroft, William Seidman, Roger Porter, and Robert Hormats.

be more integrally involved in both the work and operations of the Economic Policy Board and that the most important adjustment to accomplish this is to make the Secretary of State a member of the EPB Executive Committee. Secretary Kissinger concurs with this recommendation and has indicated that he will insure full cooperation and participation by the Department of State in the work of the EPB Executive Committee.

In my meetings with the other Executive Committee members we also discussed other possible additions to the Committee. In view of the significant involvement of the Department of Commerce in both domestic and international economic policy issues it was agreed to recommend to you that the Secretary of Commerce be made a member of the Executive Committee.

The President concurred; an executive order added the Secretaries of State, Commerce, and Labor to the Executive Committee.[38]

THE SECOND PHASE:
THE ENLARGED EXECUTIVE COMMITTEE

Adding the Secretaries of State, Labor, and Commerce to the EPB Executive Committee marked a new stage in its evolution. Previously, the Executive Committee primarily consisted of representatives from the Executive Office of the President and the Secretary of the Treasury.[39] Departments and agencies were included in considering issues directly affecting their interests. But the addition of three cabinet secretaries – first Labor, and later State and Commerce – provided more consistent representation of departmental views. Expanding the Executive Committee's membership also changed somewhat the character of the group, although "principals only" meetings remained relaxed and candid.

Adding the Secretary of State to the Executive Committee did not eliminate all procedural issues between the State Department and other

[38]   Adding the Secretary of Labor simply formalized an arrangement that had existed since February when John T. Dunlop became Secretary of Labor. Dunlop, a Harvard economist and former Director of the Cost of Living Council, had told the President he would accept the nomination as Secretary of Labor only if he were made a member of the EPB Executive Committee. The President readily agreed; EPB executive committee members were enthusiastic. Dunlop was already familiar with the workings of the EPB through his occasional attendance at executive committee meetings when issues relating to the President's Labor–Management Committee and the National Commission on Productivity were under discussion.

[39]   In this sense it resembled a slightly modified version of the Troika, although it met more frequently and operated under a much more regularized set of procedures than the Troika ever did.

members of the EPB, but it resulted immediately in improved participation and cooperation from State Department officials. Likewise, Kissinger publicly displayed a new attitude. Kissinger, meeting July 24, 1975, at the State Department with congressional representatives on his forthcoming September United Nations address on economic policy issues, stated that he was coordinating the preparation of his address within the executive branch through the EPB Executive Committee.[40]

In part, this new cooperation resulted from what one official referred to as "the feeling of now being part of the team."[41] Personnel changes also played a role. Charles Robinson, the recently appointed Under Secretary of State for Economic Affairs, was new to his job and willing to participate in the EPB's deliberations, as was the new Assistant Secretary of State for Economic Affairs Joseph Greenwald.

Adding State, Labor, and Commerce strengthened the EPB's position as a major policy conduit to the President. One cabinet member observed:

> It was really quite remarkable. When you get the State Department, at the highest levels, dealing with the Board where heretofore they wouldn't talk with anybody but the Treasury Department and God,

[40] Memorandum of Meeting at State Department, July 24, 1975.
[41] Another State Department official acknowledged:

I will say honestly that I had a lot of reservations about the EPB, in part because of misconceptions: that it was the CIEP in another guise, that it was reaching out for areas that were not previously subject to interagency coordination, that it was another form of bureaucracy. Those were perceptions that turned out to be wrong. But I think that there were a lot of reservations about it at the beginning, but they disappeared over time.

Once we were members it was different. I think probably it was from that point that things worked better because I think we felt more a part of the process than we did earlier. We were really outsiders before that.

Two major procedural questions that persisted were arrangements for interagency consultation on commodity matters and the relationship between the State Department and the Office of the Special Representative for Trade Negotiations. Indicative of the us–them attitude that prevailed during the period before State was added to the EPB Executive Committee was an internal NSC memorandum on the relationship between the Special Representative for Trade Negotiations and the White House:

There is nothing in STR's operating mandate which connects it with the Economic Policy Board. Ambassador Dent's predecessors have reported directly to the President, as called for in the governing Executive Order, through normal White House staffing. Seidman moved into the vacuum which developed during the period in which the two top jobs in STR remained unfilled, however, and Dent seems to be accepting the EPB as his channel to the President. This could come back to haunt STR and the rest of us in the foreign policy community. Sooner or later this issue will have to be joined – but on substantive rather than purely procedural matter [sic]. [NSC memorandum 3691.]

that is quite an accomplishment. We got the commodity policies into the EPB, the international energy issues, the whole North–South dialogue. The Treasury Department was happy – which it had never been happy to do before – to put tax policy into the EPB and international monetary matters, and trade matters and the STR. We had the whole range of domestic and international economic issues in one forum for the first time in history.

Refining procedures continued throughout the remainder of 1975 and 1976. Memorandums detailing decisions of the President at EPB meetings, identifying follow-up responsibility, and establishing deadlines for completing such actions, were instituted in June 1975. In late December 1975, Seidman and Frank Zarb, Executive Director of the Energy Resources Council, agreed that the overlap of issues and membership justified holding a joint EPB/ERC executive committee meeting once a week at the time of one of the regular EPB executive committee meetings.

During 1976, more and more issues were handled through options papers sent to the President without also holding a meeting with him. This occurred for several reasons. The President and top administration officials had even less time during an election year. Moreover, the administration's basic policies and economic strategy had been thoroughly discussed and were now in place. Finally, the quality of the papers continued to improve, making it feasible to rely more frequently on them alone. The President thus met less freqeuntly with his Economic Policy Board but still personally made the decisions on a broad range of economic policy issues.

In addition to formulating new policy proposals for presidential consideration, the EPB also became the forum for resolving disputes between departments. More and more, departments brought matters to the EPB to generate support or secure approval for a policy action. Over time, the President's reliance on the EPB for developing his economic policies and the EPB's own procedures – characterized by "a sense of due process," according to one participant – gave the Economic Policy Board a strong role in the Ford administration.[42]

[42] For example, after the Murphy Commission Report on the Organization of the Government for the Conduct of Foreign Policy was released in June 1975, the Office of Management and Budget solicited agency views on the report. On the crucial recommendation to enlarge the jurisdiction of the National Security Council "to include major issues of international economic policymaking," OMB reported to the President that outside of the Department of Defense and the Department of State (whose views had not yet been received), "the other agencies argue for continuation of a strong Economic Policy Board as the forum for the consideration of those issues." Memorandum from James T. Lynn to the President, November 12, 1975, on "S.2350 'to include the Secretary of the Treasury as a member of the National Security Council.'"

3

The Economic Policy Board: operation, organization, and functions

*C*rucial to understanding any White House council or committee is a sense of how it operated. What meetings did it hold and who attended? Who determined what issues were considered? What type of organizational structure (subcommittees or groups) existed? Who exercised operational control and what roles did he assume? What staff support did the council or committee have? What functions did the council perform? How did it relate to other White House and Executive Office of the President units? What range of issues did it consider?

MEETINGS AND OPERATION

The daily executive committee meeting

The heart of the Economic Policy Board was the daily executive committee meeting held at 8:30 A.M. in the Roosevelt Room of the White House. In meeting daily, it was far more active than the other four presidential coordinating and policy councils – the Office of Management and Budget, the National Security Council, the Domestic Council, and the Energy Resources Council. In actual practice, "daily" was a bit of a misnomer. The Executive Committee generally met three or four days each week for forty-five minutes to an hour, considering an average of about three agenda items.[1] (See Table 1.)

Members received the agenda a week in advance. A daily agenda incorporating any revisions in the weekly agenda was sent to members the day before a meeting along with the papers on agenda items that had not

---

[1] Meetings were not held when several members were scheduled to be out of Washington, when presidential meetings involving executive committee members such as congressional leadership meetings were scheduled at the same time, or when both Simon and Seidman were unable to attend – a case known as "the Bill–Bill rule."

TABLE 1
EPB executive committee meetings

	Number of meetings	Number of agenda items	Average number of items/meeting
October–December 1974	58	273	4.71
January–March 1975	53	164	3.09
April–June 1975	41	146	3.56
July–September 1975	37	120	3.24
October–December 1975	42	136	3.24
January–March 1976	30	79	2.63
April–June 1976	39	101	2.59
July–September 1976	33	93	2.82
October–December 1976	18	39	2.17
Total	351	1151	3.28

Source: EPB executive committee meeting minutes.

already been distributed. In addition to the published agenda, executive committee members were free to raise any issue they wished during the meeting. Papers were prepared by a department, agency, or subcabinet interagency task force for most agenda items, as shown in Table 2.

Despite heavy demands on their time and frequent commitments outside Washington, principals consistently attended. Initially, executive committee meetings were restricted to members or, if the member were out of town, his deputy. In July 1975, the Executive Committee allowed each member to bring one staff person to regular executive committee meetings.[2] Chairmen of EPB task forces and subcommittees also at-

[2] The practice of permitting principals to bring one staff person with them also applied to full board members who attended executive committee meetings. The practice arose because one member wanted it badly on personal grounds, another's staff wanted it because

TABLE 2
Papers at EPB executive committee meetings

	Number of agenda items	Agenda items with papers	Percentage of agenda items with papers
October–December 1974	273	100	36.6
January–March 1975	164	100	61.0
April–June 1975	146	97	66.4
July–September 1975	120	84	70.0
October–December 1975	136	75	55.1
January–March 1976	79	61	77.2
April–June 1976	101	82	81.2
July–September 1976	93	65	70.0
October–December 1976	39	32	82.1
Total	1151	696	60.5

Source: EPB executive committee meeting minutes.

tended to present task force reports. One meeting each week was for "principals only" with attendance restricted to executive committee members and the Executive Secretary.[3]

The EPB consistently encouraged members of the full board to attend executive committee meetings when issues affecting their departments were under consideration, and all board members were notified a week

he was slow in debriefing, and because members didn't want to prevent Paul MacAvoy or Burton Malkiel, the other members of the CEA, from attending regularly. Thereafter, attempts at additions were constant but successfully resisted. Most of the "staffers" who attended were at the assistant secretary level.

[3] The Committee also went into executive session, meaning that the room was cleared of all nonprincipals, at the end of the daily meeting if a particularly sensitive matter required consideration.

in advance of the next week's agenda items. The office of the Executive Director also contacted board members personally when an issue affecting their department or agency was scheduled. In practice, the process worked smoothly and full board members consistently participated in discussions on issues affecting their departments.[4]

Minutes were deliberately depersonalized to encourage free and candid discussion and to reduce possible leaks to the press.[5] They included the subjects and major points that emerged during the discussion, the decisions taken, and the assignments made. The Executive Secretary prepared the minutes and the Executive Director approved them before they were distributed. If there were some question on the outcome of a controversial matter, the Executive Secretary frequently reviewed the minutes with one or more members before they were put in final form. The minutes were distributed on the same day of the meeting and served four basic functions. First, from the minutes, the Executive Secretary prepared his action list to insure appropriate follow-up on Committee decisions.

Second, the minutes were the definitive record when disputes arose about decisions or what official policy was. EPB minutes acquired a prestige almost akin to that of presidential speeches, messages, and other official statements concerning the parameters of administration policy on an issue.[6]

---

[4]   A member of the full board could also request permission from the Office of the Executive Director to attend any executive committee meeting.

[5]   In contrast to the conventional wisdom that "fixed committees make the problem of reasonable press security impossible" (Bator Hearings, pp. 115–116), leaks of EPB minutes, documents, or accounts of executive committee discussions occurred only twice between September 1974 and January 1977. One involved an economic analysis of a sensitive international problem. The second involved an early draft of an EPB task force report. Neither involved the content of discussions at executive committee meetings or the content of EPB minutes.

The press speculated about executive committee members' positions on certain key issues, but as often as not, was wrong, providing amusement at more than one executive committee meeting. See "The Priority Goes to Tax Reform," *Business Week* (August 18, 1975); and Seidman letter to *Business Week* (September 10, 1975).

As one regular participant observed: "There were quite a few instances where President Ford wanted to maintain secrecy where he allowed the multiple advocacy process to operate and he didn't get burned by it. I think the general record on being able to contain things inside the advocacy system was remarkably good."

[6]   The care with which EPB minutes were scrutinized is illustrated by a letter from Under Secretary of State for Economic Affairs Robinson to Seidman formally objecting to the phrasing of a minute because it implied a level of agreement on a technical issue to which his department did not concur. He acknowledged in the letter that the matter was a minor one, and "not of sufficient importance to justify reopening the discussion," but that his bureaucracy felt strongly about it. Letter from Charles W. Robinson to L. William Seidman, July 29, 1975.

One senior OMB official observed: "I am convinced that the minutes were absolutely essential in disseminating information on what had been decided. I used them on a number of occasions to 'prove' what had been decided."

Third, the minutes were a primary information source for the executive branch economic community. Some departments distributed the unclassified minutes to virtually every senior departmental official with any economic policy responsibilities; other agencies maintained the minutes in a central location where they could be reviewed by any senior official; other departments restricted the distribution of the minutes to a small number of officials.[7]

Finally, the minutes clarified the outcome of some discussions. The discipline of committing the outcome of a discussion to paper highlighted unresolved questions, clarified decisions, stipulated the precise nature of assignments, and assigned responsibility.

Agenda items originated from four primary sources. First, any member department or agency could request that the Executive Committee consider an issue, and members' offices were contacted weekly for items. Each department and agency represented on the Executive Committee designated an individual, generally at the assistant secretary level, to work with the EPB Executive Secretary. On Thursday mornings the Executive Secretary asked each contact for agenda items for the following two weeks and arranged for distributing papers and timing the consideration of each issue. The Executive Director's office polled members on their schedules two weeks in advance to insure that agenda items were considered when the maximum number of members with a critical interest in an issue would be present. Since the Executive Committee frequently specified additional work or reconsideration of an issue in the future, many agenda items came from the Executive Secretary's action list.

Second, the Executive Committee established a series of approximately a dozen task forces that reported on a monthly, bimonthly, or ad hoc basis, depending on the particular task force. These task forces generated some agenda items themselves and were specifically assigned certain issues by the Executive Committee.

A third major source of agenda items was requests from the Executive Director to a department or agency to report on a particular subject. The Executive Director, as Assistant to the President for Economic Affairs, assumed primary responsibility for identifying issues that might merit presidential attention or consideration by the Executive Committee. These issues varied widely. Some basically lay within a single department's jurisdiction but had broader economic implications, such as a Department of Transportation regulation entailing heavy costs on a key sector of the economy. Others involved interdepartmental issues in which no single department had a compelling interest, such as a new examination of banking regulatory reform.

[7] The Executive Committee itself never had a policy on distributing the minutes within a department or agency.

Finally, some agenda items resulted from the six-month and three-month work plans. Roughly each quarter, executive committee members were polled for recommendations regarding issues they felt the Executive Committee should consider during the next three months. Task force chairmen provided an outline of their projected work during the following three months. These recommendations became part of a master work plan and responsibility for each item was assigned. The three-month and six-month work plans were particularly useful in identifying longer-term issues and generating support and resources to study such questions as capital formation and productivity.

Full board meetings

The executive order creating the EPB specified that the Executive Committee should meet daily but was silent on the frequency of full board meetings. Initially, board meetings were held monthly.[8] After the first four months, they were convened generally three or four times a year.

Board meetings served two functions. First, they informed and explained. Board meetings were used to explain the thrust and rationale behind major programs, such as the economic proposals in the President's 1975 State of the Union Address, thus helping cabinet officers in their role as advocates for administration policies. Full board meetings always included the CEA Chairman's presentation on the economic outlook, a subject that board members frequently had to discuss in their public appearances.

A second function of full board meetings was to get board members' contributions in the early stages of a major economic program's development. Board meetings were held early in the preparation of the President's first economic program, announced in October 1974, and in the preparation of the 1975 State of the Union economic proposals. The meetings included a general discussion of likely major proposals; members also suggested additional initiatives they would like considered, which were discussed at subsequent executive committee meetings. In practice, board meetings were like cabinet meetings in most administrations – occasions to exchange information, consolidate support, and solicit suggestions, not a forum for making decisions.

Economic policy reviews and special sessions

The Executive Committee also organized two types of meetings to supplement the daily morning sessions – quarterly economic policy reviews

[8] The first four board meetings were held on October 4, November 4, and December 11, 1974, and January 10, 1975.

and executive committee special sessions. The quarterly reviews assessed the overall economic outlook, reviewed the general direction of either domestic or international economic policy, and analyzed specific problem areas.[9] The reviews lasted two or three days and followed a three-part format.

First, the Executive Committee usually met with ten to twelve non-governmental economists for three hours followed by further discussion at lunch. Executive committee members asked two broad questions: What was their outlook for the economy? And, based on that outlook, what were their recommendations for the administration's economic policies? The visiting economists, spanning a wide spectrum of opinion, always produced a lively and stimulating discussion. The Council of Economic Advisers prepared a summary of the meeting, which was sent to the President.[10]

Second, the Troika II group presented a comprehensive forecast for the economy.[11] The Troika II forecast was displayed alongside the forecasts of six leading private forecasting organizations, invariably prompting a lengthy discussion of the reasons for differences between the various forecasts — the assumptions used and forecasting techniques applied — and a more general discussion on the accuracy and utility of forecasting by econometric models. The Troika II forecast provided the basis for discussing general macroeconomic policy as well as considering specific problem sectors.

Third, the quarterly reviews scrutinized particular problems, such as unemployment, and selected economic sectors, such as automobiles or construction. Interagency task forces, or, less frequently, a single department or agency, prepared papers. The papers varied from a detailed examination of the automobile industry to alternative strategies for the multilateral trade negotiations. The quarterly reviews also considered departmental or task force proposals ranging from a railroad roadbed rehabilitation program to the accelerated payment of general revenue sharing funds.

[9] During the two and a quarter years of its existence, the Economic Policy Board held four domestic economic policy reviews, two international economic policy reviews, and two review exercises in preparation for the International Summit Conferences at Rambouillet, France, in November 1975, and in Puerto Rico in June 1976.

[10] The nongovernmental economists changed membership from quarter to quarter to expose executive committee members to a variety of views and to avoid any problems with provisions in the Federal Advisory Committees Act. Frequent participants included Paul Samuelson, Paul McCracken, Walter Heller, Otto Eckstein, Arthur Okun, Herbert Stein, and Milton Friedman.

[11] The Troika II group was chaired by a member of the Council of Economic Advisers and included the Assistant Secretary of the Treasury for Economic Policy and the Assistant Director for Economic Policy of the Office of Management and Budget.

Planning and preparing for the reviews generally commenced eight to ten weeks in advance by informally canvassing departments and agencies for possible agenda topics. A review outline was then prepared under the Executive Director's supervision and circulated to executive committee members for comments and suggestions. The Executive Committee then approved a revised agenda, established task forces, made assignments, and set deadlines for papers. The quarterly review task forces were chaired by representatives of member departments and agencies, with members of the Executive Director's small staff monitoring them to insure that deadlines were being met, particularly on early drafts of the papers, so that final versions could circulate well in advance of the review.

Measured by preparation and attendance patterns, executive committee members considered these economic policy reviews useful and important. Full board members also attended the review sessions when subjects of interest to their department were on the agenda. The Chairman of the Federal Reserve Board rarely attended the daily executive committee sessions, but came regularly to the quarterly reviews. The reviews let executive committee members collectively discuss the shape of the administration's economic policies with a diverse group of respected "outsiders." These discussions provided a touchstone for the internal analyses generated by governmental economists.[12]

Freedom from the hour limit normally observed at the daily executive committee session meant longer discussions and more thorough debates of issues and proposals. The agenda's length, at least half a dozen topics, discouraged rambling discussions. But since the separate review sessions lasted a full half day, thorough and extended discussions were welcome.

The structure of the quarterly reviews and the nature of the topics discussed also helped focus on longer-range problems, trends, and developments. In short, the quarterly reviews added a different dimension to the work and activity of the EPB.

Executive committee special sessions were a second type of ancillary EPB meeting. Special sessions generally lasted from two to three hours and focused on a single issue, such as tax reform, capacity shortages, unemployment, or energy alternatives, which merited more extended discussion than was possible at the daily meetings. Sometimes special sessions were held on two or three related issues, such as aviation regulatory reform, an international aviation policy statement, and airline mergers.

---

[12] The meetings with nongovernmental economists were not the only sessions with "outsiders" at the quarterly reviews. One review was timed to coincide with a meeting of the President's Labor–Management Committee; another review included a meeting with a group of financial consultants; a third review included four panels with "outside experts" on various international economic policy issues.

The EPB Executive Committee held fifty-eight special sessions, usually on Saturday mornings or weekday afternoons, between October 1974 and January 1977 – roughly one every other week. At times of intense activity, the Executive Committee held as many as four special sessions during a two-week period. At other times, special sessions were scheduled once every six to eight weeks. Like the quarterly reviews, the special sessions permitted fuller and more detailed discussion of an issue and were used in formulating most major policies.

Presidential meetings and papers

The EPB Executive Committee met with the President frequently, averaging slightly more than one meeting with the President for every four regular meetings of the Executive Committee. During 1974 and 1975 the EPB met with the President, on average, slightly more than once a week. In 1976 the number of formal EPB meetings with the President declined, partially because of election year pressures and the transition to a new administration during the last two months, and partially because the administration's economic policies were more firmly established and economic issues were less pressing than during the previous fifteen months. (See Table 3.)

In addition, as the EPB matured, its interagency papers improved and the President made relatively more economic policy decisions using the papers alone. However, meetings were held when one or more members strongly wanted an oral discussion with the President to supplement the options paper.

In preparation for the EPB presidential meetings, the EPB sent the President a briefing paper containing a decision memorandum or information paper for each recommended agenda item. The briefing paper also included an Economic Policy Board Weekly Report normally about two pages long. The report contained: (1) issues the Executive Committee had considered during the past week with a two- or three-sentence description of each issue and any action taken; (2) a brief activity summary of each task force that had reported during the past week; and (3) major upcoming agenda items. The weekly report helped keep the President abreast of the Executive Committee's work and alerted him to major upcoming agenda issues. The Council of Economic Advisers also prepared a one-page economic fact sheet for the President as part of the briefing paper. The fact sheet succinctly summarized the most recent developments in prices, employment, production, and certain key economic sectors such as housing, with a short analysis of the statistics released during the past week.

Seidman also transmitted a decision memorandum or options paper on each issue requiring the President's decision and scheduled its discus-

TABLE 3
EPB meetings with the President

	Number of meetings	Number of agenda items	Additional Presidential meetings[a]
October–December 1974	15	64	5
January–March 1975	17	48	3
April–June 1975	15	27	7
July–September 1975	13	23	6
October–December 1975	18	20	5
January–March 1976	5	14	3
April–June 1976	5	10	—
July–September 1976	2	8	—
October–December 1976	3	5	1
Total	93	219	30

[a]"Additional presidential meetings" refers to meetings that the President held with outside groups, such as the Farm Bureau Federation Executive Committee, maritime leaders, automobile executives, the National Commission on Productivity and Quality of Working Life, and the Labor–Management Committee. The EPB Executive Director was responsible for coordinating within the White House meetings related to issues the Economic Policy Board was considering.

Source: EPB files.

sion on the agenda. The decision memorandum included a statement of the issue, background on the problem, relevant factual and analytical data, the policy alternatives the Executive Committee had considered, the advantages and disadvantages of each policy alternative, and the recommendations of each executive committee member, other interested departments and agencies, and appropriate White House offices. Seidman did not formally support any alternative in the memorandum, as other executive committee members did.

This weekly meeting with the President served a variety of functions. Its central purpose was to provide the President with an oral exchange of views on important policy decisions to supplement the written options papers. From the discussions, he could gauge the intensity of his advisers' feelings about issues, clarify his own thinking, and ask questions about matters raised in the written memorandums. Since written documents might become public, some officials preferred making certain arguments orally rather than on paper. Analyzing these meetings' impact on the President, one participant observed:

> I think the meetings helped the President satisfy himself on some questions that were raised in his mind by the papers and to get the crossfeed in an open forum between people who had different views. The meetings also helped him get a sense of the depth of commitment to a position that is very difficult to communicate on paper that he would not have had without that personal exposure.

Another reflected:

> I think the meetings were very helpful to him because there is no way of getting all of the nuances in a memorandum no matter how well written it is. The second reason they were helpful is that many times you were willing to state something orally that you don't want in a piece of paper.
> He used them on the whole quite skillfully to develop suboptions that hadn't even been explored. Also there are nuances on how strong each person feels about what option they support. And I really do think that the political considerations are appropriately left to the oral discussion.

The meetings also permitted the President to see his advisers interact. Gerald Ford enjoyed and encouraged spirited discussions. Exchanges of candid and often strongly differing viewpoints characterized his economic policy meetings.[13] The meetings also consistently included an opening discussion on the current state of the economy, useful background for many of the decision items on the agenda. In addition, the meetings helped the President indirectly in preparing for press conference questions on the economy.

---

[13] One cabinet secretary suggested that:

In some cases he [the President] almost asked for heartaches by encouraging debate among his top people to be sure what they were saying rather than to tip his hand and have them line up behind whatever decision it was that they thought he wanted. I have often said that I felt in the other administration there were indications of where we were going and people lined up behind it. That was not as true in this administration.

The economic policy meetings generally lasted an hour or an hour and fifteen minutes, but occasionally took almost two hours. The agenda included one, two, or occasionally three decision items for consideration. The Executive Director's office tried to anticipate issues that would require presidential review during the coming three or four weeks and to arrange the daily meeting agendas to insure full discussion and agreement on options papers so they could be submitted to the President well in advance of his meetings with the Executive Committee. Naturally, unanticipated problems often intruded on the careful planning of upcoming issues. But since the Executive Committee met daily, it could consider issues quickly. In practice, the system had a great deal of scheduling flexibility and allowed repeated discussion before a final decision was needed. The Board's capacity for advance planning and skill at anticipating issues improved steadily as the participants matured as a team of advisers.

The format of the meetings remained constant over time. The President invariably called on the cabinet officer with primary responsibility for the issue to begin the discussion. After this initial presentation, the President would call on others for their views until all those in attendance who wished to speak had spoken. Frequently, an individual's presentation would be interspersed with questions or comments by the President or by other participants.[14] The President then generally asked a series of questions distilled from reading the paper and listening to the discussion. Sometimes the questions clarified the President's understanding of an argument or alternative. Sometimes the President fashioned a new alternative and asked for his advisers' reaction to it. Multiple viewpoints and broad participation characterized the meetings; rarely did a single individual or viewpoint dominate the discussion. One participant observed:

> He [the President] knows how to listen to Simon or Usery . . . how to get from them what he needs to know. I have seen him change his mind during the course of a meeting, but he rarely revealed which way he was leaning.
>
> I think he is the kind of person who plays a good poker hand. He consciously, I think, goes in with what seems to be an open mind. You can't guess what he wants — that's good. It not only

[14] Usually attendance at economic policy meetings with the President was limited to executive committee principals, other cabinet secretaries with an interest in the issue, and a few senior White House staff members. The press secretary, the Assistant to the President for Legislative Affairs, the Counsellor to the President, the President's Chief of Staff, the Assistant to the President for Domestic Affairs, and the Assistant to the President for National Security Affairs, when appropriate, frequently attended the economic policy meetings with the President.

encourages debate, but it encourages people to be prepared with factual arguments. He welcomes these differing points of view. I don't know of anybody whom I feel more comfortable disagreeing with. . . . He wants to have a range of viewpoints. It is my judgment that it would offend him if he thought you were trying to guess what he wanted. He doesn't like yes men.

On less controversial issues the President often made decisions during the meeting. On more controversial issues, he frequently indicated that he wished to think about his decision overnight. On several occasions he specified that he would have a decision by a certain time later in the week. Members of the EPB generally felt that the President found the meetings useful. As one reflected during the closing days of the administration:

> The meetings with the President were helpful to him in giving him a chance to hear the issues laid out and to hear the points of view towards them. I thought that the spirit of those meetings was very good and that people did speak up candidly. It is to President Ford's credit that he encouraged a climate in which people felt free to say what they thought. I don't think anyone ever had the feeling that somebody was marking them down as wrong, or on the wrong side of things. There was a well-identified viewpoint which Frank Zarb characterized as belonging to the free marketeers but in fact there was never any inhibition against expressing a more qualified or pragmatic approach.

EPB ORGANIZATION

Executive committee members quickly recognized that, even with their personal commitment to attend daily meetings and longer special sessions on weekends, subcabinet officials and their staffs would have to do much of the detailed development of a data base, analysis, and alternatives. Sometimes committee members agreed to assign preliminary work on a problem to an individual department or agency. For example, the early stages in developing information and analysis on tax policy questions was generally undertaken by the Tax Division at the Department of the Treasury, although informal contacts between Treasury and the staffs at OMB, the CEA, and other member departments and agencies were commonplace. More frequently, the Executive Committee approved some form of interagency effort to produce a paper for its consideration. These interagency groups took three forms.

First, quasi-informal subcabinet groups convened by the Executive

Director and his small staff at the White House developed many issues. Members were selected both for individual expertise 'and to represent a particular department or agency with a clear stake in the issue. The composition of these groups shifted from problem to problem, but, over time, an informal group of half a dozen individuals, generally at the assistant secretary level, came into use. The members of this informal group shared several important characteristics: They were close to their department or agency head, could mobilize their department or agency resources quickly, and worked well together. This informal group fit Francis Bator's description of:

> A small number of people who are senior enough to marshal the resources of their agencies; not so senior as to make it impossible for them to keep up with detail, or spend the time needed for comprehensive and sustained exploration of each other's minds; and close enough to their secretaries and to the President to serve as doubled-edged negotiators (each operating for his secretary in the task group bargaining, and in turn representing the group's analyses of the issues and choices to his secretary).[15]

Second, the EPB Executive Committee established six permanent sub-cabinet-level committees, each responsible for a particular policy area or range of issues. The six permanent EPB committees were: Troika II, the EPB/NSC Commodities Policy Coordinating Committee, the EPB Labor Negotiations Committee, the EPB Subcommittee on Economic Statistics, the EPB Task Force on Small Business, and the Food Deputies Group.[16]

Third, the EPB Executive Committee also formally created a large number of interagency committees and task forces to undertake long-range studies or to develop policy alternatives on specific issues. These ad hoc committees and task forces had narrower responsibilities than the

[15]   Bator Hearings, p. 114.

[16]   A compelling political need to counter farm community perceptions that officials outside the Department of Agriculture were controlling agricultural policy making prompted the creation on March 5, 1976, of the Agricultural Policy Committee (APC). The Secretary of Agriculture was named chairman. The Secretaries of State, Treasury, and Commerce, the Assistants to the President for Economic Affairs, Domestic Affairs, and National Security Affairs, the Director of OMB, the Chairman of the CEA, the Executive Director of CIEP, and the Special Assistant to the President for Consumer Affairs were named members.

An assistant secretary level Agricultural Policy Working Group, chaired by representatives from the Department of Agriculture, was also created and replaced the Food Deputies Group. The Food Deputies Group had been chaired by a member of the Council of Economic Advisers. In practice, the Agricultural Policy Working Group met regularly, reported to the EPB, and prepared issue papers for consideration by the EPB on agricultural policy matters. The cabinet-level Agricultural Policy Committee met only twice between March 1976 and January 1977.

permanent EPB committees, coming and going as issues were resolved and others were identified. These project or ad hoc committees and task forces included:

The EPB Task Force on Antitrust Immunities

The EPB/NSC Food Committee

The EPB Task Force on Railroad Reorganization

The EPB Task Force on Capital Formation

The EPB Task Force on Services and the Multilateral Trade Negotiations

The EPB Task Force on Product Liability

The EPB Task Force on International Air Transportation Policy

The EPB Task Force on Productivity

The EPB Task Force on Fertilizer

The EPB Task Forces on Improving Government Regulation

The EPB Task Force on Questionable Corporate Payments Abroad

The EPB Task Force on Banking Regulatory Reform

The EPB Capital Markets Working Group

The EPB Task Force on Taxation and International Investment[17]

EPB task forces and committees operated under several general guidelines. First, the committee or task force was chaired by a representative

---

[17] The impetus for creating various task forces and committees occasionally came from an individual department or agency but more frequently from the Executive Director. Some of the subcabinet committees such as Troika II, the Food Deputies Group, and the Subcommittee on Economic Statistics existed when the Economic Policy Board was created and were continued or in some instances revitalized by the EPB.

The Economic Policy Board did experiment briefly with a deputies group intended to handle minor issues and to take a first cut at many policy questions before their consideration by the Executive Committee. This experiment was short lived for three reasons.

First, the regularity of executive committee meetings combined with the immediate attention required by many questions meant that large numbers of issues would simply bypass the deputies group. In this sense, the deputies group would have merely imposed an additional layer and stiffened a flexible system designed for considering and handling issues quickly.

Second, most of the key participants at the subcabinet level – Paul MacAvoy, Burton Malkiel, Richard Darman, Rudy Penner, Gerald Parsky, Jules Katz, Henry Perritt, Richard Bell, and others – attended executive committee meetings with their principal when issues of importance to them were on the agenda. Having them meet at a separate time struck many as a poor use of scarce executive resources.

Third, the Economic Policy Board already had a full system of task forces that did much of the work to prepare issues for consideration by the Executive Committee. These structural factors, combined with a lack of genuine need and a lack of interest, contributed to the short life of the experiment.

of a department or agency with a primary interest in the subject matter, not by the White House.[18] Three of the task forces were co-chaired by representatives of two departments.[19] Second, representatives of departments or agencies on EPB committees were generally at the assistant secretary level or higher. Third, the permanent EPB committees reported regularly to the Executive Committee, generally biweekly or monthly. Fourth, the Executive Committee developed a work plan for each committee and task force, roughly each quarter.

The EPB task forces and committees performed a variety of functions. Some task forces, such as Troika II, focused on forecasting developments, providing data and analysis essential in making macroeconomic policy decisions. Other task forces, such as the Food Deputies Group, the Task Force on Fertilizer, and the Labor Negotiations Committee, concentrated on monitoring specific sectors or activities and served as an early warning mechanism for the Executive Committee. Other task forces were designed to undertake longer-range studies, such as the task forces on capital formation, productivity, product liability, services and the multilateral trade negotiations, taxation and international investment, and banking regulatory reform.

Frequently, the formal task forces and subcommittees helped generate an agreed upon data base and analysis of a policy issue. Complex issues often involved interagency differences on the reliability of certain data, the appropriate base period for making calculations, the relevance and importance of particular facts, and judgments involved in making certain estimates. Several task forces spent considerable time developing a solid analytical base on complex policy issues.

The assistant secretary level task forces and committees also served as forums for resolving issues that were not of cabinet-level importance. In this sense, the task forces lightened the burden of dispute resolution on the Executive Committee. The ease with which executive committee members could place an issue on the agenda helped to prevent task force

---

[18]   While White House representatives did not chair any of the committees and task forces established by the Executive Committee, White House representatives served as members on several committees and consistently monitored their activities. Several of the committees were chaired by one of the members of the Council of Economic Advisers, a unit in the Executive Office of the President.

In contrast, the Nixon–Kissinger NSC system had the Assistant to the President for National Security Affairs chair all of the interdepartmental committees established at the level below the NSC for formulating options before they were submitted to the NSC and/or the President. Studies generated by National Security Study Memorandums (NSSMs), however, designated a specific department or agency as the lead agency for the study.

[19]   The chairmanships of the permanent and ad hoc committees and task forces were distributed as follows: Council of Economic Advisers 6, Treasury 5, Commerce 3, State 3, Transportation 2, Labor 1, Agriculture 1, Justice 1, Small Business Administration 1.

deliberations from simply seeking a lowest common denominator solution. The task force members were aware that they could appeal a decision through their cabinet secretary to the Executive Committee and ultimately to the President.

Finally, and not least, many task forces and committees devoted much time and attention to shaping policy alternatives and developing possible legislative initiatives. In some instances, the task forces played a major role in developing general policy positions. The Task Force on International Air Transportation Policy, which met for almost a year and a half, significantly contributed to a new air transportation policy. Likewise, the Commodities Policy Coordinating Committee assumed a central role in developing the administration's position on commodity issues and on North–South relations in general.

The formally established committees and task forces were crucial in performing such tasks as longer-range studies, regular forecasting, and continuous monitoring of various sectors of the economy. The subcabinet committees also facilitated the exchange of information between departments and agencies.

However, these formal task forces and committees were less useful when speed was essential, largely because of their size. Task force membership policy deliberately erred on the side of inclusion, rather than exclusion, in order to include representation from all major departments and agencies with an interest in the subject matter.[20] Over time a rough division of labor emerged between the formal committees and task forces and the informal sub-cabinet groups convened by the Executive Director. The formal committees and task forces focused on longer-range studies, the quarterly forecasting exercises, continuous monitoring of key sectors, and policy development involving relatively long lead times. The more rapidly a task had to be completed and the more closely the Executive Director wished to exercise control over the product, the more likely it was that he would form an informal group to address the problem, refine the preliminary work of a department or agency, and shape the range of policy alternatives. Thus, the EPB organizational structure had an array of formal subcabinet committees coupled with more informal arrangements for handling issues requiring immediate or sensitive attention.

THE EXECUTIVE DIRECTOR

The executive order establishing the Economic Policy Board designated the Assistant to the President for Economic Affairs as Executive Director

---

[20] Troika II was an exception and remained limited to the traditional Troika membership – Treasury, OMB, and the CEA.

of both the Board and its Executive Committee. Theoretically, it is possible to differentiate between the responsibilities of the Assistant to the President for Economic Affairs and the responsibilities of the Executive Director of the EPB. In practice, the distinction was rarely made. In his dual capacity, William Seidman performed ten basic roles.

Clerk

Responsibility for the day-to-day operation of the Economic Policy Board was his most basic function. The EPB, largely because of Seidman, operated much more formally than previous cabinet-level committees and groups dealing with economic policy issues.

It is commonplace to consider responsibility for such housekeeping functions as minutes, agendas, and schedules to be relatively unimportant. Routine clerkship functions are often viewed as essentially paper-shuffling. Well organized meetings with clear records do not make an entity successful. However, it would be misleading to conclude that attention to housekeeping functions contributes little to a group's success.

Seidman viewed his clerkship role as important in at least two respects. First, a formal agenda to help focus discussion at the meetings, papers circulated in advance, and a systematic record of the proceedings would help set the tone for the Board's work and could contribute to a feeling of time well spent. Second, regularizing the flow of paper generated on economic issues through a single channel and maintaining a consistent format for the papers submitted to the President could make him more willing to spend time on matters raised by the Board and insist that individuals not circumvent the process. Seidman, who was familiar with the style and preferences of the President, worked closely with his staff to insure such consistency in style and format. Not least, Seidman used his role as clerk to assist him in his other roles as policy manager, catalyst, and implementor.

Policy manager

Seidman viewed his role as policy manager as perhaps his most important function and his approach emphasized four basic concerns. First, he insured that all interested parties in the executive branch were included in discussing issues that affected their interests — not only to eliminate friction from people who were excluded, but also because he wanted to mobilize the best resources available in the government to address a particular problem. He felt that an inclusive policy was essential to create a climate in which departments would consistently commit their best personnel and resources to the EPB's work.

Second, he considered deciding which issues should go to the President as a major responsibility and consistently resisted individuals who wanted to take narrow or minor issues to the President. He also sought to insure that bureaucratic compromises between competing interests did not bury basic issues.

Third, Seidman repeatedly reminded the Executive Committee that one of its central responsibilities was to define differences rather than to seek a consensus. Both in executive committee meetings and in meetings with the President, he worked to clarify differences rather than move the group toward a compromise.

Fourth, Seidman sought a balanced and fair presentation of analysis and alternatives on an issue while exercising control over the quality of the materials that ultimately went to the President.

Catalyst

Closely associated with his functions as policy manager was his role as a catalyst. To identify issues meriting EPB attention, Seidman spent considerable time scanning daily governmental operations, keeping abreast of developments in various economic sectors, and monitoring trends.[21] His interest was vital in stimulating support for longer-range studies of such issues as capital formation, productivity, taxation and international investment, and banking regulatory reform. He initiated contingency studies that had a dual effect on the policy process. First, announcing a group's formation focused attention at the highest levels on an issue's importance. Second, the group's report, which was placed on the Executive Committee agenda, stimulated serious discussion of the problem.

Seidman's role as catalyst also involved reaching down into a department or agency and pulling issues up out of the bureaucracy that would not necessarily come to the attention of the President or of the Economic Policy Board otherwise. Finally, as catalyst, he pressed for movement on issues stalled in a subcabinet bureaucratic morass, generally by calling a meeting of the officials involved to get a status report on the issue or by simply placing the issue on the Executive Committee agenda and getting a commitment to complete work by a specific date. Since Seidman's interest in an issue was widely interpreted as an indication of presidential interest, he was remarkably effective in producing a response. The fact that the Executive Committee met daily was important in aiding Seidman to move many issues simultaneously.[22] In summary, Seidman was an

[21] Seidman regularly read the White House Daily News Summary and Treasury News, a thirty- to sixty-page daily compilation of economic-related articles in newspapers and magazines, in addition to reading several private forecasting and trade publications.

[22] A good example of his influence is the grain reserves case. Formally, determining the

effective catalyst. Because of his clout and his information network, he could get departments to commit their resources to specific problems and could break up bureaucratic logjams.

Implementor

Seidman was also responsible for seeing that presidential decisions were implemented. He developed an elaborate system of charts, deadlines, and weekly monitoring after the President's first major economic policy address on October 8, 1974. Because this system imposed such heavy time demands on the Executive Director's limited staff, responsibility for following up on later major economic programs – for example, the proposals in the 1975 State of the Union address – was assigned to the Office of Management and Budget, which provided a weekly computer printout of the status of each proposal in the program.[23]

Seidman's general approach to implementation was to provide clear directives through the minutes and Economic Policy Decision Memorandums (EPDMs) to all appropriate senior officials supplemented by personal spot checks. He then relied heavily on self compliance, with informal monitoring by other agencies such as the Office of Management and Budget. His office's periodic spot checks showed a high level of compliance with the President's decisions.[24]

U.S. position lay within the jurisdiction of the International Food Review Group (IFRG), nominally a cabinet-level body chaired by the Secretary of State. Largely because of an impasse among officials in the subcabinet IFRG Working Group, the cabinet-level IFRG, created in November 1974, met only twice in the first nine months of its existence.

Seidman got an acceptable resolution by holding private meetings with the chief protagonists in coordination with OMB Director James Lynn, and by placing the issue on the EPB Executive Committee agenda. Here, as usual, he got cooperation because the principals saw him as expediting the outcome, not pushing his own position on the issue.

[23]   In cases where implementing a decision involved some formal participation by the President (a message to the Congress or issuing an executive order), Seidman oversaw preparing the document and coordinated its clearance before the President signed it. For example, formal presidential action is required in all escape clause cases that are sent by the U.S. International Trade Commission to the President for his determination. Seidman and his staff worked closely with the White House Staff Secretary's Office and with the Chief Clerk of the White House on such matters.

[24]   It is instructive to compare the EPB approach to implementation with Richard Neustadt's list of five factors that encourage compliance with presidential orders. (1) Assurance that the President has spoken. The formal Economic Policy Decision Memorandums (EPDMs), minutes, and other memorandums from the Executive Director to appropriate department and agency officials were generally phrased to eliminate ambiguity: "The President has determined that . . . ;" "The President has approved. . . ." Equally important, decisions were normally reached only after the executive branch officials responsible for implementing the decision had met with the President and were personally aware of his decision on the issue. (2) Clarity about the meaning of the request. Seidman and his staff

Mediator

Disputes between departments and agencies with competing interests are inevitable. Many of these disputes are minor and can be resolved at relatively low levels. Other conflicts escalate until they come to the White House for resolution. Naturally, it is neither possible nor feasible for the President to become personally involved. For one thing, there are too many issues. For another, they are not sufficiently important to warrant his attention. Furthermore, many are so technical that it would take too long for the President to become sufficiently familiar with the details to make an informed judgment.

Many disputes, admittedly minor, gravitate to the White House because it is viewed as neutral territory by the parties to the dispute. One assistant secretary explained:

> I can go to the White House for a meeting to resolve a problem with a reasonable degree of flexibility in my negotiating position. If I don't come away with everything we would have liked I can always explain to my bureaucracy that this was a decision made by the White House. That is invariably a decision they will accept.
>
> However, I could not return from a meeting at another department with the same compromise and offer an acceptable explanation. It would be viewed as having capitulated. One needs a neutral meeting place and a mediator often times for both sides to be flexible enough to reach an agreement.

Many of the disputes that came to Seidman involved jurisdictional questions rather than differences over policy positions. Typically, one of the parties would inform him of the dispute and solicit his assistance in resolving it. Seidman made an initial decision about whether the issue merited the President's attention. If not, then he generally met with both parties separately to hear their side and to assess what they considered their most vital interests at stake. Frequently, he would develop a pos-

carefully drafted options papers, decisions in the minutes, and EPDMs to state what the options were and what the President had decided. Thus, the President knew what he was being asked to decide and those expected to carry out the decisions knew what their responsibilities were. (3) Publicity. The minutes and EPDMs were sent to between six and twenty people who were also informed of the other officials who had received a copy. This wide internal publicity within the executive branch was an impetus to implementation. (4) The actual ability to carry out the decision. This factor generally presented few difficulties. (5) The sense that what the President wanted was his by right. This also did not present an obstacle, partly because the departments and agencies expected to implement the decision participated fully in the process leading up to the President's decision. Advising the President on the matter represented their acknowledgement that he had a right to decide the issue. See Richard E. Neustadt, *Presidential Power: The Politics of Leadership* (New York: Wiley, 1960), pp. 19–27.

sible solution that he would present to each side. If the disputing parties did not agree on his proposed solution, he would bring them into his West Wing office together. Usually this meeting hammered out an agreement that was subsequently written up by a member of Seidman's staff, approved by both parties, and on more controversial issues, was subsequently ratified by the EPB Executive Committee.

In his role as mediator, Seidman not only sought to find common ground and arrangements that were acceptable to both sides, but he preserved the President's time for major issues. This issue weighing inevitably involved some subjective judgments. Seidman's experience gave him exceptional skill in sensing the President's interest in becoming personally involved in such disputes. Over time, the impulse to refer disputes to the President was replaced by a pattern of resolving more disputes without recourse to the Oval Office.

Arbitrator

The counterpart to Seidman's role as mediator was that of arbitrator. Sometimes the parties to a dispute could not reach a mutually satisfactory solution and required arbitration. In such cases, when he considered the matter "not of presidential importance" and when he had exhausted all efforts at mediation, Seidman did assume the role of arbitrator, though somewhat reluctantly. Such instances were rare and involved minor matters because he felt that successful mediation reduces the need for arbitration, and conversely, that the more frequent the recourse to arbitration, the less flexible the parties become in seeking mediated solutions.

In cases of arbitration, there was always an expressed understanding that either cabinet officer could appeal the decision to the President if he wished. In practice, few decisions were appealed.

Presidential sentinel

Seidman was a primary figure in keeping the President informed on economic developments, a responsibility he shared with Alan Greenspan, Chairman of the Council of Economic Advisers. The CEA continued its practice of providing the President with periodic memorandums assessing key economic indicators – growth of the money supply, wholesale prices, unemployment, consumer prices, housing starts, the balance of payments, international monetary developments, and so forth – when the statistics were released each month or each quarter. The written CEA memorandums were sometimes supplemented by oral discussions between the President and Greenspan on the current state of the economy and on the meaning of recently released statistics.

A rough division of labor between Seidman and Greenspan soon emerged. Greenspan kept the President informed on movements in key economic indicators and provided the President with his assessment of their meaning. Seidman kept the President informed on such day-to-day developments as potential strike activity, large grain sales abroad, summaries of important speeches by key business and labor leaders, the progress of major labor negotiations, and the New York City financial situation. Both Greenspan and Seidman were comfortable with this division of responsibilities.

As presidential sentinel, Seidman had three basic tasks. First, he informed the President on the activities of the Economic Policy Board through the EPB Weekly Report. Second, he informed the President on day-to-day developments through information memorandums and personal meetings. In preparing economic information memorandums for the President, Seidman and his staff worked closely with EPB members and their staffs and used the daily executive committee meeting to consider which developments should be reported to and analyzed for the President. A review of the files indicates that Seidman sent the President an average of eight to ten information memorandums each month.[25] Finally, Seidman coordinated the preparation of questions and answers on economic issues for the President's briefing book used to prepare for his press conferences and interviews with media groups. The questions and answers were updated every week to ten days. As a presidential sentinel, Seidman sat astride one of the main information conduits flowing to the President, summarizing and filtering to preserve the President's time while seeking to insure that he was not left uninformed about major developments in the economy.

Presidential guardian

Closely related to his role as presidential sentinel was Seidman's role as presidential guardian. The essence of the guardian's role is to protect – in this instance, the integrity of the work that went out under the President's name and the integrity of what the President said on economic

---

[25] For example, during July and August 1976 the information memorandums sent from Seidman to the President included: TWA Flight Attendants Strike, Federal Seasonal Assistance Loans to New York City, Economic Developments, Westinghouse Negotiations, Tax Bill, Report on Task Forces to Improve Government Regulation, Coal Strike, Rubber Strike Status, Sugar Policy Review, Meat Import Situation, Tax Reform Bill, and five memorandums on the California Cannery Strike.

policy issues. Seidman's role as presidential guardian involved three principal tasks.

First, he and his staff took pains to insure that formal and informal communication in the President's name was accurate. Speechwriters, press office spokesmen, and congressional liaison personnel cannot be expected to assimilate and understand the details of complex and unfamiliar issues without assistance. Someone within the White House itself must be responsible for insuring that the economic content of presidential speeches, messages to the Congress, fact sheets, and statements issued to the press are accurate. Seidman and his staff were deeply involved in reviewing, clarifying, rewriting, and approving the stream of documents on economic policy issues that flowed from the White House. Seidman also spent countless hours with press spokesmen and congressional liaison personnel explaining and clarifying the President's position on particular issues or briefing them on how to explain the President's decision on a controversial problem.

A second task was developing speeches. Sometimes Seidman's interchange with speechwriters involved less checking than generating. Commitments on the President's behalf to address a particular group – the U.S. Chamber of Commerce, the Business Council, the AFL–CIO, the U.S. Conference of Mayors – are frequently made because the group represents a good forum for a presidential address or the address will help shore up support from a particular constituency. Often, what the President will say is not considered until after the commitment is already firm. "What can the President say to this group?" and "Isn't there something that the President can announce in a major speech next week?" are words often on the lips of presidential speechwriters.

Such circumstances usually invite intrusions by individuals anxious to secure quick approval for a pet idea that would appeal to the group being addressed. In such situations, Seidman not only tried to safeguard the President from being subtly committed to something undesirable, but he also used such occasions to define and explain the thrust of the administration's economic policies.

Third, Seidman participated in the White House staffing system on enrolled bill memorandums providing his comments and frequently the comments of his colleagues on the EPB Executive Committee as a way of insuring that the President's economic policy interests were raised and integrated in his decisions.

Presidential representative

Seidman also represented the President in executive committee meetings. At times this role involved emphasizing a perspective important to the President that was receiving little attention. At other times, it involved informing the Executive Committee of the President's desires or views expressed in meetings with congressmen or private groups. One of Seidman's responsibilities as Assistant to the President for Economic Affairs was to attend meetings that the President held with interest groups, congressional delegations, governors and mayors, and to attend the regular GOP and bipartisan congressional leadership sessions when economic policy issues were scheduled for discussion. Seidman thus served as an invaluable link between the President and the EPB Executive Committee.[26]

Seidman, as Assistant to the President for Economic Affairs, also served as the principal White House liaison with several cabinet officers on matters that did not necessitate the President's personal or immediate attention. As presidential representative, Seidman also handled presidential correspondence on economic policy matters, not only preparing much correspondence from the President on economic policy issues but also responding on the President's behalf when a White House, but not a presidential, letter was considered most appropriate.[27]

White House link to the outside world

Seidman viewed his role as larger than mobilizing the best information, resources, and analysis within the executive branch. He also considered strengthening the links between the Economic Policy Board, the White House, and the "outside world" – business, labor, academia, state and local governments, and the Congress – as an important part of his portfolio. His frequent contacts with individuals and groups outside the executive establishment served, in his view, several purposes.

[26] Seidman was not the only member of the Executive Committee who served to some extent as a presidential representative. James Lynn, Alan Greenspan, and William Simon also attended many of the meetings that the President held with groups relating to economic policy issues. Yet it was Seidman who worked consistently in executive committee meetings to bring the President's views into the discussion. Daniel J. Balz, in his account of the Economic Policy Board, based in part on his attendance at some executive committee meetings, noted: "It is Seidman more than anyone else there who brings 'the President' into the discussions. The President would like to know this, the President would like to know that. We should get this put together for our meetings with the President, Seidman says." Balz, p. 426.

[27] The White House at the time was receiving slightly over two million pieces of mail annually. Approximately 185 people, by far the largest single component of the White House staff, initially handled the routing. A small fraction of the mail received a presidential response; much of it was farmed out to executive branch departments and agencies for response; the correspondence unit itself answered many of the letters; and some mail was sent to various White House offices – congressional liaison, the counsel's office, the press office.

Seidman's office handled most of the economic-related letters not sent to departments and agencies. A major function of the CIEP staff secretariat was preparing correspondence for Seidman's signature. The volume of mail sent out from Seidman's office ranged from twenty to fifty pieces a day.

First, these discussions sensitized him, and, through him, sensitized the Board to the views that various elements of American society took of administration policies.[28] Second, the discussions provided outsiders' insights on problems the Board was then considering. Frequently, these insights took the form of information and analysis that Seidman would have his staff or appropriate departments and agencies review. Third, Seidman's contacts with outside groups and individuals often alerted him to new issues the EPB should address and to the results of recent research and studies. Finally, these contacts communicated that the White House was once again responsive to a wide spectrum of views, in part a deliberate reaction against the tone of previous administrations. A review of Seidman's telephone logs and daily schedule reveals that he averaged over a score of such contacts each week.

Advocate and spokesman

In delineating Seidman's roles as Assistant to the President for Economic Affairs and as EPB Executive Director, it is revealing to examine two additional roles frequently assumed by senior presidential assistants that Seidman consciously and consistently did *not* assume.

The first was the role of policy adviser and advocate. Proximity, particularly for those officed in the West Wing,[29] provides frequent access to the President for many senior aides. In the Ford White House's relatively open atmosphere, Seidman and other senior presidential assistants were no exception.[30] Seidman had an unquestioned opportunity to carve out a significant role as a policy adviser and advocate.

However, despite his strong personal views on many issues, Seidman eschewed advocacy, not only in executive committee discussions with the

---

[28]   Seidman, of course, was only one of many on the Board who maintained and cultivated extensive links with the "outside world." Members of the Executive Committee frequently related information and impressions received from meetings with private sector groups and individuals or with senators and congressmen.

Interestingly, the Ford administration, although a Republican administration, was not top-heavy with leading officials experienced in business. Thus, Seidman's extensive business experience and contacts were one of the main links between the administration and the business community.

[29]   Seidman and Porter had offices in the West Wing of the White House from February 1975 to January 1977.

[30]   The organization of the Ford White House announced in February 1975 designated nine individuals – Donald H. Rumsfeld (Chief of Staff), Henry A. Kissinger (Assistant to the President for National Security Affairs), L. William Seidman (Assistant to the President for Economic Affairs), James M. Cannon (Assistant to the President for Domestic Affairs), Philip W. Buchen (Counsel to the President), Ronald H. Nessen (Press Secretary to the President), John O. Marsh, Jr. (Counsellor to the President), Robert T. Hartmann (Counsellor to the President), and James T. Lynn (Assistant to the President for Management and Budget) – as having direct reporting relationships and access to the President.

President, but also in the memorandums that went from the EPB to the President, and, for the most part, in the daily executive committee meetings. In those meetings he generally drew attention to neglected interests or considerations, emphasized the importance of devoting resources to particular problems, facilitated coordination between two or more members or departments, reported conversations he had held with representatives or groups in the private sector, and suggested further analysis before presenting an issue to the President. Rarely did he identify with a particular option or alternative. Even on matters within his own technical expertise, such as tax policy questions, he generally refrained from advocacy. He did, from time to time, work closely with the staff at the tax division of the Treasury. But, the thrust of his efforts was posing difficult questions or suggesting ways of improving the quality of the analysis.

Seidman's willingness to accept relative anonymity surprised and perplexed many other White House and executive branch officials. He resisted the lure of becoming a principal spokesman for and defender of the administration's economic policies by maintaining a low public profile, particularly during late 1974 and 1975 when the EPB was in its formative period. He happily deferred to Simon, Greenspan, and others as the main public spokesmen. His appointment as EPB Executive Director did not require Senate confirmation or testimony before congressional committees.

Seidman felt that if he became an active public spokesman for the administration's policy, it could limit his ability to preside impartially over the policy development process. In short, Seidman viewed the roles of advocate and, to a somewhat lesser extent, public spokesman as conflicting with his most important responsibility of honest broker and policy manager.[31]

STAFF

The Executive Director's immediate staff resources remained modest despite frequent pressures to increase its size and periodic attempts to establish the Economic Policy Board by statute complete with its own

---

[31] It is interesting to compare Seidman's roles as Assistant to the President for Economic Affairs with David K. Hall's description of the roles typically assumed by the Special Assistant to the President for National Security Affairs. Hall maintains that the Assistants to the President for National Security Affairs have increasingly assumed the roles of "policy adviser–advocate" and "policy spokesman–defender," and that these roles have conflicted with their role of overseeing the development of policy advice to the President through the NSC. David K. Hall, "The Special Assistant for National Security Affairs," in U.S. Commission on the Organization of the Government for the Conduct of Foreign Policy, *Appendices* (Washington, D.C.: GPO, June 1975), Vol. 2, pp. 100–119.

professional staff. The office of the Assistant to the President for Economic Affairs, technically part of the White House staff, numbered about ten individuals – roughly half professionals, half support personnel.[32] This White House–based staff, working almost exclusively on Economic Policy Board–related matters, was supplemented by the staff of the Council on International Economic Policy (CIEP), which processed most of the correspondence that went through Seidman's office. CIEP also assisted in coordinating specific issues, played a major role in organizing the international economic policy reviews, assisted in coordinating the domestic economic policy reviews, and provided support services for putting together the international summit conference briefing books.

However, CIEP staff members served on interagency committees as CIEP representatives and often participated in discussions as advocates. CIEP was recorded on memorandums as having an institutional position on several international economic policy issues. The Executive Director of CIEP was a member of the Economic Policy Board and the EPB Executive Committee. However, despite this independent institutional existence, the CIEP staff was considered a support staff for the EPB.[33]

Seidman maintained a relatively small staff for three reasons. First, he was concerned about the influence of staff size on his image as an honest broker. Most assistants to the President responsible for organizing advice over a broad policy area built relatively large personal staffs. The Kissinger National Security Council, Erlichman Domestic Council, and Peterson–Flanigan Council on International Economic Policy staffs had ranged from approximately 40 to 110 members.[34] Seidman was anxious to avoid the label of empire builder and to differentiate himself from this pattern.

Second, Seidman was convinced that EPB member departments and agencies would view a relatively large staff in his office as a competitor resulting in less cooperation.

Finally, Seidman reasoned that it would be easier to build his staff

[32]   As part of the White House staff, Seidman's office could and frequently did draw upon the White House correspondence unit during evenings and on weekends.

[33]   In practice, during 1976, two professional members of the CIEP staff spent the majority of their time working on EPB matters with the EPB Executive Secretary. During 1976 the CIEP staff included, in addition to the Executive Director, twelve professionals and twenty-two support staff. "Report to the President on the Activities of the Council on International Economic Policy," Appendix A in the *International Economic Report of the President, January 1977* (Washington, D.C.: GPO, 1977).

[34]   Even these figures may be somewhat understated because individuals from a department or agency were sometimes detailed without appearing in any formal accounting of the staff size. See Destler, *Presidents, Bureaucrats, and Foreign Policy*, p. 126. See also the *International Economic Report of the President* from 1973–1977. These figures usually involve about half professional and half support staff.

later, if he found his staff resources inadequate, than to live with or pare an oversized staff. Seidman was also sensitive to: the personal demands on his time involved in managing a relatively large staff; the potential communication problems caused if large numbers of people dealt with departments and agencies for his office; and the tendency for capable, underused staffers to generate work of their own.

The decision not to try to establish the Board statutorily grew out of the same philosophy. Serious consideration of whether to seek such legislation commenced early in 1975 when it became apparent that the Economic Policy Board's responsibility for formulating all foreign and domestic economic policy greatly weakened the rationale for a separate Council on International Economic Policy. One alternative to having a small Economic Policy Board staff supported by a larger CIEP staff on international economic policy issues was to seek legislation formally establishing the Economic Policy Board by statute and to fold CIEP into it. In early 1975, Ford tentatively approved the idea of a statutory EPB and authorized the preparation of draft legislation; by March he agreed with the overwhelming consensus of his advisers and Seidman's judgment not to go forward with it. Seidman and the other members of the Executive Committee resisted the idea for three reasons.

First, establishing the Economic Policy Board by statute would give the EPB its own budget separating it from the White House staff. The National Security Council, the Domestic Council, and CIEP, all of which had their own budgets, had grown several times larger than the EPB staff. The temptation for the staff size to grow if the EPB were established by statute would be great.[35]

Second, any legislation creating the Economic Policy Board would raise the issue of CIEP's status. Most senior officials felt that creating the EPB had made CIEP anachronistic. But legislation creating the EPB and eliminating CIEP would entail, in the eyes of the Congress, substituting the EPB for CIEP.

The CIEP Executive Director was confirmed by the Senate and periodically testified before congressional committees on international economic policy issues. CIEP also prepared an annual report to the Congress and other reports on demand.

---

[35] The National Security Council was established by the National Security Act of 1947 (61 Stat. 496; 50 U.S.C. 402), amended by the National Security Act Amendments of 1949 (63 Stat. 579; 50 U.S.C. 401 et seq.). The Council on International Economic Policy was authorized by the Congress in the International Economic Policy Act of 1972 (86 Stat. 646; 22 U.S.C. 2841 et seq.), as amended. The Domestic Council was established by Reorganization Plan 2 of 1970, effective July 1, 1970. The reorganization authority under which the Domestic Council was created had expired and thus it would require legislation to establish the EPB by statute.

The Treasury Secretary, the CEA Chairman, and the OMB Director were investing a large share of their time and staff resources preparing and delivering testimony before congressional committees on economic policy issues. If the EPB Executive Director were expected to comply with a similar level of requests plus prepare reports, he would need a much larger staff. The Congress had a pattern of seeking Senate confirmation of key Executive Office officials. There didn't seem to be any way to avoid the confirmation requirement, especially since legislation was the only way to establish the EPB by statute, the President's reorganization authority having lapsed.

Finally, there seemed no compelling need for such a move. The EPB did not lack access to staff resources. Its status and prestige were tied to its relationship to the President, not to whether it was established by statute or by executive order. On balance, Seidman and the rest of the members of the Executive Committee concluded that there was little to gain and much to lose; in March 1975, the idea was quietly dropped.

The EPB did not need a larger staff because existing arrangements were working well. Seidman and his small staff had developed excellent relationships with Treasury, CEA, and OMB. Simon had instructed his Treasury staff that a request for information or analysis from Seidman was to be considered a request from him. Seidman and his staff had essentially the same working relationship with the staffs at the Council of Economic Advisers and the Office of Management and Budget. Neither Greenspan nor Lynn considered Seidman a threat, although some of their bureaucrats did at the beginning. Similar arrangements developed with the Departments of Labor, Commerce, and State after they joined the Executive Committee. Seidman and his staff also worked closely with the National Security Council, CIEP, and the Domestic Council staffs on certain projects. His ability to draw freely and extensively on staff resources elsewhere permitted Seidman to operate with a very small personal staff throughout the two and a half years of the Ford administration.

FUNCTIONS

Economic Policy Board members considered advising the President on economic policy issues their most important collective function; they focused on identifying issues meriting presidential attention, generating an agreed upon set of facts and analysis, developing alternatives for the President's decision, coordinating the flow of economic information to the Oval Office, generating ideas and themes for presidential speeches, and clearing the stream of economic statements and messages issued from the White House.

But the EPB also performed several other functions. Exchanging information was one of the most important. Most cabinet officials are expected to master a wide range of issues. Their need to keep current on many policy issues limits the amount of time they can devote to any one problem. Their position at the top of their departments means that much of the information they receive has been summarized and sanitized on its way up the departmental ladder. Moreover, many cabinet officials depend heavily on what their own bureaucracy prepares for them. The analyses they receive often reflect the interests and the perspectives of those in their own department.[36]

The EPB helped the exchange of information among cabinet officials in a number of ways. The daily executive committee meetings included discussion of current developments; members could ask their colleagues for appraisals of a recently released statistic or efforts to deal with a particular problem. This type of information exchange was extended less frequently to all members of the EPB at full board meetings and in the periodic briefings held by the EPB for groups of subcabinet officials. Not least, executive committee members also exchanged a large number of information papers on a wide range of issues.[37]

The daily executive committee meeting also indirectly played an important role in coordinating administration presentations to congressional committees. House and Senate committees commonly call several administration witnesses to testify on a given subject. Not infrequently, the committees try to discover or to promote a difference of opinion among administration officials. An official not fully aware of an administration policy and its rationale can be severely embarrassed and give the impression of an administration in disarray when skillfully questioned by a congressman or senator.

[36] One of the problems with this pattern of summarizing and sanitizing is the process of substituting judgments or inferences for facts, which John C. Ries has called "uncertainty absorption." Ries argues convincingly that "through this process, communications moving upward tend to get sugarcoated. A subordinate is much more likely to report improvements and successes than failures." John C. Ries, *The Management of Defense* (Baltimore: Johns Hopkins, 1964), pp. 49–50.

[37] During 1975 an average of eleven information papers per month were distributed to executive committee members through the EPB Executive Director's office. They ranged from "Changes in Unemployment Compensation Legislation" to "The Current Economic Situation in the United Kingdom." The papers were included in the packet of materials sent each day to executive committee members. The daily packet included the final agenda for the next executive committee meeting, the minutes of that morning's executive committee meeting, papers for upcoming agenda items, as well as the information papers described above.

Having an accurate opening statement is only the first step in making a coherent and convincing presentation of administration policy before a congressional committee. It is also necessary to understand its details and background. As one member remarked:

> I find that I am constantly drawing on information and arguments that I pick up in the discussions at the EPB meetings in responding to questions I get on the Hill. It makes a difference to know that you sat through the same meetings with one of your colleagues who is also scheduled to testify before the same committee. Many committees are anxious to drive wedges between different people in an administration if they can, but we have had little of that on economic policy questions.

The Executive Committee also cleared legislation occasionally. For many years, the Bureau of the Budget and the Office of Management and Budget have cleared proposed legislation and draft testimony by executive branch agencies on behalf of the President,[38] frequently discovering conflicts between agencies, which OMB seeks to resolve in accord with the program of the President. On approximately half a dozen occasions when interagency meetings with subcabinet officials failed to resolve a dispute, OMB's Legislative Reference Division requested the EPB to consider the issue and see if some agreement could be reached at the cabinet level. The EPB was generally willing, and invariably the disputes were more easily resolved once they were elevated to the cabinet level.

Over time the Economic Policy Board developed a feeling of collective responsibility for overall economic policy among its members that let it raise issues generally regarded as within a single department's jurisdiction. Sometimes the EPB served as the ally of a cabinet secretary anxious for high-level White House support for internal changes within his department. For example, repeated EPB discussion of motor vehicle safety standard 121 requiring computerized braking systems on certain trucks, buses, and other vehicles contributed to the National Highway Traffic Safety Administration's (NHTSA) reevaluation of the procedures used in calculating the economic costs of regulations. Ultimately, the Secretary of Transportation, with the backing of the EPB Executive Committee, secured a major revision in NHTSA's procedures.

The EPB was also instrumental in establishing three task forces to improve government regulation, which undertook in-depth analyses of the regulatory procedures and practices of the Export Control Adminis-

---

[38] See Richard E. Neustadt, "The Presidency and Legislation: the Growth of Central Clearance," *American Political Science Review* 47 (1954): 641–671; also R. S. Gilmour, "Central Legislative Clearance: A Revised Perspective," *Public Administration Review* 31 (1971): 150–158.

tration in the Department of Commerce, the Occupational Safety and Health Administration in the Department of Labor, and the Federal Energy Administration. Since several EPB members were concerned, the Treasury delayed its regulations on taxing international investment until an interagency study provided information that resulted in modified regulations. In all these instances, the Economic Policy Board was the vehicle through which issues previously under the effective control of a single agency were placed in an interagency forum for discussion.

The EPB also maintained liaison between the White House and a variety of economic-related commissions and councils, including the Council on Wage and Price Stability, the President's Labor–Management Committee, the Trade Policy Committee, the National Advisory Council on International Monetary and Financial Policies, the East–West Foreign Trade Board, the National Center for Productivity and Quality of Working Life, and the National Commission on Supplies and Shortages. Many of these commissions and councils made periodic status reports to the EPB Executive Committee and occasionally brought issues to it for resolution. The President's Labor–Management Committee coordinated closely with the White House and the Treasury. Simon, Seidman, and on occasion other members of the EPB, attended the meetings of the President's Labor–Management Committee (LMC) and LMC meetings with the President.

From time to time, the EPB also monitored and evaluated existing programs. Frequently, the EPB's interagency evaluations occurred when a program was due for termination unless renewed, as in the case of the inflation impact statement program.

In short, while the EPB's primary role was organizing the pattern of advice to the President on economic policy matters, it also cleared speeches and messages, exchanged information, coordinated administration presentations to congressional committees, cleared legislative initiatives, raised issues embedded in a single department for interagency consideration, and evaluated existing programs.

RELATIONSHIPS WITH OTHER COORDINATING BODIES

The Economic Policy Board was one of five formal entities responsible for advising the President over a broad range of public policy. The National Security Council, the Domestic Council, the Office of Management and Budget, and the Energy Resources Council were the other four. No matter how one slices the public policy pie, assuming that more than one entity reports to the President, overlaps are inevitable. The lines between national security, budgetary, economic, and domestic issues are rarely clear. Almost any issue involves budgetary matters, and most issues can be defined as economic.

While the potential for jurisdictional battles among White House policy councils is great, two factors traditionally serve to reduce such conflicts. First, the principal actors acknowledge and accept the primacy of one set of concerns or range of interests. Developing a policy on arms sales abroad may have significant impact on the domestic economy and the balance of payments, but national security and foreign policy considerations would likely give lead responsibility to the National Security Council.

Second, tradition and precedent define some issues as part of a particular entity's domain. Distributing food aid under the PL-480 program, a series of decisions involving foreign policy, economic, and budgetary interests, is firmly rooted in an OMB-chaired interagency body closely tied to the budgetary process. Tradition and precedent are sometimes challenged, occasionally successfully, but on many issues, they add stability as issues are divided among the major policy-making bodies in the Executive Office.

Widespread agreement on who should have responsibility for an issue and the momentum of precedent determine the distribution of most issues, particularly after an administration's settling-in period. Dividing the remaining issues depends on institutional strength, interest, and the personal relationships among the principal actors.

In the Ford administration, coordinating assignments between the principal policy bodies occurred at two daily meetings in the White House. The first was the White House senior staff meeting presided over by the President's chief of staff. Approximately twenty people, including the heads of the five coordinating bodies, attended. It clarified assignments and responsibility for dealing with current problems. The chief of staff met with the President immediately afterward and thus could get the President's decision on those rare occasions when jurisdictional questions were not resolved.

The EPB executive committee meeting, held immediately following the senior staff meeting, also frequently sorted out responsibility for issues among the coordinating bodies. Sometimes discussing an EPB agenda item ended with assigning responsibility for the issue to the NSC, the Domestic Council, or OMB. Sometimes the Domestic Council or OMB would bring an issue to the EPB to get the views of the "economic types" on the matter.

Since the EPB was the only coordinating body that met daily, the speed with which it could consider an issue meant that a large number of issues gravitated to it. Even more importantly, the EPB executive committee meetings included representatives from all of the other coordinating bodies, improving communication and hence reducing duplicated effort. Because individuals could not claim that they were excluded from discussing an issue, the process did not usually generate jurisdictional conflicts.

Another helpful factor was the close proximity and good personal relationships between the directors. Occasionally, jurisdictional questions were resolved by joint coordination of an issue. The EPB and the NSC commenced a study on East–West economic relations and established two joint committees – the EPB/NSC Commodities Policy Coordinating Committee and the EPB/NSC Food Committee, which was responsible for negotiation of the U.S.–U.S.S.R. long-term grain agreement. In some instances, two coordinating entities submitted joint papers to the President. The EPB and the NSC jointly coordinated the preparations for the Rambouillet and Puerto Rican summit conferences.

Energy policy also witnessed a high level of coordination between economic and energy interests. During the development of the President's energy program in 1974 and 1975, the EPB and the ERC worked closely together and frequently held joint economic and energy meetings with the President. After December 1975, the EPB and ERC held a joint executive committee meeting approximately once a week.

Although the Director of OMB was a member of the EPB and its Executive Committee, many career civil servants at OMB viewed the Economic Policy Board as a potential threat. Some felt the EPB might "recapture" the power and prestige that OMB had wrested back from the Domestic Council after John Ehrlichman's departure. As one senior OMB official explained:

> I know that people at OMB were very sensitive to preserving their own bureaucratic turf. They were very worried from time to time that the EPB would replace the testimony clearance function of OMB. But although that was the big worry of different people, I think, in fact, that the EPB enhanced OMB's role. I know that there were a number of occasions when Jim Lynn or I found out about testimony that in the absence of the EPB might not have been cleared through OMB. The ones that OMB knew about they could insist on their usual clearance role, but these were ones that we otherwise would not have found out about.
>
> At OMB you had the typical bureaucratic tendency to think that an issue should go the EPB less often than it probably should. And there Lynn was incredibly strong about taking things to the EPB. I know that he insisted that we take many things to the EPB that

otherwise would not have been taken there. And that happened many, many times when he was really the guy who pushed the thing.

Once again, personalities and a willingness at the top to make the system work with a minimum of turfsmanship contributed to the smooth relationships of the major coordinating entities.

SCOPE OF ACTIVITIES

Examining the agendas, minutes, and papers considered at Economic Policy Board meetings helps answer questions about what the EPB did and how it worked. What range of policy issues did it consider? What portion of its efforts was devoted to which policy areas? What kinds of special problems or crises did it undertake? Which departments and agencies took lead responsibility on which issues and the preparation of papers? Did one or more agencies dominate the economic decision-making process?

The Economic Policy Board's explicit responsibility for overseeing the formulation, coordination, and implementation of all U.S. economic policy, foreign and domestic, was an unusually broad mandate by historical standards. Several post–World War II presidents had established cabinet-level councils and committees to deal with foreign economic policy issues – the Truman administration's Executive Committee on Foreign Economic Policy, the Eisenhower administration's Council on Foreign Economic Policy, the Johnson administration's Cabinet Committee on the Balance of Payments, and the Nixon administration's Council on International Economic Policy.

These same presidents had likewise created a variety of councils and committees to deal with domestic economic policy issues – the Eisenhower administration's Advisory Board on Economic Growth and Stability and the Cabinet Committee on Price Stability for Economic Growth, the Kennedy administration's Cabinet Committee on Economic Growth, the Johnson administration's Cabinet Committee on Price Stability, and the Nixon administration's Cabinet Committee on Economic Policy. Moreover, beginning in the Kennedy administration, a group known as the Troika – the Secretary of the Treasury, the Chairman of the Council of Economic Advisers, and the Director of the Bureau of the Budget – assumed responsibility for advising the President on macroeconomic policy issues. Interestingly, the Troika rarely if ever considered microeconomic or sectoral issues. In short, during the last quarter of a century, most cabinet-level interagency bodies dealing with economic policy have addressed a relatively narrow range of issues.

Most recent administrations have organizationally separated responsibility for domestic and foreign economic policy issues. Among the predecessors of the EPB, only the Council on Economic Policy, established early in the second term of the Nixon administration, had a mandate that included both domestic and foreign economic policy. But the Council on Economic Policy rarely met as a body; neither was its principal function to advise the President, in part because Nixon wasn't actively interested in many economic policy decisions. Thus, the Economic Policy Board was unique among economic policy entities in the level of its activity and the breadth of its mandate.

Its mandate covered three general types of activities: (1) devoting continuous attention to a wide range of policy areas; (2) addressing special problems or crisis issues; and (3) undertaking longer-term studies and projects.

Regular policy areas

A breakdown of the agenda items considered at regular EPB executive committee meetings is found in Table 4. Sixteen of the twenty-three policy areas had at least twenty-five agenda items during the twenty-seven month period from October 1974 to January 1977, an average of once a month or more. As Table 4 shows, the EPB regularly not only considered domestic and foreign economic policy issues, but several other major policy areas.

Macroeconomic policy agenda items included regularly assessing the pattern of economic activity to determine an appropriate level of proposed federal spending, developing economic assumptions for use in the federal budget, and monitoring the price outlook and capital investment as well as overall strategy for dealing with inflation and the recession, and the appropriate mix of fiscal and monetary policy.

Procedural issues included internal organizational questions such as establishing subcabinet-level task forces or committees, or considering which issues to raise with the President. Agricultural policy issues considered at executive committee meetings included: meat import policy; foreign agricultural sales and export policy; loan rates and target prices for wheat, corn, soybeans, and dairy products; the relationship of wholesale prices, margins, and consumer prices for meat; the crop supply and demand outlook and its impact on farm income and the consumer price index; an international grain reserves system; sugar supply and demand conditions and policy alternatives; and the economic effects of marketing orders for agricultural products.

Tax policy issues included tax reform, capital formation tax incentives, individual and corporate income tax reductions, and estate and gift

TABLE 4
Policy areas considered by the Economic Policy Board

Policy area	Agenda items	Percentage of total agenda items	Number of months issues in policy area considered
Macroeconomic policy	174	15.1	27
Procedural issues	130	11.3	22
Agricultural policy	116	10.1	21
Tax policy	98	8.5	25
Energy policy	96	8.3	23
Employment–unemployment policy	58	5.0	17
International economic policy	53	4.6	22
Trade policy	52	4.5	22
Government regulation	47	4.1	22
Domestic economic policy	40	3.5	20
Government operations	37	3.2	15
Labor policy	36	3.1	17
Third World economic relations	35	3.0	18
Urban policy	32	2.8	12
Maritime policy	26	2.3	15
Finance and banking	25	2.2	16
Transportation policy	22	1.9	13
International investment policy	17	1.5	11
Housing policy	14	1.2	6
Statistics	12	1.0	11
International monetary policy	11	1.0	8
Environmental policy	11	1.0	8
International aviation policy	9	0.8	7
Total	1151	100.0	

Source: EPB executive committee minutes.

taxes. Energy policy issues ranged from discussing the economic impact of alternative energy conservation measures to natural gas deregulation and ways of cushioning the impact of the President's energy program for various sectors of the economy.

Employment and unemployment policy issues included job creation initiatives, the minimum wage, the unemployment compensation system, public service jobs, and structural unemployment. International economic policy agenda items included assessments of the outlook for the world economy, codes of conduct for multinational corporations, the economic aspects of the Law of the Sea Conference, and preparations for the international economic summit conferences in Rambouillet and Puerto Rico.[39] Among the trade policy issues considered were the Generalized System of Preferences, strategy for the multilateral trade negotiations in Geneva, the U.S. response to Canadian restrictions on American cattle and beef exports, certain countervailing duty cases, and major escape clause cases such as footwear and specialty steel.

Government regulation issues included inflation impact statements, banking regulation, financial institutions reform, antitrust policy, transportation regulatory policy, and the work of special task forces to improve government regulation by examining the regulatory activities of various executive agencies. Domestic economic policy agenda items included considering measures to benefit small businesses, stockpile sales, the EDA revolving fund, and advancing general revenue sharing payments. Government operations issues included governmental accounting practices, government-sponsored loans in leverage leases, and federal procurement policy.

Labor policy included monitoring wage settlements, strike activity and collective bargaining negotiations, and benefit adequacy requirements. Issues considered regarding economic relations with the Third World included U.S. policy on several international commodity agreements and expropriation policy. Transportation policy included railroad revitalization and problems facing the automobile and airlines industries.

International investment policy included issues involving both foreign investment in the United States and taxation of U.S. international investment. Statistical issues included reviewing departmental priorities in expenditures on statistics, and examining several specific statistical problems and alternatives for reorganizing the federal statistical system. These examples illustrate the wide variety of agenda items considered by the EPB.

---

[39] The international economic policy and domestic economic policy categories in Table 4 are general categories that include a host of miscellaneous issues.

Special problems and crisis issues

The Economic Policy Board also coordinated executive branch elements to meet special problems and crises including the New York City financial situation, the Arab boycott, questionable corporate payments abroad, negotiations for a long-term grain agreement with the Soviet Union, preparations for the international economic summit conferences, and international monetary problems involving Italy and Great Britain.

While the Economic Policy Board did not spend large amounts of its time on crisis management, the President or his chief of staff assigned it responsibility for many special problems with primarily economic implications, because it met regularly and brought together the major economic officials in the executive branch.

Long-term projects and studies

During 1975 and 1976, the Economic Policy Board organized several long-term projects on a wide variety of subjects, generally by a subcabinet level task force or committee. They included studies of productivity, capital formation, product liability, railroad reorganization, services and the multilateral trade negotiations, sugar, international air transportation policy, banking regulatory reform, antitrust immunities, taxation and international investment, the organization of the federal statistical system, and East–West economic relations.

Departmental participation

Departmental participation was broad and involvement in EPB executive committee meetings was high, as shown in the breakdown by department of lead responsibility for EPB agenda items in Table 5. The weekly agendas distributed to EPB members identified a department or agency as responsible for each agenda item. Lead responsibility generally involved preparing and presenting a paper distributed to members in advance of the meeting. For other agenda items, the lead department or agency made an oral presentation rather than preparing a paper in commencing discussion of the issue.

Table 6 gives a breakdown by department of papers prepared for EPB agenda items. A dozen entities had lead responsibility for twenty-five or more agenda items; over two dozen agencies were involved in preparing and presenting issues at executive committee meetings.

Four members – Treasury, OMB, CEA, and the Assistant to the President for Economic Affairs – presented over 60 percent of the agenda items and prepared almost 60 percent of the papers considered at the

TABLE 5
Lead responsibility for EPB agenda items

	Number of items	Percentage
Department of the Treasury	254	21.5
Assistant to the President for Economic Affairs	236	19.9
Council of Economic Advisers	135	11.4
Office of Management and Budget	108	9.1
Federal Energy Administration	68	5.7
Department of Labor	67	5.7
Department of State	44	3.7
Council on International Economic Policy	39	3.3
Council on Wage and Price Stability	38	3.2
Department of Commerce	33	2.8
Troika II	29	2.4
Department of Agriculture	25	2.1
Department of Transportation	19	1.6
Special Representative for Trade Negotiations	16	1.4
White House Offices	16	1.4
Domestic Council	12	1.0
Department of Housing and Urban Development	8	0.7
Department of Justice	8	0.7
Department of the Interior	7	0.6
Federal Reserve Board	5	0.4
Miscellaneous (NSC, NASA, CIA, EPA, SEC, FPC, ERDA, HEW, Eximbank)	17	1.4
Total	1184ᵃ	100.0

ᵃThe total exceeds the number of agenda items considered because it includes 33 agenda items for which two departments or agencies shared responsibility for presenting the agenda item.

Source: EPB executive committee minutes.

TABLE 6
Papers prepared for EPB agenda items

	Number of papers	Percentage
Department of the Treasury	160	22.2
Council of Economic Advisers	109	15.2
Assistant to the President for Economic Affairs	75	10.4
Office of Management and Budget	74	10.3
Department of Labor	39	5.4
Federal Energy Administration	35	4.9
Department of Commerce	28	3.9
Department of State	26	3.6
Council on Wage and Price Stability	26	3.6
Council on International Economic Policy	24	3.3
Troika II	22	3.1
Department of Agriculture	19	2.6
Special Representative for Trade Negotiations	18	2.5
Department of Transportation	13	1.8
White House Offices	12	1.7
Domestic Council	9	1.3
Department of Housing and Urban Development	7	1.0
Department of Justice	6	0.8
Department of the Interior	5	0.7
Federal Reserve Board	3	0.4
Miscellaneous (NSC, NASA, EPA, ERDA, OTP, FPC, FHLBB)	9	1.3
Total	719ᵃ	100.0

ᵃThe total includes 23 papers jointly written by two departments. Task forces and committees formally established by the EPB prepared 122 of the papers. Except in the case of Troika II, the department (or departments) serving as chair of the task force is credited with having prepared the paper.

Source: EPB executive committee minutes.

meetings. This pattern reflects the Executive Committee's composition since it consisted of these four members and the Executive Director of CIEP when the EPB was created on September 30, 1974. Their prominence was also reflected in the large number of EPB committees and task forces they chaired. Yet no single department or agency dominated the work of the EPB, which remained accessible and receptive to a broad spectrum of views and options.

SUMMARY

This survey of the operations, organization, and functions of the Economic Policy Board reveals several distinguishing characteristics. The EPB was an extremely active entity, meeting 520 times and considering 1,539 agenda items during the two and one-quarter years of its existence. (See Table 7.) Moreover, the EPB operated more formally than its predecessors had. Agendas and papers distributed before meetings, minutes, options papers on issues for presidential decision, decision memorandums for implementing presidential decisions, and quarterly work plans were all part of the daily life of the EPB.

The Executive Committee functioned through an organizational structure that included twenty subcabinet-level committees and task forces, quarterly domestic and international policy reviews, and special sessions in addition to the regular executive committee meetings and meetings with the President.

The EPB members as a group had regular and frequent access to the President. The Executive Committee met with the President nearly a hundred times and was the conduit through which the President made virtually all of his decisions on economic policy matters.

An Assistant to the President for Economic Affairs working from a base in the White House ran the EPB. Seidman not only had the President's confidence and support, but the other members of the EPB viewed him both as a peer and as an honest broker. Not least, he had no departmental or agency responsibilities and devoted his full time and energies to overseeing the EPB decision-making apparatus. The EPB staff of half a dozen generalists worked closely with the staffs of member departments and agencies.

While the EPB's primary function was organizing the flow of information and advice to the President for his decisions on economic policy issues, the Executive Committee also produced and cleared presidential speeches and messages, exchanged information among the administration's leading economic officials, coordinated administration presentations to congressional committees, resolved disputes between member

TABLE 7
Economic Policy Board meetings

	Number of meetings	Number of agenda items
Executive committee meetings	351	1151
Meetings with the President	93	219
Special sessions	58	75
Quarterly reviews	8	53
Full board meetings	10	41
Total	520	1539

Source: EPB files.

departments and agencies, coordinated the activities of several statutory councils and committees, and served as the place where the major White House policy-making entities responsible for advising the President met and coordinated their activities.

Finally, the EPB exercised responsibility for both domestic and international economic policy, considering a wide variety of issues. Moreover, the members of the EPB developed a sense of collective responsibility for a broad range of issues transcending their more narrow departmental concerns.

The following three chapters turn from the EPB's general operations to examine in detail its handling of three specific policy issues.

4

The 1975 State of the Union
tax proposals

*O*n January 15, 1975, Gerald R. Ford delivered his first State of the Union message to a joint session of the Congress, declaring that the state of the nation was not good and proposing a $16 billion temporary antirecession tax reduction, $30 billion in energy conservation taxes and fees coupled with $30 billion in permanent tax reductions made possible by the energy taxes and fees, and a one-year moratorium on new federal spending programs. Many called his proposed reduction in individual and corporate income taxes a "180 degree turn" from his temporary surtax proposal and summons to mount a fight against inflation three months earlier. The story behind his State of the Union economic proposals illustrates the process by which a major macroeconomic policy change was shaped.

When Gerald Ford assumed the presidency in August 1974, the nation was experiencing double-digit inflation. Economists pointed to a variety of possible causes – the quadrupling of oil prices, skyrocketing food prices due to drought-induced food shortages, persistent and growing federal deficits, a rapidly expanding money supply, and the aftermath of wage and price controls. However, they no more agreed on a solution than on the causes – except to concede that the economy was a major problem for the President and the country.

As Vice President, Ford had called inflation public enemy number one. Three days after he was sworn in, addressing a joint session of the Congress, Ford repeated that "inflation is domestic enemy number one," and accepted the recommendation of Senate Resolution 363 for a White House summit meeting on the economy.[1]

---

[1] "Address to a Joint Session of the Congress, August 12, 1974," *Public Papers of the Presidents, Gerald R. Ford, 1974* (Washington D.C.: GPO, 1975), pp. 6–13. See also "Remarks on Signing the Council on Wage and Price Stability Act," August 24, 1974, *Ibid.*, p. 48; "The President's News Conference," August 28, 1974, *Ibid.*, p. 63.

While most of his rhetoric focused on inflation, Ford emphasized his concern about unemployment in speaking to labor leaders during the Conference on Inflation.

We must also exercise care to prevent our recently overheated economy from cooling off too rapidly. We must, at all costs, avoid a damaging recession. . . . I recognize the concern of many that unemployment might rise because of the policies we must follow to fight inflation. I am watching the unemployment rate very, very closely. This administration, as I said the other day, will act with compassion. We will not permit the burden of necessary restraint to fall on those members of society least able to bear the cost. The unemployment rate in August, announced last Friday, was 5.4 percent. But we certainly cannot be complacent about any American lacking work. The present situation calls for full use of currently available tools and dollars. As a consequence, I have instructed the Department of Labor to accelerate the obligation of currently available funds under the Comprehensive Employment and Training ACT (CETA).[2]

The President's first economic program, presented in an address to a joint session of the Congress on October 8, 1974, was produced in ten intense days in the wake of the Conference on Inflation. Ford's address made combatting inflation the nation's foremost economic priority. His thirty-one point program concentrated on ten areas for action including food, energy, restrictive practices, capital formation, "helping the casualties," stimulating housing, international interdependency, federal taxes, and federal spending. The media and the public identified the October 8 program with one memorable proposal – a one-year surcharge on corporate and upper-level individual incomes. The President explained that the estimated $5 billion the surtax would raise "should pay for the new programs I have recommended in this message." The purpose of the tax was to make the overall program fiscally neutral. The result of the pro-

---

[2]   "Remarks at Conference on Inflation," September 11, 1974, *Ibid.*, pp. 116–117. Ford went on to announce that by the end of the month the Secretary of Labor would disburse $415 million to finance eighty-five thousand public sector jobs in state and local governments. Added to the almost $550 million obligated for public service employment in June and $50 million in prime sponsorship funds, this "will provide approximately 170,000 public service jobs this coming winter," effectively doubling the number of federally funded public service jobs.

The President's Message to the Congress on Legislative Priorities of September 12, 1974, also reiterated the theme of his concern over possible increased unemployment. *Ibid.*, p. 130.

posal was that it became the cornerstone of the President's economic program in the public mind.[3]

The President proposed two major programs to "help the casualties" – temporarily broadening and lengthening unemployment insurance benefits and creating a new temporary public service employment program to take effect if unemployment exceeded 6 percent nationally.[4] The President and his administration spokesmen, however, publicly emphasized that the program was to reduce inflation. The economy, they declared, was not in a recession. At a time when double-digit inflation persisted with no slackening in sight and the unemployment rate was less than 6 percent, the state of the economy seemed to justify this emphasis.[5]

The administration's macroeconomic policy evolved through four

[3] The proposed tax excluded from the surcharge those families with gross incomes below $15,000 a year. As the President made repeated efforts to explain in subsequent speeches and news conferences, the tax applied only to the top 28 percent of the taxpayers in the country and that for a family of four with a $20,000 gross income, the additional tax would be $42 or 12 cents a day.

[4] In the October 8 speech, the President emphasized that helping the casualties was "a very important part of the overall speech." Specifically, the two elements of the program included:

First, 13 weeks of special unemployment insurance benefits would be provided those who have exhausted their regular and extended unemployment insurance benefits, and 26 weeks of special unemployment insurance benefits to those who qualify but are not now covered by regular unemployment insurance programs. Funding . . . would come from the general treasury, not from taxes on employers as is the case with the established unemployment programs.

Second, I ask the Congress to create a brand new Community Improvement Corps to provide work for the unemployed through short-term useful work projects to improve, beautify, and enhance the environment of our cities, our towns, and our countryside.

This standby program would come alive whenever unemployment exceeds 6 percent nationally. It would be stopped when unemployment drops below 6 percent. Local labor markets would each qualify for grants whenever their unemployment rate exceeds 6.5 percent.

State and local government contractors would supervise these projects and could hire only those who had exhausted their unemployment insurance benefits. The goal of this new program is to provide more constructive work for all Americans, young or old, who cannot find a job.

The purpose really follows this formula: Short-term problems require short-term remedies. I therefore request that these programs be for a 1-year period. [Ibid., pp. 228–238.]

[5] In the President's news conference the day following his October 8 address he affirmed: "I do not think the United States is in a recession. . . . We have to be very, very careful to make sure that we don't tighten the screws too tightly and precipitate us into some economic difficulty. And at the same time, we had to have provisions and programs that would meet the challenge of inflation." Ibid., pp. 245–246.

stages from October 1974 to January 1975: first, the focus on inflation and the assertion that the economy was not in a recession; second, recognizing and acknowledging that the economy *was* in a recession while maintaining that current policy, the October 8 program, was adequate and appropriate to deal with both recession and inflation; third, determining the need for new initiatives and proposals to deal with the recession; and fourth, refining the details of the new proposals.

The first phase lasted for most of the month of October. As with many newly announced major initiatives, the President and his spokesmen actively sought public and congressional backing for the thirty-one point program. The President, who spent a good deal of time campaigning for party candidates in the November elections, used his numerous speaking engagements to urge support for his economic program. But inside the White House some officials noted the first signs of a new set of difficulties for the economy. On October 16, Troika II, using the recently released third-quarter GNP figures, gave the EPB Executive Committee a disquieting forecast: the unemployment rate would rise from 5.8 to the 7 percent level.[6]

In the following two days, the Executive Committee met with the President to review the third quarter GNP figures and the current state of the economy. There was little inclination to consider fundamental policy changes based on a single forecast, but the first warning had been sounded. A week later, on October 25, the Executive Committee spent a good part of the daily morning meeting discussing how to answer queries about whether the economy was in a recession, queries prompted by the recently reported 2.9 percent (annualized) decline in the GNP and 1.2 percent September increase in the Consumer Price Index (CPI).

Many felt that the term "recession" sounded unsettling and that the present data did not indicate a recession. Conceding a recession, they argued, could do little good and possibly much harm. Instead, administration spokesmen could emphasize elements in the October 8 program designed to strengthen the unemployment compensation system and to provide public service jobs for the long-term unemployed. This theme of publicly shifting the rationale for the October 8 program, as designed to

[6] Since the early 1960's the Troika was a three-by-three group involving: (1) three agencies – the Treasury, the Office of Management and Budget (formerly the Bureau of the Budget), and the Council of Economic Advisers; and (2) three levels – a staff level, a middle level (a member of the CEA, the Assistant Secretary of the Treasury for Economic Policy, and an assistant director of OMB), and a senior level (the three agency heads). The staff level was widely referred to as Troika III, the middle level as Troika II, and the senior level as Troika I. After the creation of the Economic Policy Board, the EPB Executive Committee assumed Troika I's role with Troika II reporting to it. A good, concise description of the functioning of the Troika during the Kennedy and Johnson years is found in Okun, pp. 9–12.

meet any deterioration in the economy while combatting inflation, was taken up in the Executive Committee's weekly meeting with the President later that day.

On October 29, the index of leading indicators reported the largest decline in any single month in twenty-three years. That morning at the President's nationally televised news conference, reporters asked him if this would prompt him "to amend [his] economic program to put more emphasis on fighting recession rather than fighting inflation?" The President responded:

> The 31-point program that I submitted to the Congress and the American people did take into recognition the problems of some deterioration in some parts of the economy and at the same time recognized the need to do something about inflation. It was a finely tuned, I think, constructive program to meet both of these problems . . . at this point, I still believe the plan or program, as I submitted it, is sound, both to meet the challenge of inflation and any deterioration in the economy.[7]

During the following fortnight the continued deterioration in the economy (the unemployment rate rose from 5.8 to 6.0 percent) prompted a review of the outlook for automobiles and housing, discussion of economic forecasting procedures, and an appraisal of the adequacy of current forecasting models. Alan Greenspan, Chairman of the CEA, was assigned to construct a new forecasting model with Troika II advising him.[8] The Executive Committee also discussed at length the upcoming State of the Union address, agreeing that it would set the pattern for the

---

[7] *Public Papers of the President, 1974*, p. 482. Later in his news conference the President was pressed on the issue of whether or not the economy was in a recession.

Q. Administration officials have been avoiding the word "recession." Would you apply that term to our economic condition now?

The President: "Recession has been defined. I think the national bureau of economic research (Bureau of Economic Analysis) actually is the authority on this matter. It is my understanding they are going to come up with some answer on this question in the very near future.

But let me make an observation of my own, if I might. We are facing some difficult economic circumstances. We have too many people unemployed, and we want to do something about it. And my economic package that I submitted to the Congress and the American people will do something about it.

The American people are concerned about inflation, and my economic program would do something about inflation. So, what we have tried to do, instead of getting into semantics, is to offer constructive proposals to meet the problem. Whether it is a recession or not a recession is immaterial. We have problems. The plan I submitted is aimed at solving these problems. [*Ibid.*, pp. 487–488.]

[8] Minutes, EPB executive committee meeting, November 5, 1974.

new administration, that the address would likely center on the economy, and that the group needed to develop an array of alternatives for the President, including a review of tax policy.

As the week ended, the Executive Committee discussed again the press's persistent question: Is the economy in a recession? After considerable discussion a consensus emerged. Data since September suggested that the economy was softening. As of September, the economy was not in recession, but the last official data would lead one to believe that the economy was moving in that direction. Following the EPB's November 11 meeting with the President, Press Secretary Ron Nessen acknowledged in his daily White House briefing that the most recent data seemed to support an assessment that the economy was in the early stages of a recession.[9]

While administration officials acknowledged the onset of a recession, the President and his advisers were firm that the situation did not require any departure from the program announced on October 8. As the President explained at his November 14 news conference:

At the time we put together the 31-point program that I submitted to the Congress on October 8, 1974, which was a finely tuned program to meet the challenges of a softening economy – and there were definite signs at that time – and on the other hand, to tamp down inflation, we believed then, and I believe now, that the plan is sound, that it is constructive, that it will meet the two problems that we face. . . .

I happen to think we have got two problems – a weakening economy and inflation that is too high. The proposals that I submitted, 31 in number, try to meet both, and at the moment, I see no justification for any major revisions.[10]

---

[9] Later that day the President met with the Labor–Management Committee (LMC). The LMC members confirmed the view of his advisers that the economy was in the beginning stages of a recession. Ironically, there was more bad news for the President on the economic front with the announcement of a coal strike.

[10] *Public Papers of the Presidents, 1974*, p. 601. The President not only supported his thirty-one point program in general but also, in subsequent questioning, stood firmly behind his controversial surtax proposal.

I would hope that the Congress would take a serious look at this constructive proposal which would affect only 28 percent of the personal income taxpayers, with 72 percent of the income taxpayers not being affected at all. And even a person with a $20,000 a year taxable income would only have to pay an additional $42, or 12 cents a day. I think somebody making $20,000 a year would be willing to make that kind of sacrifice if that would be helping the people who are less fortunate who need some help during this transition phase from a recession to a healthier economy. It

Acknowledgment that the economy was in the early stages of a recession coincided with agreement among executive committee members on the need to develop contingency plans if the economy deteriorated faster or further than expected. On November 18, Seidman met with Troika II to discuss plans both for closely monitoring the pattern of economic activity and for developing alternatives for dealing with a sharp downturn. Of the executive committee members, Seidman expressed the most concern over the possibility of a rapid deterioration and the need to make contingency plans.

On November 21, Alan Greenspan reviewed the most recent statistics at the executive committee meeting. He concluded that progress in easing inflation had been made but the problem had not been solved. He counseled the President: "We have not yet broken the back of inflation." The following day brought bad news. Ford Motor, American Motors, and General Motors announced a total of over 60,000 temporary layoffs due to the lack of demand for automobiles. U.S. Steel and Bethlehem Steel also announced plans to lay off 6,800 workers because of the coal strike.[11]

On November 25, Secretary Simon, interviewed on the "Today" program, predicted that inflation would be 9.5 to 10 percent by the end of the year, that unemployment might reach 6.5 percent, but that predictions of 8.5 to 9 percent unemployment were "not supported by the facts." During the same interview, Simon strongly supported the proposed 5 percent surtax as "an extremely healthy tax" but acknowledged that it had not been "properly explained to the American people."[12]

Simon, Seidman, Ash, and Greenspan met after the November 25 executive committee meeting to discuss what the President might do to reassure the country about the economy. Two days later they expressed their concern to the President. While the CEA was not yet prepared to alter their forecast for the economy during 1975, recent developments had moved their estimates of economic conditions during the first half of the year toward the bottom of the range that appeared plausible earlier.

---

is a good proposal. I hope the Congress does take affirmative action. [*Ibid.*, pp. 605–606.]

This position was also reflected in the "President's Message to the Congress on Legislative Priorities, November 18, 1974," *Ibid*, pp. 619–621.

[11] A settlement was reached in the coal strike two days later.

[12] The following day, the Associated Press, in a story carried by both NBC and CBS, quoted Simon as saying that the United States was experiencing a recession that might be "the longest and worst recession since World War II." Simon was quoted as saying that unemployment would reach 7 percent by late spring but that he predicted an economic upturn next summer.

The Executive Committee told the President that the economy was in the midst of "a marked contraction in production, employment and incomes," that GNP could be expected to decline in both the current quarter and in the first quarter of 1975, and that this would be reflected in "pronounced increases in unemployment over the next few months." The CEA predicted "a significant increase in unemployment in November" (announced during the first week in December). At the time the CEA felt that unemployment would go to "the 7 to 7.5 percent area" during the first half of 1975. Finally, the President was told that while "we expect a bottoming during the first half of next year, we cannot rule out the possibility of a more extended slide. In any event, it is difficult to envision an economy that would be strong enough in the second half of 1975 to reduce the rate of unemployment."[13]

The group agreed that the economy deserved special treatment along with the President's Far East trip at his next news conference. Accordingly, on December 2 the President divided his news conference in two, each begun with an opening statement.

The opening statement on the economy acknowledged that the country was facing three serious domestic challenges – inflation, recession, and energy – and then urged congressional action on the President's program announced October 8 that "was designed to meet all three of these challenges." The President's statement asserted that his program "was balanced to deal with an already rampaging inflation and already anticipated recessionary forces." He urged special, immediate congressional attention on four measures, including the national employment assistance act "to provide useful work for those who had exhausted their unemployment benefits" and the tax reform bill with needed tax relief for low-income citizens. Yet, the new emphasis on combatting recession did not include a public retreat from the surtax proposal. The President added, under questioning, that he hoped "the Congress would be responsible and pass legislation that would provide the revenue to pay for the Unemployment Act extension that I recommended and the public service program that I recommended. . . . I think it would be irresponsible for the Congress to add expenditures and not provide any additional revenues."[14]

Two days later, at the December 4 executive committee meeting, Alan Greenspan reported the likelihood of sharp unemployment increases. The November figures, released the following day, showed a jump to 6.5

[13] Memorandum from Alan Greenspan to the President, "Current State of the Economy," November 26, 1974.

[14] *Public Papers of the Presidents, 1974*, p. 689. The President had returned on November 24 from an eight-day, seventeen-thousand-mile trip to the Soviet Union, Japan, and the Republic of Korea.

percent. The executive committee meeting on December 5 was one of the most heated in weeks. Seidman pressed the need to take more seriously the threat of a major recession and the possibility of much higher unemployment rates. He also urged committee members to listen to – and perhaps adopt – the views of nongovernment economists calling for a major shift in fiscal policy.

William Eberle reported that George Meany was incensed about the shift of the Labor–Management Committee meeting with the President from December 16 to January 10 because of a change in the President's schedule. The LMC members were particularly upset because by January 10 the President would probably have already made the major policy decisions that would be reflected in his State of the Union address. Seidman, anxious that the President hear the Labor–Management Committee as soon as possible, secured committee agreement to urge a December meeting between the LMC and the President. When informed of the circumstances, the scheduling office arranged a meeting for December 18. The Executive Committee, again at Seidman's urging, also agreed to meet with a group of Republican senators and congressmen to review their suggestions for economic policy.

During the week following release of the November unemployment figures, the President met with his economic advisers, the transition team, and the bipartisan congressional leadership, spending a good deal of time on the economy. During this week, he became convinced the economic situation had deteriorated so rapidly and the prospects for recovery were so faint that additional measures were necessary.

As is often the case in presidential decision making, a presidential speech before a major group frequently becomes an action-forcing event. The President's December 11 speech to the Business Council provided the opportunity for those anxious for a public commitment to a shift in policy and new proposals to press their case. By December 11, the President was convinced:

> We are in a recession. Production is declining, and unemployment, unfortunately, is rising. We are also faced with continued high rates of inflation greater than can be tolerated over an extended period of time.

He downplayed both the sense of crisis and the expectation of a quick reversal:

> I cannot and will not promise you a sudden change for the better. There is no prospect that I can discern for instantaneous improvement in the economy. Without enumerating them, you and I know that today's difficulties stem from policies and developments of

past years. The effect of policies adopted today would not be felt for months to come.

But he explained that the situation required new proposals:

> I intend to keep my experts working over the holidays, translating into specifics a number of new or alternative measures to augment and update the economic package that I will place before the Congress within the next two months. We will meet the changing priorities of our present based on future realities. I will have new proposals on the desks of the new Members of Congress when they convene in mid-January, if not sooner.[15]

Earlier that day the full Economic Policy Board held its monthly meeting reviewing the current state of the economy, discussing the budget outlook, and inviting all cabinet officers to submit their recommendations for economic initiatives in the State of the Union message. Seidman told cabinet officers that the upcoming quarterly economic policy review would consider their proposed initiatives.[16]

The following week on December 18, the President met with his Labor–Management Committee.[17] The Committee members expressed unanimous concern over the economy's rapid deterioration and the need for immediate fiscal stimulus. At the meeting they urged a quick, temporary tax cut for working and low-income taxpayers, coupled with an increase in the investment tax credit to spur business investment in plant and equipment. The LMC urged that these tax cuts total about $20 billion with about three-fourths going to individuals and one-fourth to corporations. The Committee had not completed the details of their recommendation by the meeting time, but promised to send them to the President within a week.

Later that week the EPB held its quarterly review, including a lengthy meeting with nongovernment economists on December 19 and a full-day session on December 20, considering taxes, fiscal and monetary policy,

---

[15] *Ibid.*, pp. 733–735.

[16] During December, the President continued to meet with a variety of outside groups on economic-related issues. For example, on December 12, 1974, he met with representatives of the four major automobile manufacturing corporations and the United Auto Workers to discuss the current situation and near-term outlook for the automobile industry and to listen to their recommendations.

[17] This was the third meeting of the Labor–Management Committee with the President. He had met with them on October 3 and November 8. At the November 8 meeting, Ford indicated an interest in soliciting their views prior to his State of the Union message. John Dunlop served as the neutral coordinator of the LMC, which consisted of eight business and eight labor leaders. All the members of the LMC, with the exception of Arnold Miller, who was ill, attended the December 18 meeting.

unemployment, food, housing, automobiles, public utilities, productivity, and other issues. A strong consensus favoring a tax cut emerged at the meeting of nongovernment economists. The following executive committee discussion of macroeconomic policy confirmed support for a temporary tax cut.

On Saturday, December 21, the President held two economic policy meetings. He first met with a group from the Senate Republican Conference that presented an "Economic Policy Statement and Initiatives" with recommendations related to jobs and employment assistance, energy, food, and productivity. Secretary Simon, William Seidman, and Alan Greenspan represented the EPB Executive Committee at the meeting and agreed to integrate the congressional recommendations with the EPB presentation to the President.[18]

Later that afternoon, the President met with the EPB Executive Committee on the results of the quarterly review. The meeting, which lasted for almost two and a half hours, helped solidify the President's thinking and establish the basic framework that the administration would follow in its macroeconomic policy.[19] The meeting began with a review of the economic outlook followed by a discussion of the budget situation and detailed review of a tax proposals and options paper.

The economic outlook showed at least short-run deterioration. Insured unemployment was up substantially and the household unemployment survey was expected to rise sharply in December. Within weeks the economy would probably record the highest absolute number of layoffs. Fear of becoming unemployed accounted for much of the pullback in retail purchases and a loss of confidence in the capital goods markets. The Executive Committee informed the President that they expected a rapid decline in the spring months with recovery commencing sometime during the second half of 1975. "We will likely hit 8 percent unemployment with layoffs peaking in January or February. Automobiles and housing can be expected to bottom in the first quarter of 1975. An anticipated slow reaction in the capital goods markets will likely dampen somewhat the recovery."

The budget discussion focused on the deficit for the current fiscal year (FY 1975) and the expected deficit for FY 1976. OMB Director Ash

[18]   The Senate Republican Conference statement was prepared by Senators John Tower, Jacob K. Javits, Paul J. Fannin, Carl T. Curtis, Ted Stevens, Charles H. Percy, and Howard H. Baker, Jr.

[19]   The attendees at the meeting included the President, the Vice President, Secretary Simon (Treasury), Alan Greenspan (CEA), Roy Ash (OMB), Secretary Lynn (HUD), Arthur Burns (FRB), William Seidman (WH/EPB), Albert Rees (CWPS), Donald Rumsfeld (WH), Kenneth Cole (Domestic Council), William Eberle (CIEP), Richard Cheney (WH), Ron Nessen (WH), Roger Porter (WH/EPB), and Milton Friedman (WH speechwriter).

explained that the increase in the FY 1975 deficit was almost exclusively due to increased unemployment, which had caused an increase in outlays for unemployment compensation and a decline in revenues from the lower level of economic activity.

Most of the meeting was spent reviewing the Executive Committee's tax proposals. The "Tax Proposals and Options" paper provided for the President's consideration outlined six issues requiring his decision regarding a tax cut for temporary economic stimulus and nine issues requiring decisions regarding a crude oil tax and tariff, coupled with a permanent income tax cut. The paper proceeded from a consensus that "despite the enormous budget deficit in prospect for FY 1976 and the continuing serious inflation problem, the weakness of the economy and the anxieties of the American people lead to the recommendation that a tax cut is necessary to provide short term fiscal stimulus to the economy."

The issues presented for the President's consideration included the size, duration, form, and distribution (between individuals and business) of the tax cut and whether it should be tied to offsetting expenditure restraint or a moratorium on new spending programs. The options relating to a tax and tariff on crude oil, coupled with a permanent income tax cut, came from a consensus that "the need for more effective incentives for Americans to conserve energy calls for a tax and tariff on crude oil. To keep the impact on overall economic activity approximately neutral, the oil tax increase is balanced by a major income tax cut."

On twelve of the fifteen issues presented to the President, the EPB Executive Committee had outlined two options, on one of the issues they had outlined three options, and on two of the issues the Executive Committee indicated that additional work was necessary before they were prepared to make a recommendation. On each of the thirteen issues with options the Executive Committee made a recommendation. In ten instances there was a consensus recommendation and on three issues the President was informed that there were "mixed opinions."[20]

The discussion on the tax proposals began with a detailed review of all fifteen issues, including the Executive Committee's recommendation and its rationale. The President asked a number of clarifying questions, then after the options had all been explained, he asked different members of the Executive Committee for their individual comments and asked what would happen if he did nothing on taxes.[21]

[20]   The "Tax Proposals and Options" paper was originally prepared by the Department of the Treasury with votes tabulated after the issues were discussed at the daily executive committee meetings. The first three issues in the paper (the size, duration, and distribution of a temporary tax cut) were the three issues with mixed recommendations.

[21]   Burns, Ash, Simon, Greenspan, Seidman, Lynn, the Vice President, Rees, Cole, Eberle, and Rumsfeld participated actively in the discussion.

Those who were most enthusiastic about a tax cut and who favored a relatively larger aggregate reduction argued that all of the tax cut would not add to the deficit because the stimulation would provide revenue from the income generated, concluding that "if we are to reduce the deficit it will not be by expenditure restraint but by increased revenues from greater economic growth." Those less enthusiastic about a tax cut suggested that a tax reduction would increase the deficit, helping in the short run but possibly "deepening the difficulty in the long run." The discussion included what the nongovernmental economists and the President's advisers considered were the economic merits of proposing a tax cut, and also whether "the opinion makers" would support the tax cut and how it would affect the public's confidence that the President was providing "a sense of hope and direction." Later, the advisers examined whether a tax cut would help secure congressional agreement on fiscal restraint and its contribution in "breaking the back of the growth of federal spending."

Eventually, the discussion took up the options paper proposal of linking a tax cut with a moratorium on any new federal programs entailing additional expenditures. Near the end of the discussion the President, who had spent most of the time asking questions and soliciting individual opinions on specific points, declared that he wanted the State of the Union message to deal with the problem of taxes and spending, that he supported the notion of a tax cut, but that "we can forget any new programs." He said that his mind "was pretty well made up" and that his State of the Union message would "not be a shopping list."

He then made tentative decisions on the first three issues in the options paper, before the meeting had to end. The President stressed the need for confidentiality and promised they would resume their discussions at Vail, Colorado, over the Christmas holidays.

During the next five days, two members of Seidman's staff and Treasury officials revised the options paper. The revised paper was longer, contained more details on the advantages and disadvantages of various alternatives, and added two options on the possible form of a temporary tax cut for individuals, one made by former Federal Reserve Board member Andrew Brimmer and one by former CEA chairman Arthur Okun that had been mentioned during the meeting with nongovernment economists.

The Executive Committee also considered the latest Troika II forecast and requested Troika II to make several forecasts on alternative stimulus measures. A document summarizing the results of the quarterly economic policy review was distributed to executive committee members on December 26, the day before their early morning departure for Vail.

The first of the two days at Vail was spent on energy alternatives using materials prepared by the Energy Resources Council.[22] All of the President's major economic policy advisers were present, had received the papers before the meeting, and could comment on the economic impacts of the various proposals. Much of the discussion focused on the economic impact of the energy program.

While the group agreed that the nation had an energy problem, they differed widely on how fast the administration should implement measures designed to encourage conservation. As one adviser put it: "This is not a particularly good time to be swinging a $30 billion shillelagh around with the economy in the shape it is now." Others countered: "There is never a good time to do difficult things." Whatever the merits of their respective positions, the meeting did provide the President with the perspectives both of those whose principal interest was in developing a "comprehensive and meaningful" energy program and of those whose principal concern was the accelerating deterioration of the economy.

The following day's four and a half hour session focused on economic policy.[23] The meeting covered three broad subjects: (1) a general review of the economy, budget outlays, and reconsideration of whether the President should propose a temporary tax cut and a moratorium on new federal spending programs; (2) various economic sectors such as housing, automobiles, and agriculture, wage and price restraint, and government as a lender of last resort; and (3) the specifics of the President's tax program.

Despite the President's tentative decision on December 21 to propose a temporary tax cut, three advisers raised the issue of whether a tax cut was advisable in light of the large anticipated FY 1976 deficit. The hour and a half discussion probed how much of the deficit could be attributed to unanticipated expenditure increases for automatic stabilizing programs like unemployment compensation, and how much could be linked to lower revenues because of the economic downturn, the difficulties of financing a large deficit, the economic impact of no tax cut, and the value of a tax cut in reviving consumer and business confidence. The spirited exchange, involving a wide spectrum of advisers and differing opinions, concluded with the President's decision to propose a temporary tax cut and a moratorium on new spending programs in 1975.[24]

[22]   The meeting was attended by the President, Rogers Morton (Interior, and Chairman of the ERC), Frank Zarb (FEA), William Simon, Alan Greenspan, William Seidman, Roy Ash, James Lynn, Russell Train (EPA), William Eberle, Thomas Enders (State), Donald Rumsfeld, Ron Nessen, Kenneth Cole, Eric Zausner (FEA), John Hill (FEA), Roger Porter, and Milton Friedman.

[23]   The Vail economic review was attended by the President, Simon, Seidman, Greenspan, Ash, Lynn, Rumsfeld, Burns, Eberle, Cole, Zarb, Enders, Nessen, Cheney, Porter, and Friedman.

[24]   Those more concerned about the size of the anticipated deficit wanted to link any

The meeting then examined several individual sectors of the economy and administration policy in light of the "no new spending programs" limitation. During the course of the meeting, the President made thirty decisions, fourteen on nontax issues and sixteen on his tax proposals.

After the Executive Committee's return to Washington, Seidman and his staff prepared a detailed "Summary of Decisions" and a list of assignments; both were distributed at the executive committee's first meeting after returning to Washington.

During the following week, the daily executive committee meetings and two three-hour special sessions focused on details of the tax program. Simon and Seidman reported on the Labor–Management Committee recommendations and Treasury reported on their assignments structuring the tax cut proposals. This sequence of meetings produced another "Tax Proposals and Options" paper that the Executive Committee reviewed with the President during a three hour and ten minute meeting Saturday afternoon, January 4. The paper included the Executive Committee's recommendations and the recommendations of the Labor–Management Committee.

The January 4 meeting reviewed the distribution of the temporary personal tax cuts, the kind and amount of investment tax credit restructuring, allocating the tax reductions between individuals and corporations, the form and speed of the temporary tax reduction, and similar issues regarding the permanent tax cuts rebating the revenues derived from the energy taxes and import fees. In general, the issues reviewed at the January 4 meeting involved more detailed aspects of the questions discussed at the December 21 and 28 meetings.

Once again, the meeting began with some members raising indirectly the feasibility of a tax cut, voicing their concerns about the shortness of the debt structure, the serious financial situation, and the possibility that a large federal deficit would create severe pressures on financial markets. The President asked if these advisers were now suggesting that he not propose a tax cut. He was told that his advisers remained unanimous in recommending a tax cut, and the subject was dropped.

During the remainder of the meeting, the President made decisions on five tax cut issues and six energy tax issues. The detailed nature of most of the President's decisions and the absence of any deferred issues gave the session a ring of finality. Seemingly, the package of economic and energy proposals was set.

Over the weekend, however, several of the President's economic ad-

tax cut to an equivalent reduction in federal spending. While the idea of linking tax cuts and spending reductions was not adopted, the seed was sown for what eventually became the President's October 6, 1975 proposal of a $28 billion tax reduction coupled with a $28 billion reduction in the expected growth in federal spending.

visers shared their concerns about the impact on the economy of the energy taxes, fees, and rebates. After two lengthy executive committee sessions on Monday and Tuesday, they decided to raise the issue again with the President. The energy tax package would increase prices significantly resulting in major adjustment costs, even though the increased prices were accompanied by offsetting tax reductions.

The Executive Committee discussed two possible modifications: (1) timing the permanent tax reductions to coincide with or to precede the increase in energy costs, except in the case of the tariff, or, in other words, to cushion the adjustment costs by providing some additional fiscal stimulus on the front end; and (2) phasing in the energy package over a longer period to permit a more gradual adjustment.

After much discussion and development of the figures on what the phase-in might look like, the Executive Committee decided that the point was worth pressing with the President; Seidman scheduled a meeting for the late afternoon of Tuesday, January 7. Those primarily responsible for energy policy did not favor the modifications but attended all the executive committee discussions on the issue and actively participated in the meeting with the President.

The President listened to the arguments once more, indicated that he was aware of the potential impact of the energy proposals, but reaffirmed that his mind was made up and his decisions were firm.

At his January 10 meeting with the Executive Committee, the President approved a slight raise in the temporary tax cut proposal – $15.0 to $15.9 billion – because of some revisions in Treasury estimates and the structural decisions he had made on January 4, and a revised scheme for rebating the energy taxes. By the end of the January 10 meeting, both the economic and energy tax proposals seemed set. The President would recommend a temporary, one-year, across-the-board 10 percent reduction in individual income taxes totalling roughly $12 billion. He would also recommend a temporary increase in the investment tax credit to 12 percent (up from 4 percent for utilities and from 7 percent for all other corporations) plus temporary restructuring of income limitations for utilities, estimated to total roughly $4 billion in lost revenues.

On Saturday, January 11, the President met with members of his transition team, a group of political advisers that periodically provided an assessment of how things looked from outside the White House. The core of the group was the original transition team that the President had announced the afternoon he was sworn in as president with others added over the months.[25]

---

[25] The January 11 meeting included Donald Rumsfeld, John Marsh, Rogers Morton, William Scranton, Senator Robert Griffin, David Packard, John Brynes, Philip Buchen, and William Seidman.

During the meeting, Seidman explained the elements of the tax package that the President was getting ready to announce. The discussion centered on the advisability of a straight 10 percent temporary tax cut for all taxpayers with no limit on the amount that any individual could benefit. David Packard quickly figured out the rebate he would receive from his estimated 1974 taxes – a considerable sum – and after much discussion, the President agreed with his transition team advisers that he should include a "cap" of $1,000 per person.

Seidman contacted the Treasury after the meeting and requested them to prepare estimates of the percentage reduction that the President could propose with various "caps" – no maximum, $1,500 maximum, $1,000 maximum, $750 maximum, $500 maximum, and $350 maximum – given the constraint of a total revenue loss of approximately $12 billion.[26]

After discussing the issue at the January 13 morning executive committee meeting, the Executive Committee met, reviewed the issue with the President, and presented the Treasury estimates. The President reaffirmed his decision to include a $1,000 "cap" and the package was complete.

That evening, pressured by reports that Democrats in the Congress would upstage his fiscal stimulus package, the President delivered a nationally televised address on the economy outlining the highlights of his temporary tax cut proposal. Two days later, the full details were revealed in his State of the Union message.

EVALUATING THE PROCESS: CHARACTERISTICS

The process of formulating the President's January 1975 tax reduction proposals exhibited two general characteristics: (1) it was incremental and occurred over several weeks; (2) it involved many sources within and outside the executive branch.

The decision to propose a tax reduction and then to determine its design and size evolved through several stages: recognizing the change in the economy, determining the need for a policy shift, and refining specific proposals. Each stage involved a sequence of meetings between the President and the EPB Executive Committee, and the President and "outside" groups. As is frequently the case with major policy changes on complex issues, the formulation of the January 1975 tax proposals involved a

[26] The President had previously determined that the total size of the temporary tax cut package would be approximately $16 billion, divided with roughly three-fourths for individuals and one-fourth for corporations.

number of meetings with opportunities to reconsider and revise previous decisions.

The incremental decision-making process contributed to the President's involvement in making a large number of detailed decisions on the specifics of the proposals. From the outset, the President was willing to invest a great deal of time, never suggesting that any specific decision was nonpresidential. This willingness encouraged the Executive Committee to seek the President's approval on successive refinements, even when they were in accord on a proposal. This pattern characterized the EPB's operation during its early months. Later, the President and his economic advisers were more accustomed to one another and the Executive Committee had developed more confidence in making judgments on what issues merited presidential time and attention.

While the process was incremental, it was not disjointed or chaotic. The EPB Executive Committee coordinated the pattern of advice without excluding other participants and advice. It prepared and submitted the options papers for the President and provided a high degree of continuity throughout the entire decision-making process.

In making his decisions, the President relied on several sources for advice: the EPB Executive Committee, a group of nongovernment economists, the Labor–Management Committee, the congressional leadership, and the transition team. The pattern of multiple sources of advice, however, had two features that provided continuity and order. First, the internal advice from within the executive branch came through a group rather than an individual representing the group or from advisers meeting one-on-one with the President. Moreover, this group of advisers remained constant. The half dozen principal advisers spent lengthy sessions over an extended period discussing the state of the economy and the range of alternatives available before reviewing the issues with the President. All the executive committee members knew each other's views and the arguments and analysis each was giving the President. This openness, encouraged by the President, did not stifle differences of opinion. While a general consensus ultimately emerged, there was no unanimity of opinion at the outset.

Second, the Executive Committee, at Seidman's urging, supplemented their own thinking by seeing that the President had advice from other sources. But, these other sources did not operate in isolation from the primary conduit to the President through the EPB. The Executive Committee organized the December 1974 quarterly economic review to include nongovernment economists. The Executive Director and the Secretary of the Treasury served as links between the EPB and the President's Labor–Management Committee. Seidman was also a member of the President's transition team and, along with several other executive committee members, attended meetings the President held with congressional leaders on the economy. Thus, while neither the Executive Committee as a whole nor any of its members individually tried to control the advice the President received from other sources, the Executive Committee kept fully informed on it and gave him their evaluation of it.

EVALUATING THE PROCESS: STRENGTHS AND WEAKNESSES

Masked by inadequate inventory statistics, the White House economic decision-making apparatus failed to foresee the approaching precipitous economic decline and the need for additional stimulus. However, considering the available information, statistics, and state of the art of economic forecasting, the process alerted the President in time to reshape his macroeconomic policy in a deliberative, noncrisis atmosphere.[27]

Major policy changes often occur gradually, after sufficient time to think, rethink, and refine ideas. Presidents must rely on others for much of the data and preparatory analysis – in this case, the EPB Executive Committee. It studied macroeconomic policy early and continuously. During the EPB's first sessions Seidman organized contingency planning. Thus, when developments convinced the President that a policy change was needed, the permanent government apparatus was ready to respond.

The agendas of the President's economic policy meetings during October, November, and December 1974, show many minor issues accompanying the central focus on macroeconomic policy. Participants at the meetings remember occasional rambling and unproductive discussions, but on balance, the process of deciding to seek a tax cut let the President consider alternatives carefully; pressure from less important issues did not force a quick or uninformed decision.

The process, by including multiple sources of advice from outside as well as within the executive branch, gave the President both a broad spectrum of views and analysis, and a sense of how the Congress and the business and labor communities would react. In short, he had a reasonably clear vision of economic and political realities in making his judgments and weighing the trade-offs. This feel for political reality – how his proposals would be perceived by the public and various interest groups – principally came from sources outside the EPB Executive Com-

---

[27] After the January 1975 tax proposals were developed, the Economic Policy Board directed its subcommittee on economic statistics to study the problem of inadequate inventory statistics. The subcommittee's report led to several improvements in the quantity and quality of inventory statistics collected by the federal government.

mittee, which instead focused on the substantive merits of various alternatives.

The Executive Director's role was crucial in managing the pattern of advice to the President. As a catalyst, he created opportunities for input from outside sources and served as a link between the Executive Committee and the other sources of advice. Seidman suggested a meeting between the Executive Committee and a group of nongovernment economists as part of the December 1974 quarterly review because he was anxious to provide the President with alternative views to those held by executive committee members and their staffs.

Likewise, Seidman worked to have the President meet with his Labor–Management Committee in December rather than in January while the situation was still fluid and the LMC's advice could still have an impact. In these efforts to broaden the advice the President received, Seidman secured executive committee approval for each step. Thus, he maintained his credibility and reputation for managing a fair and open process with executive committee members while seeking to expand the range of views reaching the President. Likewise, in organizing contingency planning to encourage a reexamination of the administration's economic policy, Seidman acted with executive committee approval.

One of the most persistent challenges facing policy makers is how to integrate related policies. The nexus between economic and energy policy is one of the clearest and most obvious of such interrelationships. Integration of the 1975 Ford economic and energy proposals was vastly helped because the Energy Resources Council, which had lead responsibility for developing an energy program, had the same core membership as the EPB – Treasury, OMB, CEA, and the Assistant to the President for Economic Affairs. During this period the ERC, like the EPB, operated collegially, although the FEA played a more dominant role in developing the energy program than any single agency played in developing the economic tax proposals. Moreover, there was considerable overlap among those who advised the President on the two problems. Simon, Greenspan, Ash, Seidman, and their staffs were consistently involved in both efforts.

Second, the EPB Executive Committee's daily meeting was a frequent forum for discussing energy issues, particularly the economic impact of various energy alternatives. Frank Zarb, the Executive Director of the ERC, was invited to attend executive committee meetings and frequently raised issues there for discussion with the "economic policy community."

During the last three months of 1974, the EPB Executive Committee discussed energy issues thirty-four times. On twelve occasions, the Executive Committee discussed issues directly related to the overall energy program; many sessions analyzed forecasts of the economic impact of major oil import reductions on unemployment and inflation. As one veteran staffer later observed: "Most of the important macroeconomic and some of the important microeconomic aspects of energy policy were discussed and coordinated with the balance of the administration's overall economic policy. In this respect the EPB performed a highly useful and productive function."

The decision-making process insured that all interested departments and agencies could make their inputs without one viewpoint or interest dominating. It expanded the range of views presented to the President by including nongovernment economists, business and labor leaders, and congressional leaders, as well as outside political advisers. Finally, the economic decision-making process was well integrated with the decision-making process for the energy program. Not surprisingly, those in the economic policy community brought a perspective to the discussion of the energy problem different from that of the energy community. However, the process itself took the burden of integrating the two sets of proposals from the President.

Formulating the 1975 State of the Union tax proposals occurred during the early months of the EPB's operation. Most new entities refine their procedures and improve their work product over time; the Economic Policy Board was no exception.

In its more mature period, the options papers that the EPB Executive Committee sent the President typically included the following elements: (1) an opening section defining the issue under consideration and clarifying what decision or decisions the President was being asked to make; (2) a section providing relevant background information to place the issue in context; (3) a section providing factual information and analysis; (4) a section outlining alternative courses of action with the advantages and disadvantages of each option; and (5) a section identifying which departments, agencies, and individuals supported which alternatives.

The options papers prepared for the President on the January 1975 tax reduction decisions were more primitive than later papers in three ways. They included little general analysis, little detailed discussion of each alternative's advantages and disadvantages, and either a single recommendation from the EPB Executive Committee or an indication of "mixed opinions."

Much of the substance of issues and the positions of individual advisers was left to discussion. While the written papers identified a large number of specific and often technical issues for the President's decision, they did not outline the advantages and disadvantages of various alternatives in detail. Thus, the papers were a good framework for discussion but not documents from which one would feel comfortable making decisions without a supplementary meeting.

Since the early decision-making process relied heavily on meetings between the President and his advisers, they consumed large amounts of the President's time. The numerous meetings meant additional opportunities for raising old issues and re-arguing the administration's basic economic policy strategy. But the process, while extended and time consuming, was open; all participants had equal access to the President and equal opportunity to make their arguments. It was a process that resulted in a program that was truly the President's.

5

The U.S.–U.S.S.R.
grain agreement

On July 11, 1975, Paul MacAvoy, a member of the Council of Economic Advisers and Chairman of the Economic Policy Board's Food Deputies Group (FDG), presented the regular biweekly report of the FDG to the EPB Executive Committee. The previous day the Department of Agriculture July crop report had forecast record 1975 wheat and corn crops, 22 percent and 30 percent above 1974 levels, respectively. MacAvoy's review noted that the corn crop forecast was much less certain than the wheat crop forecast, that the USDA had reduced their estimates of the Soviet grain crop, and that the Russians had begun negotiations with U.S. grain exporting firms. Two questions dominated the Executive Committee discussion. How much grain from abroad did the Soviets need and want and how quickly would they seek to purchase it?

OMB Director James Lynn reminded his fellow executive committee members of the President's commitment that he would not restrain agricultural exports. MacAvoy observed that, while there was no formal export authorization system in place, he understood that the Department of Agriculture had informally authorized U.S. grain companies to sell the Soviets up to five million tons of wheat and five million tons of corn.

Secretary of Labor John T. Dunlop probed to clarify the precise situation regarding U.S. government monitoring and authorization of large export orders; MacAvoy told him that U.S. grain export firms were formally required only to notify the Department of Agriculture within twenty-four hours *after* they had made a sale. Dunlop expressed concern at the possibility of "another 1972–73 mess" and urged that the Food Deputies Group prepare a report exploring the U.S. and Soviet crop situation in detail and reviewing the present export monitoring system for executive committee consideration early the following week. The Executive Committee approved Dunlop's recommendation and instructed

MacAvoy to report the following Tuesday, July 15, on procedures for monitoring grain sales and on "the range of error around the estimates."[1]

The U.S.–U.S.S.R. Maritime Agreement was also briefly discussed and the Department of Commerce was requested to prepare a report on the status of the agreement and the potential for expanding the use of American vessels if there were additional large shipments of grain.

DEFINING THE PROBLEM

Over the weekend, MacAvoy and Edward Schuh, a senior staff member of the CEA, prepared Food Deputies Report No. 21, "The Soviet Grain Situation," for the Tuesday, July 15, executive committee meeting. The report claimed that on Friday, July 11, the Department of Agriculture "informally authorized U.S. dealers to sell the U.S.S.R. seven million tons of wheat and seven million tons of corn – an increase from the five million tons of each that had previously been authorized." Moreover, the report surfaced an interagency difference on the price effects of selling fourteen million tons of grain to the U.S.S.R.: "The USDA estimates that U.S. exports of 14 million tons to the Soviets would have basically no effect on prices from their present levels. The CEA believes that exports of this magnitude would result in upward pressure on prices." The report recommended asking the Soviets for information about their worldwide purchase intentions, noting that "our concern over extremely large purchases has been communicated to the Soviets." It further recommended that the "EPB review the authorizations (informal authorizations to U.S. companies to sell to the Soviets) for economic implications before they are changed by USDA." The report concluded:

> The USDA has informally authorized the grain companies to sell to the Soviets up to 7 million tons of wheat and 7 million tons of feed grains. No communications on possible limitations on purchases have been made directly to the Soviets, although it is believed that the grain companies pass this information on to the Soviets. Changes in authorizations are made informally by USDA, presumably on the basis of changes in their U.S. crop forecasts.
>
> RECOMMENDATION: Our authorization policies should be revised. Changes in authorizations should be made only after approval within EPB.

Paul MacAvoy began the July 15 executive committee meeting by reviewing various assessments of the size of the Soviet purchases and their

[1] Executive committee minutes, July 11, 1975.

estimated impact on prices. He suggested that if Soviet purchases went to seven million tons of wheat and seven million tons of corn, then U.S. inventories would decline to 1973–74 levels and could increase the food consumer price index a couple of percentage points. He also observed that forecasts of the Russian crop were in "a stampede to lower levels."

Richard E. Bell, Assistant Secretary of Agriculture for International Affairs and Commodity Programs, acknowledged that USDA had not received authority from or consulted with anyone outside the department in increasing the informal authorization level to fourteen million tons. However, he pointed out that the increase had not come until after the favorable July crop report and defended his department's approach to Soviet sales as responsible and cautious. Apparently, from information provided by the grain dealers negotiating with the Russians, the Soviets didn't seem "interested in anything like 7 + 7." Yet several members remained uneasy. As one participant observed: "Practically speaking, we won't get information from the Russians on their buying intentions." The uncertainty was strong enough to produce agreement that the EPB would review any further informal authorizations of grain sales to the Soviet Union.

By the next day, Wednesday, July 16, Cook Industries Inc. advised USDA that it had completed negotiations for the sale of two million metric tons of hard red winter wheat; later, Cargill Inc. advised USDA that their European subsidiary had negotiated a Soviet sale of 1.2 million metric tons of hard winter wheat.[2]

MacAvoy, Bell, and Schuh prepared a seven-page memorandum on "Soviet Grain Purchases" that the EPB Executive Committee considered on July 17. The paper provided some historical perspective by detailing how widely fluctuating Soviet grain purchases had destabilized international markets in recent years; it compared the 1972–73 purchases – when U.S. stocks were large – with the current situation, and summarized the most recent information on world crops and Soviet purchases. While American crop prospects were bright, elsewhere the weather was taking its toll. Floods in Eastern Europe and drought in Northern Europe had damaged the grain crops in both areas. Moreover, the Soviets were moving into grain markets around the world. Yet no one knew what Soviet intentions were and Russian officials were uneasy about the publicity their purchases had generated.[3]

---

[2] U.S. *Department of Agriculture News*, July 17, 1975.
[3] The paper explained:

There has been no direct contact between U.S. and Soviet Government officials regarding the likely size of Soviet purchases of grain from the 1975 U.S. crop. The Department of Agriculture (USDA), however, has reviewed the United States supply

The discussion at the July 17 meeting centered on how the administration would authorize further sales to the Soviets. The previous October the administration had instituted a "prior approval" system for grain sales in the wake of the cancellation and renegotiation of Soviet wheat and corn purchases totalling 3.2 million tons at a time when U.S. supplies were tight and when there were indications that the Soviets were in the market for at least 2 million additional tons. The following March, the President agreed to end all prior approval requirements while retaining a monitoring system requiring grain companies to report all sales in excess of 100,000 tons within twenty-four hours. Having been "burned" the previous autumn and with the 1972–73 "grain robbery" still fresh in many officials' minds, a tone of caution and restraint characterized the discussion.

Secretary of Agriculture Butz reminded executive committee members of the President's commitment at Sioux City, Iowa, that the administration would pursue a policy of full production with no restraints on exports. Given the President's commitment and the large anticipated U.S. crop, the administration would face a difficult situation in the farm belt if it did anything that resembled export controls. He explained that each of the U.S. grain firms received specific authorization and instructions from Assistant Secretary Bell to insist on spreading the deliveries out. Furthermore, he said, there was evidence that the Russians understood the informal authorization of "7 + 7" and that, in his view, it would be unfortunate to formally establish a ceiling now. The grain companies, he concluded, were bending over backwards to cooperate.

Secretary Dunlop said he was not interested in cutting across contracts as in October 1974, but that the administration must have a better monitoring system. He suggested that the Economic Policy Board limit authorization for corn sales to the Soviet Union to the 4.5 million tons under active negotiation until after evaluating the August crop report. He said he was more concerned about the corn crop than the wheat crop, which was reasonably assured, and that he had no objection if wheat sales went up to the seven million ton level already informally authorized. The session concluded with an agreement to discuss the issue with the President on Friday, the following day, at his meeting with the EPB Executive Committee.

situation with all export firms known to be potential sellers of U.S. grain to the U.S.S.R.

Firms that have negotiated with the Soviet buyers report the negotiations have been unusually difficult with the Soviets obviously annoyed with the publicity given to their purchase prospects. As a consequence of this publicity, the Soviets for the present may well scale down their earlier purchase plans and postpone purchases for 30 to 60 days.

FIRST STEPS

The Friday, July 18, meeting with the President was crucial in establishing the context and identifying many of the interests and objectives that would dominate the issue of grain sales to the Soviet Union during the following thirteen weeks.[4] Secretary Butz began the discussion by noting that the market had dropped thirteen cents the day before because the Russian wheat sales were not as large as the market had anticipated. He reviewed the prospects for a bumper U.S. crop and indicated that the grain companies were "cooperating beautifully" in handling export sales.

The extended discussion revolved around two themes: the need to improve the system of monitoring grain sales within the executive branch; and the potential for diplomatic leverage offered by the Soviet crop shortfall and the anticipated bumper U.S. crop. The President remarked that he kept reading "rumors" regarding the amount of Russian sales and indicated that he wanted the EPB and himself notified of all such sales. Secretary Kissinger pressed for and succeeded in securing agreement that USDA would not authorize, formally or informally, any additional grain sales to the Soviet Union without EPB review.

On the issue of leverage, Secretary Kissinger argued that the U.S. grain crop was a tremendous asset, mainly because there was no substitute for it in the world. Merely pouring out the grain for "gold" was "very painful" when appropriately managed sales could buy a year or so of good Soviet behavior. He cited the skill with which the OPEC nations used their oil resources, urged that the administration maintain an "element of uncertainty," and cautioned against excessive eagerness in dealing with the Soviets.

Secretary Butz countered: The President had made a commitment of no export controls and, furthermore, the United States did not have the monopolistic control over grain that the OPEC nations had over oil.

Kissinger persisted: The administration should maximize its leverage by letting the Soviets know they could not have uncontrolled access to U.S. grain markets.

Secretary Butz acknowledged that during the previous major grain sale to the Soviet Union in 1972–73, the U.S. had tremendous stocks; low 1975 stock levels made the current situation very different. Further-

---

[4] The meeting was attended by the President, the Vice President, Simon, Seidman, Kissinger, Dunlop, Butz, Lynn, Greenspan, MacAvoy, Burns, Zarb, Marsh, Cheney, Nessen, Porter, Deputy Secretary of State Robert Ingersoll, Deputy Assistant to the President for National Security Affairs Brent Scowcroft, Assistant to the President for Legislative Affairs Max Friedersdorf, Deputy Press Secretary John Carlson, and Joseph Kasputys, Department of Commerce.

more, he agreed with Secretary Kissinger about the advantages of using a bumper U.S. crop for diplomatic leverage. The discussion ended with a crucial link established between agricultural and foreign policy and with presidential support for elevating responsibility for export authorizations to the Economic Policy Board.

The meeting then considered the maritime situation. Secretary Dunlop emphasized the wide disparity between the tonnage shipped in American and Soviet vessels – the U.S. percentage was well below the one-third specified in the U.S.–U.S.S.R. Maritime Agreement.[5] The President probed for the reasons, then stated that he considered the maritime issue as important as the grain export issue, that the U.S. had a commitment to carry one-third of the cargoes in U.S. flag vessels, and that he wanted the appropriate departments to deal with the problem immediately. He requested Secretary Dunlop to monitor the situation closely for him.[6]

What had begun as the Council of Economic Advisers' concern about the potential price effects of a major grain sale to the Soviet Union before the U.S. crop was assured, had quickly expanded into an issue involving foreign policy interests and U.S. maritime interests.

Early the following week, Secretary Dunlop traveled to Bal Harbour, Florida, to address the International Longshoremen's Association (ILA) convention. While at the convention he met with AFL–CIO President George Meany and ILA President Teddy Gleason and became aware of the intense feelings developing within the labor movement on the question of selling and shipping grain to the Russians. Significantly, Meany seemed personally interested and was supporting those who wanted to do something. The AFL–CIO's interest in the issue was a departure from the past. On two occasions in the previous decade when the issue of shipments to the Soviet Union had arisen, the issue was perceived as essentially a maritime industry problem.

Before the convention ended, the ILA adopted a resolution declaring that since the Russians and large American grain companies had profited

[5] Signed in October 1972, the agreement provided that American- and Soviet-flag ships would each have access to a substantial (defined as a minimum of one-third of the total tonnage) share of the cargo moving between the two countries and that they would maintain parity (measured by weight) in the shipment of grain. But during the first six months of 1975, U.S. vessels had carried less than a quarter of the tonnage (345,000 metric tons representing 24.9 percent) while Soviet vessels had carried nearly half of the tonnage (646,800 metric tons representing 46.8 percent). The imbalance resulted in part from a dispute over an acceptable freight rate for carrying grain on American-flag vessels and from improper cargo offerings by the Soviets. Under the agreement, however, the Soviets were obligated to offer U.S. vessels sufficient grain cargoes to offset the imbalance by December 31, 1975.

[6] Both Secretary of Commerce Morton and Assistant Secretary of Commerce for Maritime Affairs Robert Blackwell were unable to attend the July 18 meeting. Joseph Kasputys represented the Department of Commerce at the meeting.

in the past at the expense of American farmers, consumers, and taxpayers, the ILA would refuse to load grain destined for the Soviet Union until the interests of the American public were adequately protected.

On July 24, with 9.8 million tons of grain already contracted, the Department of Agriculture requested exporters to give advance notice of sales to the U.S.S.R. and indicated that the government expected no more sales before the August 11 crop report.

The next day, Seidman sent the President a status report containing five key assessments: First, the Soviet harvest would likely fall thirty million tons short of the earlier forecast and the Russians would try to import approximately twenty-five million tons. Second, U.S. production would account for over 90 percent of the increase in the world supply of wheat and feed grains in 1975. Third, sales already made to the Soviets had not increased grain prices significantly. Fourth, the CEA was uncertain what selling an additional ten million tons would do, although the USDA predicted no material price effect. Finally, waiting for the wheat and corn harvests later in the summer would eliminate uncertainty over the price effects, and the administration might avoid price increases altogether by spreading out export commitments. The report encouraged caution because of overall economic considerations even though it appeared the Soviets were in a bind and that the U.S. possessed possible leverage.

A week later, the AFL–CIO Executive Council issued two statements from Chicago on "Russian Grain Purchases" and on the "U.S. Merchant Marine – A Victim of Detente," harshly criticizing the 1972 grain sales and declaring that the ILA had refused to cooperate in loading grain destined for the U.S.S.R. until three safeguards were provided the American public: (1) information from the Soviets regarding their import intentions; (2) a policy to protect American companies from unfair competition with state-owned monopolistic economies the size of the Soviet Union; and (3) a policy to take the offensive against commodity cartels such as OPEC, including determining the extent U.S. corporations were participating in and supporting them.

The July 23 ILA resolution and the July 31 AFL–CIO Executive Council statements signaled the administration and the Russians that American labor was unalterably opposed to any deals reminiscent of 1972–73. Despite the rhetoric, however, a longshoremen's strike remained a threat, not a reality, for the time being.

A STRATEGY EMERGES

The USDA hold on additional sales to the Soviet Union, at least until after the August 11 crop report, temporarily placed the issue on the back burner. Meanwhile, a staff-level interagency group with representatives from the Departments of State and Agriculture and the Council of Economic Advisers was considering ways to capitalize on the apparent leverage that the Soviet predicament gave the U.S.

On Tuesday, August 5, Seidman sent a draft memorandum prepared by MacAvoy on the U.S. and Soviet crop situation to Secretaries Butz and Dunlop, Alan Greenspan, and Under Secretary Robinson, indicating that he wanted to discuss it the following morning. The memorandum noted a slow-down in Russian demands for U.S. grain, recent dry weather in the western corn belt that had probably reduced the U.S. corn crop by as much as five million tons, and Soviet purchases of approximately fourteen million tons of grain in international markets, including the 9.8 million tons from the U.S. On the price side, USDA expected a third quarter surge in food prices of about 4 percent, while the CEA forecast that increased sales to the Soviets of five to ten million tons could lead to a 2 percent increase in the food-at-home component of the Consumer Price Index (CPI). The memorandum urged continuing "informal" limits on Soviet purchases: authorizing sales of three million tons more in August, and if the September crop report were favorable, three to five million tons more in September. However, the paper warned that sales beyond fifteen million tons could "impose sizable economic costs on the U.S. economy." The memorandum suggested that since larger sales to the Soviets involved "political and economic costs, one approach would be to extract political and economic concessions from the Soviets in exchange for the larger sales of grain this year." The memorandum also revealed that:

> A number of alternatives are now under review by an interagency task force. Among them are: (1) a commitment to provide crop forecast information and worldwide buying intentions each crop year; (2) longer-term purchase commitments by the Soviets so as to stabilize their export demands on world markets; and (3) a long-term tie-in agreement involving Soviet sales of petroleum to the United States in exchange for a long-term commitment of U.S. grain sales.

The August 6 meeting focused on the steps to be taken following the August 11 crop report. Three considerations dominated the discussion. First, the August crop report would be helpful but not conclusive: It was still too early in the season to predict with confidence the final size of the 1975 crop.

Second, U.S. estimates of the Soviet crop coupled with communications from high-level Soviet officials to Secretary Kissinger about large additional purchases during the 1975 crop year, revealed the outlines of a serious Soviet predicament. The apparent desperateness of the Soviet situation and the position of the United States as the residual world supplier meant that suspending sales to the Soviets for a few more weeks likely would not result in lost sales for American farmers, assuming the expected bumper crop materialized. A cautious export policy, however, would protect American consumers from steep price increases if large sales were made to the Soviets now and continued drought in the western corn belt seriously lowered the anticipated crop.

Moreover, many State Department officials felt that the Soviet predicament provided the U.S. substantial leverage. Some State Department memorandums during this period envisioned a grain-oil deal structured to provide the U.S. with clear-cut price advantages both for grain (higher than market prices) and for oil (lower than OPEC prices) as well as securing longer-term grain market and oil supply assurances. Furthermore, they felt that the mere process of negotiation would provide implicit linkages to general foreign policy objectives.

Third, the difficulties posed by the longshoremen's stand against the sales effectively meant that even if the grain were sold it could not be delivered.

The group agreed that at the time of the August crop report Secretary Butz should issue a statement that the United States would continue to supply its regular foreign customers but would not authorize additional sales to the Soviet Union at this time. Butz succeeded in securing agreement that his statement should include the caveat that the temporary suspension did not foreclose additional Soviet grain sales later in the year and that he should assure normal U.S. customers that the position vis-à-vis the Soviets was an exceptional case.

On Friday, August 8, Seidman sent the President a memorandum on the grain situation, accompanied by a proposed statement for Secretary Butz to make on suspending Soviet grain sales, and a status report on the "Maritime Unions and Shipment of Grain to the Soviet Union," with a note that Secretary Dunlop wanted to speak with the President as soon as possible on the subject. The following day, the President approved the proposed statement for Secretary Butz to make at his press conference on the August crop report, and Seidman informed Butz of the President's approval.

The August crop report forecast a decline of 3 percent in the corn crop from the July estimate and a decline of 2 percent in the wheat crop from the July estimate. Don Paarlberg, chief economist at the Department of Agriculture, acknowledged that the rains since August 1, when the sample was taken, had been "sparse and scattered," and that overall, there had been "some continued stress since August 1." USDA officials at the press conference also disclosed that they had revised their estimate of the Soviet crop down to 180 million tons and that the crops in Canada and Australia were "so-so."

On Monday, August 18, developments moved forward on several fronts. At the morning executive committee meeting, the group agreed that the administration should not rescind the suspension on additional Soviet grain sales before an evaluation of the September 11 crop report. That afternoon at the Iowa State Fair, the President praised America's farmers, declared that his administration would continue a policy of full production, indicated that he anticipated further sales to the Soviet Union, and emphasized the temporary nature of the current suspension on sales to the Russians.

In Washington, George Meany announced that the ILA was acting on its threat to refuse to load grain bound for the U.S.S.R., and the long-shoremen went on strike. That evening, MacAvoy, Porter, and Schuh completed the most comprehensive and detailed memorandum to date, "An Analysis of Additional Sales of Grain to the Soviet Union," which a courier carried to Seidman and the President in Vail.

The paper outlined the Soviet predicament – a production shortfall between thirty-six and fifty-one million tons with import needs possibly as high as twenty-five to thirty-five million tons, which could result in additional demands from the U.S. of ten to fifteen million tons. The paper traced the impact in the U.S. of further sales, estimating that selling an additional eight million tons would increase the CPI by 0.5 percent the following year and that selling fifteen million additional tons could increase the CPI by more than 1.0 percent. It reviewed several remaining uncertainties that could result in higher prices – poor weather in the U.S., a shortfall in the Asian rice crop – and noted that hog inventories were at a near forty-year low and that cattle feeding was 20–25 percent below the previous year. The paper warned that, if these risks materialized, consumers would inevitably blame the resulting sharp price increases on "mismanagement" of the Russian sales. It concluded with an EPB recommendation that the administration make no additional commitments to the Soviets until after a reassessment following the September 11 crop report. Seidman reviewed the memorandum with the President in Vail; the President concurred with the EPB recommendation.

Meanwhile, the subcabinet-level interagency machinery continued to discuss the notion of a long-term agreement with the Soviet Union, an idea the Russians had suggested in 1973 at a meeting between Secretary Kissinger and Foreign Minister Gromyko in Moscow. When Secretary Kissinger returned to Washington, he asked the Department of Agriculture to evaluate the idea. At the time, USDA officials concluded that its potential negative effects on relations with traditional customers outweighed the benefits. The 1973 soybean short supply and embargo, the 1974 short U.S. feedgrain crop, and now the tremendous Soviet shortfall made USDA officials reevaluate the usefulness of a long-term agreement with the Soviets.

Over the August 23–24 weekend, USDA officials completed the draft of a "Proposal for Future Trade in Grain Between the U.S. and the U.S.S.R." It pointed out the tremendous fluctuations in Soviet grain production and trade; Russia had shifted from being a net exporter to being a net importer of grains, a problem complicated by the lack of adequate storage capacity in the Soviet Union. The paper projected anticipated Soviet needs, assuming both a significant stocks build-up and continued expansion of their livestock industry. Bell and Don Novotny, who drafted the paper together, envisioned average annual shipments of twelve million tons, or sixty million tons over a five-year period. The proposal included provision for twice yearly consultations, a minimum amount that the Soviets would be obligated to take in any year (eight million tons), and a maximum amount that the U.S. would be required to supply in any one year (sixteen million tons). The paper concluded:

> If the agreement were to be useful for both maximizing Soviet ability to increase their livestock industry and maximizing the assured export market for U.S. grain, the total quantity to be traded over the five-year period should be set as high as possible, and there should be little or no excuse for shortfall.

Elsewhere in the executive branch, the idea of a long-term agreement was acquiring support and further definition. On Saturday, August 23, at Secretary Dunlop's request, Lynn, Dunlop, MacAvoy, and Porter, representing Seidman, who was out of town, met in Lynn's office. Dunlop, concerned about the short-run potential price effects of additional sales, argued that, with the Soviets "between a rock and a hard place," the administration should turn a short-run problem into a long-run asset by negotiating a long-term agreement with the Soviets.

DEALING WITH LABOR

The July ILA and AFL–CIO resolutions and the August 18 longshoremen's strike resulted from a confluence of two quite separate but harmonious interests pursued by the maritime union leaders and George Meany. The industrial relations element of the situation centered in three sources of discontent widely shared by the maritime union leaders and their members.

First, the Soviet Union was making increasing inroads in the shipping industry worldwide, largely at the expense of the United States merchant marine. Second, the Soviets were failing to abide by the provisions of the 1972 U.S.–U.S.S.R. Maritime Agreement stipulating that U.S. and Soviet vessels would each carry a minimum of one-third of the grain cargoes between the two countries. Finally, the Soviets had refused to offer shipping rates high enough to bring out of lay-up large numbers of American vessels that could not operate profitably at the current low world rates. In short, the maritime unions saw the Soviet need for American grain as an opportunity for leverage in redressing their grievances with the Russians on shipping matters.

The AFL–CIO supported the maritime union position, however, largely because of George Meany's overriding concern with food prices. Inflation in recent years had hit hard at union members, as consumers, and food prices had risen rapidly during the past three months. Moreover, they remembered that the 1972–73 grain sales were followed by rapid agricultural price increases. These grain sales were an opportunity to dramatize the broader public policy issue of food prices and inflation. While the maritime and federation labor leaders agreed that the Russians were a problem, they did not agree on which interests and objectives they should press most ardently.

As early as the July 18 meeting, the President had instructed John Dunlop to monitor the maritime situation and to handle personally relations between the administration and the union leaders. While Dunlop had stayed in touch with union leaders on the grain issue during the last two weeks of July and the first two weeks of August, and was aware that "there was a major problem brewing," neither Meany nor ILA President Teddy Gleason told Dunlop precisely what they were planning to do.

However, once the longshoremen went on strike, Dunlop moved quickly. The following evening, August 19, he discussed the situation and his plans in a private meeting with the President. Earlier in the day, a U.S. District Court judge had ordered the longshoremen back to work and Dunlop was anxious to resolve the issue nonjudicially. The President agreed to have him arrange a meeting between the President and the labor leaders to discuss the issue.

The first meeting between the President and the labor leaders, on August 26, was not intended to "solve" the problem, but to let Meany present his concern about the food price issue, and the other union leaders their views on maritime matters, directly to the President.[7]

Administration officials were pleased that the union leaders were primarily interested in drawing administration and public attention to a

[7]   The labor leaders attending the August 26 meeting included: George Meany, President of the AFL–CIO; Lane Kirkland, Secretary–Treasurer of the AFL–CIO; Teddy Gleason, President of the International Longshoremen's Association; Mel Barisac, Secretary–Treasurer of the National Maritime Union; Paul Hall, President of the Seafarers International Union of North America; and Jesse Calhoun, President of the National Marine Engineers Beneficial Association.

serious problem, not in pressing for a specific solution. Having a government entity market U.S. agricultural products to the Soviet Union might be one way of dealing with Soviet raids on U.S. markets, but it was far from a "feet in concrete position" by union leaders, as one administration official put it. The union leaders saw themselves as elevating the problem. It was up to the administration to solve it.

SECURING AGREEMENT TO SEEK
A LONG-TERM ARRANGEMENT

During the first week of September, the concept of a long-term grain agreement with the Soviet Union began to secure wide support throughout the executive branch. In fact, the idea seemed to occur simultaneously in several places. During August, officials at the Departments of State and Agriculture, the Council of Economic Advisers, and Labor Secretary Dunlop all formulated various long-term approaches to control the fluctuations in Soviet purchases. By the end of August several strands throughout the executive branch came together at the highest levels.

On Tuesday, September 2, after briefly reviewing the latest developments with Under Secretary of State Robinson, Seidman called a meeting to discuss the situation. Robinson reported that the State Department was exploring a general swap arrangement with the Soviets involving five million tons of grain and ten million tons of oil. Preliminary soundings revealed Soviet resistance to any oil purchase agreement below OPEC prices, or to swapping grain for oil. Any grain, oil, or shipping agreement must stand on its own. Those attending the meeting felt the administration should seek several provisions in a grain agreement: commitment of Soviet purchases at a given level for a specified number of years, an escape clause to protect against a U.S. crop shortfall, and a Soviet commitment to increase their stock reserves.

The following day, Under Secretary of State Robinson hosted a luncheon at the State Department to consider alternative strategies for dealing with the problem. Contacts between the State Department and Soviet officials "at the highest levels" had confirmed that the Soviets were anxious to purchase an additional eighteen million tons of grain from the 1975 U.S. crop. The State Department viewed the situation as an opportunity to "get something" for helping the Soviets out of a predicament. The payoff might come in the form of Soviet cooperation in the Middle East or in the SALT talks. It might come through Soviet participation in a world grain reserve, an objective more strongly held by the State Department than by other executive branch agencies. The Soviet difficulty also provided the basis for securing a multiyear commitment from the Soviets to purchase a given quantity of grain each year.

The group reconvened Thursday evening, September 4, at the State Department to discuss specific elements of a long-term grain agreement and to review two documents. One paper, prepared by the CEA, analyzed the level of grain exports the United States could reasonably "guarantee" the Soviets in future years as a base figure for negotiations. The paper urged caution on the size of the desired purchase commitment and recommended securing an escape clause in the event of a U.S. crop shortage. The group also reviewed a draft long-term agreement prepared by Jim Mitchell and Paul MacAvoy.

Six possible provisions in an agreement were discussed: the time duration, the size of a minimum purchase requirement, the size of a maximum purchase privilege, a Soviet obligation to erect storage facilities, an escape clause for the U.S., and a Soviet obligation to provide more detailed crop information. At the conclusion of the meeting, MacAvoy and Porter agreed to develop a memorandum for the President on the issue for consideration early the following week.

While officials within the executive branch were working out the principles underlying a long-term grain agreement, Secretary Dunlop was taking steps to resolve the shipping impasse. He quickly concluded that increasing the shipping rate to give U.S. vessels equal cargoes would not solve the industrial relations problem by itself. The issue raised by the union leaders transcended the U.S. merchant marine difficulties; unless action were taken, the Soviets would continue to disrupt world grain trade by their erratic purchases.

Dunlop divided the problem into two stages: first, allaying union concerns to get them back to work; and, second, negotiating a long-term Soviet agreement — an effort that would involve considerable time. Accordingly, he had drafted a crisp, six-point "Program for Grain" that would provide the foundation for negotiating a long-term agreement, continue the suspension on sales while negotiations on the long-term agreement were underway, resume shipping the grain already sold, and negotiate shipping rates to assure that at least one-third of the tonnage was carried in American ships.

Over the weekend of August 29, Dunlop had explained his ideas on how to deal with the problem to AFL–CIO President George Meany and Secretary–Treasurer Lane Kirkland. There were considerable operational difficulties in having a government corporation market American grain abroad, and a proposal for a government grain corporation would face stiff congressional opposition. However, Dunlop acknowledged that the pattern of erratic Soviet purchases presented a genuine problem and suggested the approach of seeking a long-term purchase agreement as a means of smoothing them out. Meany and Kirkland seemed generally receptive to his idea.

The next week, Dunlop wrote out his six-point program long-hand and met with Kirkland and Meany on Thursday, September 4, ultimately securing their general concurrence. Meany emphasized that in ratifying the agreement to load the ships he did not want a series of meetings with the President. If there were another meeting with the President, Meany wanted "something to happen."

Seidman was still out of town, so Dunlop called Jim Lynn on Friday, September 5, to get his advice on how best to secure rapid agreement on his six-point program within the administration and to obtain presidential approval. Lynn contacted Richard Cheney, Deputy Assistant to the President, and deputy to White House Chief of Staff Donald Rumsfeld.[8] Cheney arranged for a Saturday morning meeting at the White House involving Dunlop, Lynn, Greenspan, and Robinson.

At the meeting, Dunlop explained that if the President would agree to negotiate a long-term Soviet agreement, with the understanding that if the negotiations were successful the U.S. would sell the Soviets some more grain from the 1975 crop, then Dunlop felt he could get an agreement from Meany and the labor leaders to load the grain. Lynn, Greenspan, and Robinson found the six-point program both an excellent approach to solving the longshoremen's strike and a framework for commencing negotiations with the Soviets.

Dunlop then outlined the next steps — securing the President's approval, holding a meeting between the President and the labor leaders to formally ratify the understanding settling the strike situation, publicly releasing the six-point program, and commencing negotiations with the Soviets. Informed of the outcome of their meeting, Cheney arranged for some time on the President's schedule the following Tuesday to meet with the labor leaders.

The Monday morning executive committee meeting spent a good share of its time discussing a new development. MacAvoy reported that Eastern European purchases of U.S. grain had picked up markedly in recent days, threatening to undermine the suspension on Soviet sales. Not only were Eastern European countries well ahead of their usual purchases from the United States, but they were increasing the absolute levels of their purchases. Poland, which traditionally purchased roughly two million tons annually from the United States, had already contracted

---

[8] Rumsfeld was with the President on a two-day trip to Washington, Oregon, and California.

for 4.5 million tons from the 1975 crop. At the same time, the Soviets had reduced their sales to Eastern Europe from five million tons to two million tons. The demand had simply shifted from the Soviet Union to Eastern Europe.

The group agreed on three options to present to the President: extending the suspension on grain sales to include Eastern Europe; limiting Eastern European sales to traditional levels; and continuing the present policy – differentiating between the U.S.S.R. and Eastern Europe and approving additional requests by Eastern European countries.

The Executive Committee unanimously approved recommending to the President that he "authorize the commencement of negotiations with the Soviet Union for a five-year agreement for the United States to export a fixed amount of grain to the Soviet Union each year as suggested in Secretary Dunlop's 'Program for Grain' paper."

The group also discussed a third issue for presentation to the President – the administration's policy on additional sales to the U.S.S.R. from the current crop year. Four options were considered: (1) if the September crop report were favorable, announcing removal of the suspension up to a specified amount; (2) continuing the current suspension and announcing that there would be no change before evaluating the October crop report; (3) continuing the current suspension and tying it to resolving the longshoremen's problem; and (4) continuing the current policy and tying it to the negotiation of a long-term agreement.

The hour-long meeting with the President on Monday afternoon primarily focused on selling additional grain to the Soviet Union and to Eastern Europe during the current crop year.[9]

The President approved exploring the possibilities of a long-term Soviet grain agreement, establishing an EPB/NSC Food Committee to monitor the negotiations, and extending the present suspension on grain sales to the Soviet Union until mid-October when additional information on world supplies and demand would be available. On the most sensitive and controversial issue, sales to Eastern Europe, the President indicated that Secretary Butz and the Department of Agriculture should continue monitoring grain sales to Eastern Europe and that Secretary Kissinger should request the Poles and other Eastern Europeans to hold their purchases to normal amounts. In short, the President agreed with those advisers who argued that if the grain leakage problem were not solved, it could undermine U.S. leverage against the Soviets. However, sensitive to farmer hostility toward any form of export controls, the President ap-

---

[9]   The attendees at the meeting included the President, Simon, Dunlop, Lynn, Seidman, Kissinger, Butz, Rumsfeld, Robinson, Scowcroft, Cheney, Greenspan, MacAvoy, and Porter.

proved a quiet, nonpublic approach of requesting the Poles through diplomatic channels to hold their purchases to normal amounts.[10]

On Tuesday afternoon, September 9, the President met with George Meany and five other labor leaders in a pro forma meeting to ratify the six-point program.[11]

However, there had been little thought given to the procedure for releasing the six-point program. Dunlop had envisioned simply a written statement on the program released by the White House press office without any individual's name identified with it. In his view, a low-key announcement was sufficient and preferable. But when Seidman, at the conclusion of the brief meeting with the labor leaders, asked who was going to announce it to the press, the President said he assumed Dunlop would. Seidman asked whether it would look right if the Secretary of Labor made the announcement on his own, when so many other interests were also involved. The President then suggested that Seidman accompany Dunlop. It was almost 4 P.M. when the meeting ended and there was little time to make other arrangements. Dunlop made the announcement, and then Dunlop and Seidman briefed the White House press corps on the statement and the meeting.

Wednesday morning, September 10, Seidman convened a meeting at the White House to discuss the parameters of a long-term agreement to serve as the basis for Robinson's initial negotiating instructions. There was consensus that the U.S. delegation[12] should seek seven provisions in a U.S.–U.S.S.R. grain agreement: (1) a five-year duration; (2) a minimum annual Soviet purchase of five million tons of grain; (3) a maximum annual purchase of eight millions tons of grain (with additional purchases if both governments agreed); (4) determination before the planting season in a given crop year of the amount, between five and eight million tons, that the Soviets wished to purchase; (5) a requirement that

[10] The sensitivity of the issue was revealed by the unusual practice of distributing numbered copies of the options paper at the meeting and collecting them at its conclusion.

[11] The meeting was attended by the President, George Meany, Lane Kirkland, Teddy Gleason, Paul Hall, Jesse Calhoun, Shannon Wall, President of the National Maritime Union of America, Dunlop, Seidman, Porter, and Ron Nessen. Administration participation in the meeting was limited to Dunlop, Seidman, Porter, and Nessen for two reasons. First, the meeting was merely a pro forma session and there was no substantive need to involve any other officials. Second, the meeting was a reconvening of the August 26 meeting and therefore it was appropriate simply to involve the same individuals.

[12] It was agreed at the September 8 meeting that the United States delegation should consist of representatives from the Departments of State and Agriculture. Under Secretary Robinson headed the small delegation that included his deputy Deane Hinton, and Donald Novotny, Director of the Grain and Feed Analysis Division of the USDA Foreign Agricultural Service.

the Soviets construct additional off-farm storage facilities; (6) provision for better information on Soviet crops; and (7) an escape clause in the event of a U.S. crop shortfall. Moreover, there was consensus that the initial U.S. negotiating posture should not involve any commitment to additional 1975 sales. That decision would follow a reassessment of the U.S. crop in mid-October. By Wednesday evening, Robinson and his small party had left for Moscow.

THE FARM COMMUNITY ERUPTS

The farm community's reaction against the Tuesday announcement was swift and sustained. On Wednesday, September 10, Secretary Butz arranged a meeting for Monday with the President and the Executive Committee of the Board of the American Farm Bureau Federation (AFBF), the largest farm organization in the United States with some 2.3 million members. At the Monday, September 15, meeting the AFBF Executive Committee was blunt and candid.[13] They told the President that the farm community was furious at the labor movement dictating agricultural export policy. One farm executive used the analogy that the farmers felt like their escort was going home with a different date – George Meany – and they were unhappy about it. As far as the farmers could see, Meany, not the Department of Agriculture, was making grain export policy.

The President emphasized that Secretary Butz was fully involved in the administration's internal deliberations about a long-term Soviet agreement and added that if the farm community thought the State Department was happy with Mr. Meany, they were totally misinformed. But hearing that USDA was an active participant in the administration's internal decision-making process did little to ease the farmers' irritation.

What incensed the farmers more than the suspension on sales (prices remained at relatively high levels) and the quest for a long-term agreement, was the public perception that agricultural policy was in the hands of officials and groups outside the Department of Agriculture. This perception was bolstered by the wide press coverage given the two meetings between the President and the labor leaders, announcement of the formation of an EPB/NSC Food Committee nominally co-chaired by Secre-

---

[13] The American Farm Bureau Federation delegation was headed by its president, William J. Kuhfuss, and included Roger Flemming, secretary–treasurer, and Allen Lauterbach, general counsel and assistant secretary–treasurer. They constituted the Executive Committee of the AFBF Board of Directors. The administration representatives at the meeting included Secretaries Butz and Dunlop, Seidman, Greenspan, Scowcroft, Bell, Porter, and John Carlson, Deputy Press Secretary. Robert Hartmann joined the meeting after it began.

tary of the Treasury Simon (EPB) and Secretary of State Kissinger (NSC), and the State Department's dominant role in conducting the grain agreement negotiations with the Soviets. The Secretary of Agriculture was a member of the Food Committee, and the Department of Agriculture was represented on the negotiating mission to Moscow, but symbolically the impression was conveyed that the Department of Agriculture was playing a supporting, not a lead role.

REFINING THE DETAILS

The September 11 crop report showed a further deterioration in the U.S. crop, supporting those who had urged caution on further sales.[14] The Food Deputies Report reviewing the September crop report detailed evidence that the Soviets had reduced grain exports to Eastern Europe, causing greater demands on U.S. markets.[15]

Mid-September assessments of the Soviet position firmly concluded that, even with major reductions in livestock feeding, the Russians genuinely needed more grain than the approximately sixteen million tons they had already purchased on world markets. Despite the apparent Soviet predicament, the President told his cabinet as early as September 17 that because of farm community pressures "we will have to announce an agreement earlier than if there were no such pressures."

On September 18, the EPB/NSC Food Committee met to discuss the first round of negotiations with the Russians. Under Secretary Robinson, recently returned from Moscow, reported his initial discussions: the Soviets were receptive to the framework of a long-term grain agreement along the lines developed by the EPB, and accepted the link between a long-term grain agreement and additional sales during the current crop year far more easily than the notion of a parallel oil agreement.

The State Department was almost alone in its desire for a grain and oil swap. Some State Department officials viewed a swap agreement as "terribly important to detente" and felt that it would represent a "real signal to OPEC" by demonstrating a balancing of oilpower with agripower. However, for an oil agreement to achieve the desired effect, it required a price below the world market. Most leading officials in the economic policy community doubted that the Soviets would agree to such an arrangement. Moreover, even if they agreed, the practical diffi-

---

[14]   The wheat crop estimate was down 0.2 percent, soybeans down 1.1 percent, and corn down 2.8 percent. In absolute terms, the forecast feed grain production (corn, sorghum, oats, and barley) declined six million short tons.

[15]   Minutes, EPB Executive Committee, September 15, 1975. A memorandum on the "East European Grain Situation" was sent to the President later that day.

culties of implementing it outweighed the relatively negligible amounts involved – roughly 215,000 barrels a day.

On September 19, Robert Blackwell, Assistant Secretary of Commerce for Maritime Affairs, returned from Moscow carrying a new shipping rate agreement that committed the Soviets to a $16 a ton rate through December 31, 1976, coupled with an escalator clause based on changes in world market rates that Blackwell was confident would substantially increase during the coming months. Blackwell acknowledged that the Soviet crop shortfall and their large import needs had materially strengthened his negotiating position. The successful negotiations on a shipping rate agreement further vindicated those who had argued that caution and patience would result in significant gains.

Throughout September and October, the President was much more enthusiastic, publicly and privately, about a long-term grain agreement than about an oil agreement. In his numerous speeches and press conferences he explained his interest in and the rationale behind a long-term grain agreement with the Soviet Union, noting that he was personally giving the agreement "priority attention."[16] The President did not refer to an oil agreement a single time in any of his prepared remarks during the period and, when the question came up in his press conferences, he downplayed it as far less important than a grain agreement. Moreover, he discouraged the perception that the two agreements were linked.[17] In short, both in his meetings with the EPB on the grain agreement and in his public statements, the President was lukewarm at best to a parallel oil agreement.

On Monday, September 22, an Associated Press report on the previously unpublicized suspension on grain sales to Poland sent farmer dissatisfaction to new heights. The report claimed that the Department of Agriculture had been excluded from the grain policy decision-making process, adding insult to injury in the agricultural community:

A Department of Agriculture official, who asked not to be identified, said the Polish suspension order was handled entirely by the State Department. He said Agriculture Secretary Earl L. Butz was told informally of it shortly before he met with Poland's Minister of Agriculture midday. The Minister, the source said, asked Mr. Butz specifically about the sales suspension. Mr. Butz was quoted as telling the Polish Minister that the suspension was "very tem-

[16] "Remarks at Republican Fundraising Dinner," Chicago, Illinois, September 30, 1975, *Weekly Presidential Documents* Vol. 11, No. 40, pp. 1086–1089.
[17] "President's Interview with KMOX-TV," St. Louis, Missouri, September 12, 1975, *Ibid.* p. 992.

porary" and "I want it understood that it did not come from the Department of Agriculture."[18]

That same day, Seidman called a meeting of the Food Committee to review the negotiating posture with the Soviets. Secretary Butz raised the Associated Press report emphasizing the tremendous resentment toward the administration this would produce throughout the agricultural community. Under Secretary Robinson brought in the draft agreement, which was reviewed provision by provision.

EBBING LEVERAGE: THE WAITING GAME

There was no question that the furor in the farm community subtly, yet decisively, altered U.S. negotiating strength. Time was now on the side of the Russians. Farmers, already skeptical that the suspension on sales to the Soviet Union represented a unique act to deal with a unique case, now saw their skepticism justified when the suspension extended to Poland.

As the fourth week in September drew to a close, it became apparent that the Soviets felt that U.S. leverage was ebbing. Each passing day made it more difficult for the administration to deal with the farm community. Clearly, extending the suspension past the end of October would entail heavy political costs for an administration facing an election in twelve months. Moreover, the Soviets had combined retrenching at home with the purchase of almost three million tons of feed grains and wheat from non-U.S. sources, increasing their total purchases for the year to more than twenty million tons.

The second round of negotiations in Moscow had been scheduled to resume on Saturday, September 27, but now the Soviets delayed. The President and other administration officials had publicly stated the U.S. intention to sell the Soviets more grain from the 1975 crop; to do otherwise would be politically untenable.[19] Some within the administration suggested that the Russians were gambling on scraping up enough grain from non-U.S. sources so that, combined with the five million tons or so that the President would have to let them purchase, they could survive without having to sign a long-term agreement.

On Monday, September 29, the EPB morning meeting considered sev-

[18] "U.S. Grain Sales to Poland Suspended," *New York Times*, September 23, 1975.

[19] See "Remarks at the Oklahoma State Fair," September 19, 1975, *Weekly Presidential Documents*, Vol. 11, p. 1034; "Remarks at the White House Conference on Domestic and Economic Affairs," Omaha, Nebraska, October 1, 1975, *Ibid.*, p. 1096; "Remarks and a Question and Answer Session with Participants at a White House Conference on Domestic and Economic Affairs," Knoxville, Tennessee, October 7, 1975, *Ibid.*, pp. 1136, 1141.

eral grain export issues. Secretary Butz raised again the question of the suspension on sales to Poland, arguing that it had hurt the administration badly among what he referred to as "our constituency," and that those in the farm belt felt the President had "sold them out." His comments prompted a vigorous and spirited exchange between Butz and those whose primary substantive concern was the threat of sharply rising domestic food prices the following year. But in the end, Butz alone wanted to lift the suspension on sales to Poland. Later that day, Under Secretary Robinson and a five-man delegation departed for Moscow and the second round of the negotiations.[20]

The following Monday, October 6, the Food Committee met once again at the White House to discuss the escape clause and what leverage Robinson now had to get an oil agreement. It was apparent that U.S. leverage was ebbing, despite a recently revised downward estimate of the Soviet grain crop, widespread use of unripened grain for forage purposes, and the beginning of distress slaughtering of Soviet livestock.

Two days later, Robinson in Moscow reported an impasse. The Soviets were prepared to sign a five-year commitment to purchase six to eight million tons of grain, with provision that the U.S. could lower the amount unilaterally in years of severe shortage. But they were not willing to sign a letter of intent obligating them to conclude within thirty days a deal to sell the U.S. 200,000 barrels of oil a day at prices discounted 15 percent from the world market prices. The refusal came from the highest Soviet levels.

Both countries were under considerable pressure. The Soviet crop was poor and apparently still deteriorating. The USDA October crop report was scheduled for release on October 10. If the crop report were favorable and the negotiations remained stalled, grain prices could break. Secretary Butz felt that he could keep the farm situation stable for about a fortnight – if he could lift the suspension on sales to Poland – but farm pressures were expected to intensify rapidly.

At the meeting several executive committee members articulated their dissatisfaction with the oil part of the package. Neither Frank Zarb nor Alan Greenspan had been very enthusiastic about an oil agreement from the outset, partly because it might mean establishing a government import purchasing authority – an idea with considerable congressional support that the administration had consistently opposed.

Three basic alternatives were considered: (1) bringing Robinson home and trying to wait the Soviets out, a strategy that involved the risk that

[20] The five-man delegation included Robinson, Richard E. Bell, Hinton, Mark Feldman, Deputy Legal Advisor at the Department of State, and Joseph Bell, Assistant General Counsel for International Conservation and Resource Development Programs at the Federal Energy Administration.

the Soviets could stand the pressure better than the U.S. could; (2) insisting on the 15 percent oil discount, but cooperating with the Soviets in disguising the discount in shipping costs and credit terms; and (3) accepting the negotiated grain agreement as it stood and abandoning efforts to negotiate an oil agreement.

The discussion of negotiating strategy revealed the underlying differences in the objectives of various departments and agencies. Those pressing for an oil agreement, principally the State Department and the NSC, saw political advantages in demonstrating that the United States could use its agripower to get a price break on oil, however symbolic the quantities.[21] Those who wanted to abandon the oil deal emphasized its small economic advantages and the problems of creating a public purchase entity to handle the transaction.

While the President was not yet prepared to abandon an oil agreement, he realized that the point of maximum U.S. leverage had passed. Farm community pressure was building daily. There was one way of easing the pressure from farmers and buying some time – lifting the suspension on sales to Poland. The idea, which had a single supporter ten days earlier, Secretary Butz, now quickly picked up support within the administration.

On Friday, October 10, the EPB Executive Committee discussed the grain export issue at length, beginning with a memorandum on the current Soviet grain situation. The USDA and CIA forecasts were cautious. The Soviet situation was uncomfortable and inconvenient; but as long as they drew down stocks and altered their consumption patterns, it was not desperate.

Moreover, relatively favorable weather in recent weeks had virtually assured the U.S. crop. The Department of Agriculture would release its confidential crop report later in the day, but everyone agreed that it would not show a significant fall, as the September crop report had, in the estimated size of the final crop. The report was, in fact, up 1 percent from September. With the risk of a serious rise in prices essentially over, the Executive Committee unanimously supported Secretary Butz's request to lift the Polish suspension. Later that morning, the President approved the change and opened his national press conference that afternoon with the announcement.[22]

The next week produced no shift in the Soviet position on an oil agreement. Press reports in the United States that a grain agreement was im-

---

[21] While a disguised price break would help the Soviets present the deal well at home, the discount would become apparent in the United States when the oil was sold publicly, perhaps at an auction, and the Treasury picked up a windfall profit.

[22] "President's News Conference of October 10, 1975, held in Detroit, Michigan," *Weekly Presidential Documents*, Vol. 11, No. 42, p. 1155.

minent simply strengthened Soviet intransigence. The U.S. leverage, to the extent that it existed, had evaporated. There was little point in further delay.

On the following day, the President approved lifting the suspension on grain sales to the Soviet Union on condition that Russian purchases not exceed an additional seven million tons. On Monday, October 20, after a weekend negotiating final instructions and arrangements for its release, the agreement was announced.

EVALUATION

Two overriding factors conditioned how the EPB handled the 1975 grain export issue. First, there was the memory of the 1972–73 Soviet grain sales. The vision of rapidly rising domestic prices and massive U.S. credits subsidizing large Russian purchases contributed to the "emotionalism" Earl Butz frequently referred to, both publicly and privately. Many of those in key roles in 1975 had lived through the 1972–73 experience – Kissinger, Butz, Lynn, and Bell – and were sensitive to its association in the public mind with U.S. government "mismanagement." These memories contributed to the essentially cautious approach taken by the administration.

Second, there was the memory of the 1974 experience with double-digit inflation. The strong conviction that reducing inflation was essential to any sustained recovery from the recession added weight to the arguments of those who consistently warned about the potential price effects of additional sales to the Soviet Union. In short, the administration fashioned its grain export policy within the context of the 1972 sales and the more recent preoccupation with inflation.

Evaluating the process: characteristics

The process of making decisions and policy involved multiple centers of action and responsibility: Secretary Dunlop dealt with labor leaders and the industrial relations problem; the Department of State conducted the grain agreement negotiations; the Council of Economic Advisers and the Food Deputies Group developed and maintained a data base; and Assistant Secretary of Commerce Blackwell conducted the maritime negotiations. While each sphere had a high level of independence, they were all coordinated through the office of the Assistant to the President for Economic Affairs. In the EPB Executive Committee, those with primary responsibility for various elements of the problem came together regularly, exchanged information, received policy guidance, and secured approval for various initiatives.

Secretary Dunlop, after securing agreement from the labor leadership, cleared his six-point program through the Economic Policy Board Executive Committee. Under Secretary of State Robinson received the general parameters of his negotiating instructions – and many of the specific details – through the EPB Executive Committee and the EPB/NSC Food Committee. Assistant Secretary Blackwell reported to and maintained close contact with Seidman, Dunlop, Robinson, and Lynn to mesh the maritime negotiations with the grain export issue. Paul MacAvoy reported the analysis developed by the Food Deputies Group and the CEA to the EPB Executive Committee. As one Department of Agriculture official observed: "I think that the EPB mechanism forced us to put the parts together in a way that was more rational than if we had not had it." Yet the decision-making process was coordinated without centralizing responsibility.

In this process, executive departments and agencies represented varied interests. Many participants agreed on the same strategy for different reasons. The State Department was anxious to increase U.S. leverage for diplomatic purposes and to secure a symbolic victory for agripower. The Commerce Department and the Maritime Administration also wanted increased leverage but to benefit the shipping rate and shipping agreement negotiations. The Council of Economic Advisers and Secretary of Labor Dunlop, formerly Director of the Cost of Living Council, wanted to protect consumers against a serious near-term rise in food prices while obtaining a more stable long-term pattern in agricultural trade between the United States and the Soviet Union. The Department of Agriculture wanted to reduce dissatisfaction in the agricultural community and to negotiate a long-term arrangement that would lessen the "emotionalism" associated with U.S.-Soviet agricultural trade. The tactical considerations were sometimes different, but not the ultimate objectives. Yet a consensus shared by many principal actors did not mean one voice speaking to the President. The process presented him with a broad range of views.

Evaluating the process: strengths

The executive branch, in its handling of the 1975 grain export sales and the long-term agreement, demonstrated a number of strengths in its internal operation.[23] The EPB decision-making process provided sufficient lead time for the President to shape events rather than merely react to them. Because of thorough staff work, the EPB weighed and balanced a

[23] This view is shared by I. M. Destler in his recent book *Making Foreign Economic Policy* (Washington, D.C.: Brookings Institution, 1980), in which he compares the 1975 experience with the 1972–73 experience.

host of considerations. Not least, it coordinated several theaters of activity within the administration.

The time factor was important. Quality analysis and balanced judgment seldom occur when decision makers feel rushed. The more time for deliberation, the more likely that the most important aspects of a problem will receive adequate consideration — and the less likely that an individual or group will stampede a decision maker. The EPB Executive Committee and its subcabinet-level Food Deputies Group were an early warning system. They raised the issue of sales to the Soviet Union in early July, focusing attention on the question before events limited options. In the absence of the Economic Policy Board and of the Food Deputies Group's regular reports, it is unlikely that the issue would have surfaced as early as it did for high-level interagency consideration. Moreover, once the issue was identified, interagency machinery was already there to deal with it. As a result, the EPB, as one participant observed, was "on top of the issue from the beginning."

The decision-making process also mobilized the best analysis available and secured agreement on an appropriate and accurate body of information and analysis for presentation to the President. The EPB Executive Committee relied heavily on Paul MacAvoy, Chairman of the Food Deputies Group, to develop and organize a data base. He maintained six principal elements in his frequent revisions: (1) the U.S. crop forecast; (2) the Soviet crop forecast; (3) the accuracy of past U.S. crop forecasts at various points to define the range of error; (4) the estimated price effects of further Soviet sales based on the forecast of the U.S. crop; (5) the amount of Soviet purchases abroad and how much more they might get; and (6) estimated Soviet adjustments in their consumption and the range of their import needs.

In preparing and updating these estimates MacAvoy relied on three principal sources and three secondary sources. The Department of Agriculture was the principal source of information on the U.S. crop and a primary source on the Soviet crop. In addition, the CEA had developed its own model, a check on the USDA model's forecast.

Likewise, the Central Intelligence Agency and the Department of Agriculture independently produced forecasts of the Soviet crop. At any given time, the CIA and USDA estimates usually differed, although they consistently followed each other "down the slippery slope" as the summer gave way to autumn. The difference between them, however, served as a range of the likely Soviet crop to many executive committee members.

Supplementing the Department of Agriculture, the CEA, and the CIA, were three secondary sources — the forecasts produced by two of the large grain companies, the estimates of a major private forecaster

(Schnittker Associates), and several knowledgeable academic agricultural economists that MacAvoy consulted periodically. The data obtained from these secondary sources was used principally to check the forecasts produced by the USDA, CEA, and CIA models.

Three important features characterized the substantive analysis and the process MacAvoy used to develop it. First, the sheer quantity was impressive. During the fourteen-week period from early July through the third week in October, the EPB Executive Committee and the Food Committee considered thirty-six papers on the grain export issue. Seidman sent nineteen of them to the President. By frequently updating the information base and its analysis, the President and his advisers could make decisions on the basis of current information.

Second, EPB members considered the quality of the analysis exceptionally good. One member observed in October 1975 that the series of analytic papers prepared for EPB consideration represented the most systematic examination that he was aware of, during his six years in government, of the effects such a major transaction would have on prices. Another official with experience in two administrations commented:

> Prior to EPB discussion and during EPB discussions, the amount of staff work required by the individual staffs in town was on occasion extraordinary. The EPB mechanism worked very well and worked very efficiently in the agricultural export decisions of 1975. It was a very complicated problem as well. The reason that the mechanism worked well was partly because the principals tended to agree on what desirable policy was. Even more importantly, at the staff and the level immediately below the principal level, the people involved in the analysis of what were very difficult issues performed their job very well.
>
> In view of the problem as it developed, in view of the lack of information, the lack of knowledge, the need to examine the consequences of different courses of action, the mechanism worked very, very well. The staff work was done well even though the work was spread out over a period of three or four months.

The reputation of the CEA and the Food Deputies Group on agricultural policy issues was extremely high; members of the EPB Executive Committee trusted them. Moreover, the Food Deputies Group had reported regularly to the Executive Committee so that by the summer of 1975, executive committee members knew the capabilities of the subcabinet-level staffs on agricultural issues.

Third, those at the staff level who participated in developing the data base and assessing alternatives felt that the process itself was fair and reasonably well-balanced. The analysis was prepared openly and was available to all interested parties. The appropriate departments and agencies were involved and perceived themselves as genuine participants.

The EPB process also sorted out major issues for the President's time and attention. The regular executive committee meetings and Food Committee meetings served as the principal forums where issues were discussed, refined, and evaluated as to whether or not they merited presidential attention. Reviewing the time the President and leading administration officials spent in grain export policy meetings shows that the problem received consistent high-level attention for fourteen weeks without consuming large amounts of the President's time.

EPB executive committee members discussed the issue in formal meetings without the President seven times for every occasion that grain export policy was taken up in EPB meetings with the President. The EPB Executive Committee considered the issue at twenty meetings, the EPB/NSC Food Committee met ten times, and Seidman, as Executive Director of the EPB and as coordinator of the Food Committee, called five other meetings of top-level officials to discuss various aspects of the problem. The EPB considered grain export policy with the President at five regular meetings. The President also met with labor leaders twice and once with the leadership of the American Farm Bureau Federation to discuss the issue – a total of forty-three meetings at the cabinet or presidential level, while still saving the President's time by winnowing out issues that did not merit his attention.

This decision-making process effectively provided consideration of all major interests and values affected by the grain export issue. Each stage in the policy's evolution developed from discussing a full range of realistic options. All departments and agencies with an interest in the issue participated. No single interest or party dominated the discussions or was favored by the process. There was a reasonably good balancing of agricultural policy, foreign policy, economic policy, and industrial relations interests. Finally, the coordination of several related issues – grain exports in the current year, the quest for a long-term grain agreement, the longshoremen's strike, a shipping rate and maritime agreement, and the problem of inflation – was facilitated because a single coordinating mechanism existed, the EPB.

Seidman and his staff were aided in coordinating the series of related issues by the perception of them as honest brokers. Secretary Kissinger, who early worked through the EPB in getting interagency control of grain exports, continued to work with the EPB and the EPB/NSC Food Committee, even after the negotiations in Moscow commenced. Likewise, Secretary Butz, even though often in a minority, acknowledged that he and his department were always included in Seidman's meetings and that the process over which Seidman presided was fair. Similarly, Secretary Dunlop and the Council of Economic Advisers recognized and worked through the EPB.

The EPB's prominent role should not obscure the major independent contributions made by Secretary Dunlop's negotiations with organized labor and by Under Secretary of State Robinson and the State Department implementing the negotiating guidelines established through the EPB. Secretary Dunlop had a free hand in developing a solution to the industrial relations problem in the maritime industry. The State Department exercised some latitude, particularly the attempt at an oil agreement, in their negotiations with the Russians. Since the State Department controlled the cable traffic and led the U.S. delegation, they virtually dominated the negotiations. However, the EPB's persistence in focusing high-level attention on the grain export issue, its access to the President, and its marshaling of resources for much of the substantive work resulted in its major role in developing the President's grain export policy.

Evaluating the process: weaknesses

Within the executive branch, the decision-making process on the grain export issue functioned smoothly and efficiently. But the administration had to cope with a bitter and hostile reaction in the agricultural community, and the EPB spent little time thinking about how farmers would interpret the administration's actions.

It was not so much what the administration did as how they did it that rankled farmers. The farm community felt excluded, ignored, unconsulted. Their attention was riveted, not on the merits of a long-term agreement or the benefits of an assured export market, but on who was making agricultural policy – certainly not farm community leaders, and apparently not the Department of Agriculture. The farmers did not see the internal working of the EPB machinery. They did see several signs that suggested a peripheral role for their leaders and their department in Washington.

The community that was regularly contacted, the labor leaders, received that attention because labor support was vital if the administration hoped to implement *any* policy. The maritime unions controlled loading and shipping the grain. Positive support from the farmers, while certainly desired, was not necessary. The grain was already planted and the farmers would harvest it whatever the administration's policy.

Thus, other interests overrode consideration of how farmers would react to particular announcements. There was little conscious effort to bring the farmers along: by consulting with them early and often, by giving visibility to their representatives in Washington, or by according their leaders a prominent advisory role. Communication with the farm community concentrated on explaining to them the virtues and long-term merits of what the administration was doing, asking them to be patient, and assuring them they would approve of the result in the end.

The President's meetings with George Meany and the labor leaders on August 26 and September 9, because of their relationship to the long-shoremen's strike and opposition to loading grain bound for the Soviet Union, received wide press coverage throughout the farm belt. The President's meeting with the board of directors of the American Farm Bureau Federation, after announcing the outlines of his policy, received much less attention. As far as public relations went, it was too little, too late.

No Department of Agriculture official was present at the September 9 White House briefing on the President's program. Secretary Dunlop and William Seidman conducted it. Understandably, the farmers felt others were making policy for them. Furthermore, establishing the EPB/NSC Food Committee to monitor and develop strategy on the grain agreement negotiations sounded distinctly nonagricultural. The farmers viewed the Economic Policy Board and the National Security Council as having primarily economic and foreign policy concerns. For those inside the administration, it seemed natural for Secretary of the Treasury Simon, chairman of the EPB, and Henry Kissinger, Assistant to the President for National Security Affairs as well as Secretary of State, to serve as the nominal chairmen of the joint EPB/NSC Committee. Likewise, to insiders, it seemed natural for William Seidman, Executive Director of the EPB, to coordinate the Food Committee's staff work and to oversee the decision-making process. But what the farmers saw was their Secretary of Agriculture as a mere committee member.

Finally, a State Department official led the U.S. delegation to the Soviet Union to negotiate the agreement. A single staff-level official who could provide expert technical advice represented the Department of Agriculture. Even though he was one of the three members in the U.S. delegation and the first mission was to clear the way for later work, the farm community saw another signal that the State Department was in charge. Assistant Secretary of Agriculture Richard Bell, well known and respected in the farm community, accompanied Robinson to Moscow for the second round of negotiations, but once more it was too little, too late.

One ranking Department of Agriculture official reflected:

> It's not what we did, it's how we did it that got us in trouble with the farming community. We got ourselves into a position of coming to a conclusion without ever consulting the farm leadership on the outside. If we had it to do over I would recommend that we have a meeting with the farm leaders the same as the President had a meeting with the labor leaders.

The way we did it, it looked like it was something that was inspired and originated in the labor community which in fact it was not, and that the agricultural people were completely left out of the decision making, which they were, except for the Agricultural Department.

So we did not do a good job of getting consensus from the outside for something that they should have been for. And, as a result, we got a lot of criticism which probably was unfair. In the end I think the farming community is going to appreciate that they have the long-term agreement with the Russians on grain.

The President and his advisers did not try to exclude or alienate the agricultural community. The sequence of signals sent to the farm belt was the result, not of deliberate planning, but of insensitivity to the public relations problem. No one assumed responsibility for making the administration's policy acceptable to the public, especially to the farm community.

There were many things the administration might have done to cast the program in a different light — consulting with farm leaders before announcing the commencement of negotiations for a long-term agreement; involving Secretary Butz in the September 9 meeting and announcement of the decision to seek a long-term agreement; elevating and publicly emphasizing his role, perhaps by making him chairman of the EPB/NSC Food Committee; providing a more prominent role for the Department of Agriculture on the U.S. negotiating team in Moscow. None of these measures would have changed the policy, but they could have altered how the farm community perceived the President's policy. Who is seen as responsible for a policy is often as important as the content of that policy.

Poor public relations aside, the decision-making process, though scrupulously fair, elevated some considerations and undervalued others. In weighing alternatives on first suspending, then resuming sales to Poland, the EPB emphasized the problem of leakage and underrated the political costs to the President in the farm community.

The EPB's objectives were securing a long-term agreement and preventing rapid price increases. Political considerations received relatively less attention. No advisers with primarily political interests were regularly involved in the discussions. True, Secretary Butz attended all the meetings on the subject and argued persistently and fervently on political grounds against suspending sales to Poland, but his was a single voice closely identified with a single constituency. The President may well have personally weighed and accurately assessed the political risks involved, but the advice he received did not emphasize political considerations.

In retrospect, many of the participants attributed this blind spot to the pervasive feeling that the farm community would appreciate what the administration had done for them if the negotiations were successful. Throughout the entire exercise, administration officials, including the President, felt that they were working for the farmers' interests. The farmers' hostile reaction genuinely puzzled many administration officials.

Simply put, the President and his advisers were still thinking of the problem as intellectual when it had long since become emotional. Farmer dissatisfaction was not simply a desire for higher current prices and still larger profits. Farmers resented what they considered the administration's paternalistic attitude toward them, and reassurances that eventually they would like what the administration was doing for them sounded like patronage.

In the end, despite the highly favorable terms of the grain agreement, Gerald Ford suffered politically in the farm belt. The farmers never fully forgave the "inconsistency" of his pledging no export controls, then suspending sales to the Soviet Union and Poland. The administration's handling of the grain export issue contributed to the President's stunning defeat in the May 11, 1976, Nebraska presidential primary, where he ran far behind Ronald Reagan in rural areas of the state.

Another political consequence of the farmers' hostility was the President's choice of Kansas Senator Robert Dole as his vice-presidential running mate. While virtually all political analysts agreed that the November election would ultimately hang on a few nonagricultural states where Dole's background would not greatly help the President, Dole would help the ticket in the farm states, essential as a campaign base. Dole was also acceptable to the conservative wing of the Republican Party, which contolled a majority of the convention delegates, and he had a reputation as a hard-driving campaigner. But Dole's attractiveness in the farm belt and help there in shoring up Ford's support was a major factor in his selection.

Political need also prompted the creation on March 5, 1976, of the Agricultural Policy Committee (APC), chaired by the Secretary of Agriculture, to advise the President on "the formulation, coordination, and implementation of all food and agricultural policy."[24] In explaining his decision to establish the APC at a Farm Forum in Springfield, Illinois, the President said:

> I have felt that this particular subject [food policy] was so vital that we ought to take it out from underneath the coverage of what we

[24] Presidential Memorandum on Establishment of Agriculture Policy Committee, March 11, 1976, *Weekly Presidential Documents*, Vol. 12, No. 11, pp. 376–377.

call the Economic Policy Board where it was. And so it has been hauled out of the Economic Policy Board and made a separate economic policy committee as far as food is concerned. As far as I am concerned, the Secretary of Agriculture, as long as he stays with me and as long as I am President, will be chairman of that group.[25]

The creation of the Agricultural Policy Committee was essentially symbolic. In practice, it met but twice during the following ten months while the EPB handled the two major agricultural policy issues considered during that period – sugar and meat imports – with the full cooperation and participation of the Department of Agriculture.

Possibly some of the political consequences were unavoidable; but the decision-making process did not highlight them for the President.

A final weakness in the process showed up over the oil agreement. The analysis was less extensive and much less broadly based. The President's interest in and commitment to securing an oil agreement with the Soviet Union was never clear in his meetings with the EPB Executive Committee. Kissinger, Robinson, and some other State Department officials strongly supported the oil agreement; presumably Kissinger raised the subject from time to time in his own sessions with the President. But Dunlop, Lynn, Butz, and the other EPB members had relatively little interest in an oil deal. They wanted a more stable trading relationship in agricultural products with the Soviets. At the same time, they recognized the potential U.S. leverage with the Soviet Union on the grain issue, acknowledged Kissinger's role in shaping overall U.S.–Soviet relations, and were content to let him work for the best results. One member explained:

> Henry was the chief negotiator for the U.S. vis-à-vis the Russians. He knew what they wanted. I didn't have the slightest idea. I didn't know whether he would trade SALT talks, some problem in Africa, the Middle East, or what. And I didn't want to pry too much into that. I didn't know about it. I am a poor fellow to second-guess him. What I said was: "We have a chip here involving this grain thing. There is no doubt about it. And let's get the most we can for it."

As a result, largely on advice from a single source, the President agreed to prolong the negotiations, hoping that the U.S. leverage would result in benefits beyond the grain agreement. It is not clear what benefits, if any, Kissinger obtained in the SALT talks, Africa, or the Middle East, but the ploy to get an oil agreement at discounted prices failed. When Under Secretary of State Robinson returned to Washington on September 16, 1975, after his first round of negotiations in Moscow, the

[25] *Ibid.*, p. 344.

grain agreement, for all practical purposes, had been made. Working for an oil agreement – plus waiting for the October crop report – merely extended the negotiations.

Almost always one sees more clearly in retrospect. Decision makers should be judged on the basis of information available to them at the time they must decide. The interesting point is not whether Kissinger's advice to press for an oil agreement was wise; rather, it is the contrast between the broadly based interagency pattern of advice the President received on the grain export question and his primary reliance on a single source of advice for seeking an oil agreement.

6

The 1976 footwear import decision

$\mathcal{O}$n February 20, 1976, the U.S. International Trade Commission (USITC) sent to the White House the report of their investigation of the domestic footwear industry. All six commissioners found the industry suffering seriously from imports, although they differed as to the most appropriate remedy.

This was the largest escape clause import relief case brought under the Trade Act of 1974, or under previous law.[1] The President had sixty days to make a decision, and the timing from his standpoint was particularly bad. The election year primary season was beginning and several important primary states had major shoe manufacturing establishments. There were compelling arguments on both sides of the issue; whatever the President's decision, it would entail heavy foreign or domestic costs. This was one of those decisions that frequently come to presidents not at their invitation or choosing, and that they cannot avoid.

The President's decision and the process by which it was made further illuminates the environment of presidential decision making – the interrelationship of foreign and domestic policy considerations, the number of competing interests and factors that a president must take into account in deciding a complex issue, the pattern of interests within the executive branch, and how advice to the President can be organized.[2]

THE TRADE ACT OF 1974

The Trade Act of 1974, the first major trade legislation in over a decade
had given the President substantial new authority to reduce trade bar-

---

[1] The only larger case in terms of trade volume, a $7.5 billion automobile antidumping case, was then pending at the Treasury.

[2] A year later another president, Jimmy Carter, faced essentially the same decision. It

riers. At the same time, it significantly strengthened redress procedures for domestic producers injured by imports or by unfair foreign competition in domestic markets. Section 201 of the Trade Act provides for handling claims "for import relief for the purpose of facilitating orderly adjustment to import competition."[3]

Initiating an investigation by the USITC is the first stage in an escape clause case. "An entity, including a trade association, firm, certified or recognized union, or group of workers, which is representative of an industry" may file a petition for import relief with the USITC.[4] Alternately, the President, the Special Representative for Trade Negotiations (STR), the House Ways and Means Committee, the Senate Finance Committee, or the USITC by its own motion can also initiate an investigation "to determine whether an article is being imported into the United States in such increased quantities as to be a substantial cause of serious injury, or the threat thereof, to the domestic industry producing an article like or directly competitive with the imported article."[5]

The USITC's investigation includes public hearings and the collection of expert testimony.[6] At the conclusion of an investigation, which must be completed within six months after a petition is filed, the USITC submits a report to the President including: (1) their finding regarding whether imports have injured the industry, and (2) if so, what form of relief the industry should receive – increased tariffs, quotas, tariff-rate quotas, or adjustment assistance.

The President has sixty days from the time he receives the USITC report to make his decision. The Trade Act stipulates that the Trade Policy Committee, chaired by the Special Representative for Trade Negotiations, shall advise the President on such matters.[7] The President can either accept the USITC recommendation, decide not to provide relief if he determines that it "is not in the national economic interest," or provide a different remedy than the one recommended by the USITC.[8]

is instructive to compare the processes through which both men were advised. See David S. Broder, "The Case of the Missing Shoe-Import Option," *Washington Post* (July 23, 1977). Broder's article is based on a case study prepared by the Carter reorganization project in the spring of 1977.

[3]   P.L. 93–618. Sec. 201 (a) (1).

[4]   *Ibid.*

[5]   *Ibid.*, Sec. 201 (b) (1).

[6]   *Ibid.*, Sec. 201 (c).

[7]   *Ibid.*, Sec. 141 (b) (3) (E) and P.L. 87–794 Sec. 242.

[8]   Sec. 202 (a) (1) (A). In making his determination, the President is to take into account, among other things, the effect of import relief on consumers, on the international economic interests of the United States, and the economic and social costs that would be incurred by taxpayers, communities, and workers if import relief were or were not provided. Sec. 202 (c).

The Trade Act also provides for congressional override of the President's action under certain circumstances. If the President does not accept the USITC finding and recommended remedy, and if the USITC remedy is supported by a majority of the six commissioners, then the Congress has ninety working days to vote a concurrent resolution, with a majority of each house present and voting, disapproving the President's action and putting the USITC recommendation into effect.[9]

The USITC report sent to the President on February 20, 1976, contained a unanimous finding of serious injury to the domestic footwear industry. However, three commissioners recommended substantially increased tariffs, varying from 35 percent for the lowest priced footwear to 25 percent for higher priced footwear, phased down over five years.[10] Two commissioners recommended imposing tariff-rate quotas allocated on the basis of each country's 1974 trade share. They proposed an over-quota rate of 40 percent in the first year, phased down by 5 percent a year over the next five years. One commissioner recommended only the provision of adjustment assistance. Thus, since there was no majority among the commissioners regarding a remedy, the Congress could not override the President's determination.

HISTORY OF INDUSTRY EFFORTS
TO OBTAIN RELIEF

Since the late 1960s the footwear industry had repeatedly sought relief from foreign imports. They had nearly succeeded in obtaining quota legislation in 1970. The U.S. Tariff Commission, predecessor of the USITC, had reported a tie vote in a footwear escape clause case in 1971. President Nixon had authorized adjustment assistance for eleven shoe plants in cases where the Tariff Commission had split evenly, but the program reportedly had little effect.[11] Nixon had also sent Ambassador David Kennedy to Spain and Italy to discuss voluntary restraint of footwear exports to the United States. Neither country had imposed such restraints, although Italy monitored its exports.

The footwear industry had succeeded in getting a provision in the Trade Act of 1974 calling for establishing within the General Agreement

---

The remedies outlined in the Trade Act that the President can proclaim include: an increased tariff, a tariff-rate quota, a quota, the negotiation of orderly marketing agreements with supplying countries, or any combination of such actions. Sec. 203 (a).

[9] *Ibid.* Sec. 203 (c).

[10] The Trade Act stipulates that no remedy may extend for longer than five years.

[11] *Weekly Presidential Documents* (April 8, 1971), p. 618.

on Tariffs and Trade (GATT) an international footwear agreement.[12] Moreover, during congressional consideration of the Trade Act of 1974, several in the Congress pressed the administration for general and specific commitments on escape clause cases. The administration representatives, Special Trade Representative William Eberle, and his deputy Harold Malmgren, who sat in on the mark-up of the legislation, gave assurances that import-injured industries would receive relief unless this was contrary to the national interest. More specifically, when the legislation was nearing a vote in the Senate, Senator Thomas McIntyre (D – New Hampshire), in a letter dated December 6, 1974, expressed grave concern regarding the Trade Act's possible effect on the shoe industry. To reassure the Senate, Eberle wrote him on December 11, 1974, that the Trade Act:

> . . . contains provisions which, if passed by Congress, will allow the Executive Branch to work out suitable remedies for disruptive imports, remedies which are appropriate to the particular difficulties of industries or workers concerned.
> . . . It seems to me that the escape clause provisions . . . are ideally suited for use by the American non-rubber footwear industry. . . . If such escape clause procedures were undertaken under the new law, priority attention would be given to the matter, and if the procedures suggested the need for import relief, you can be assured that the Administration would move expeditiously to provide it.

Subsequently, Senator McIntyre introduced a restrictive amendment relating to footwear on the floor of the Senate. Senator Russell Long (D – Louisiana) successfully urged defeat of the McIntyre amendment on the ground that "it is our guess that if the shoe industry would seek relief under the terms of this Act, chances are ninety out of a hundred that it would get relief."

Eberle's successor at STR, Frederick B. Dent, met with shoe industry spokesmen during the summer of 1975 and recommended that, rather than pressing for an international footwear agreement, they seek relief through the Trade Act's escape clause provisions. Shortly thereafter, industry representatives filed an escape clause petition with the USITC that culminated in the USITC report to the President on February 20, 1976.[13]

---

[12] Sec. 121 (a) (12). This would be similar in some respects to the Multi-Fiber Textile Arrangement.

[13] During the fall of 1975, Ambassador Dent consulted with officials from key exporting countries – Brazil, Taiwan, South Korea, Italy, and Spain – with respect to the footwear import issue but was unsuccessful in securing any change in their export policies.

STATE OF THE DOMESTIC FOOTWEAR INDUSTRY
AND SHOE IMPORTS

The footwear escape clause case involved $1.1 billion of imports representing 40 percent of domestic shoe consumption. Over 600 plants employing 163,000 workers in 37 states were affected.

Between 1968 and 1975, domestic shoe production declined from 642 million to 433 million pairs while shoe imports rose from 181 million to 288 million pairs, an increase in market share from 22 percent to 40 percent of the footwear covered by the USITC finding. One major cause was the lower cost of labor abroad. Another factor that many believed contributed to the growth of imports was consumer demand for a wide variety of styles and qualities of footwear.

Domestic employment in the shoe industry had declined since 1968 by 30 percent from 233,000 to 163,000.[14] Almost half of the shoe manufacturing firms in the United States had gone out of business and approximately one-third of the total number of plants had closed.

But these aggregate figures masked a marked trend *within* the U.S. shoe industry. The largest firms were increasing their production, while the medium-sized and smaller firms were reducing production substantially or going out of business. By 1974, out of a total of 409 firms, the 21 largest firms accounted for 50 percent of domestic production.

In short, the industry had a number of efficient, highly competitive firms that were generating healthy profits. The twenty-one largest firms had averaged operating profits of 7.1 percent of net sales from 1970–74. The most recent quarterly reports of the eight largest firms showed that all of them had increases in earnings per share, some of them very large increases. While there was an overall decline in the number of shoe firms, the number of large firms (companies producing over four million pairs) increased by 31 percent between 1967 and 1974. At the same time, a second tier of the industry consisting of smaller (under 200,000 pairs annually), less efficient firms suffered from both foreign and domestic competition, with profits averaging 2.6 percent of sales from 1970–74.

As the U.S. economy recovered from the recession, the prospects for the domestic shoe industry were brightening. Compared with a year before, domestic production was up 20.8 percent, factory shipments were up 25.9 percent, production worker employment up 9.9 percent, and retail sales up 31.0 percent.[15] Moreover, there was some evidence that

---

[14]   The level of unemployment in the shoe industry has been consistently more than twice that of the average for all U.S. manufacturing.

[15]   This upturn in the domestic shoe industry was substantiated by the results of a

TABLE 8
U.S. footwear imports 1968–1975

Year	Imports as a percentage of domestic consumption (pairs)
1968	22
1969	26
1970	30
1971	33
1972	36
1973	39
1974	37
1975	40

Source: Office of the Special Representative for Trade Negotiations.

the import share of the U.S. market was stabilizing after a sharp increase between 1968 and 1972, as shown in Table 8.

Thus, the assessment of the U.S. shoe industry was mixed. U.S. producers had a significantly smaller share of the domestic market than a decade before because of cheaper labor abroad. Scores of shoe manufacturing firms had gone out of business and hundreds of plants had closed. Employment had dropped by 30 percent since 1968. But the larger, more efficient U.S. firms were making profits and seemed to be holding their own against foreign competitors and, as the recovery proceeded, the future looked somewhat brighter for these survivors.

ADJUSTMENT ASSISTANCE

The Trade Act also includes provisions for federal adjustment assistance for workers, firms, and communities hurt by imports. Workers who lose

telephone survey conducted by the Treasury of fourteen domestic shoe manufacturers. All company representatives were optimistic, reporting reactivation of plants, rehiring of furloughed workers, regular overtime work, and general increases in production over the previous year. A majority identified the second half of 1975 as the time when the decline in their operations reversed.

their jobs because of imports can receive a supplement to unemployment insurance and funds for job retraining. Firms and communities can also receive financial and technical assistance in helping cope with plant closings. By April 1976, 22,000 footwear workers had been certified eligible to apply for adjustment assistance. Seventeen footwear firms had been certified eligible for adjustment assistance. However, the program was reaching only a fraction of the potential affected workers and firms and was generally unpopular. Many recipients disparagingly referred to adjustment assistance as "burial insurance."

THE FOOTWEAR DECISION IN PERSPECTIVE

The shoe import case was only one of several pending cases brought under various provisions of the 1974 Trade Act by industries seeking relief from import competition. There were eight other pending escape clause cases involving roughly $700 million in imports, thirteen pending antidumping cases at the Treasury, five pending Section 301 cases (unfair foreign trade practices), five pending countervailing duty cases, and fourteen Section 337 (unfair competitive practices) cases. The countries most affected by the shoe decision – Italy, Spain, Brazil, Taiwan, and South Korea – were also the principal suppliers in several of these other pending cases. There were two countervailing duty cases against Brazil. Taiwan and South Korea were the nations most vitally affected by the pending stainless steel flatware escape clause case. Spain was the subject of a countervailing duty action, and the European Community was a principal supplier in fifteen of the forty-six pending import cases.

The most significant individual case that influenced consideration of the shoe decision was the specialty steel escape clause case. The USITC report on the specialty steel case reached the White House just over a month before the shoe import report; thus the President was required to make his determination on specialty steel by mid-March. Since a majority of the USITC commissioners had recommended a quota, the likelihood was strong that the Congress would override the President if he didn't proclaim an adequate remedy.

On March 16, 1976, the President "determined that import relief is to ·e provided to permit the [specialty steel] industry to recover from its ecent depressed operating levels and high unemployment rates." He diected the Special Representative for Trade Negotiations "to negotiate ·rderly marketing agreements with supplying countries" and stipulated hat "if satisfactory orderly market arrangements are not negotiated suc-:essfully, I will proclaim import quotas for a period of three years to take :ffect on or before June 14, 1976. The quotas would be set at overall levels (but not necessarily the product category or country levels) comparable to those recommended by the USITC."[16]

Foreign countries, intently watching for signs of U.S. protectionism, would view a decision supporting relief for the shoe industry as indicative of a trend. As one adviser told the President: "Your decision in this case will inevitably be seen in the light of the speciality steel decision. A decision to provide tariff-rate quota protection to shoes will be portrayed as a major step by our country toward a protectionist trade policy."

The previous November at Rambouillet the President had joined with the leaders of five other major industrial democracies in pledging support for free trade and affirming the Organization for Economic Cooperation and Development (OECD) pledge to avoid trade restrictions. In the wake of Rambouillet, the United States strongly encouraged the British not to yield to heavy protectionist pressure from labor. The British government successfully resisted labor's pressure. In two months the leaders of the industrial democracies would meet again in Puerto Rico to assess the progress toward a more stable and prosperous world economy.

If the U.S. were seen as turning protectionist, other countries could either retaliate or emulate. Retaliation for restricted U.S. shoe imports would most likely operate against U.S. agricultural exports. Moreover, the British might not be able to resist their own domestic pressures a second time. A number of European nations were facing high and in some cases growing unemployment and large trade deficits. Italy and Spain, both with economies recovering slowly from the recession, faced Communist challenges to the current governments.[17] Thus, a decision to restrict shoe imports could trigger new barriers to U.S. exports, jeopardize the multilateral trade negotiations, and set back economic recovery efforts in the industrial world. From a foreign policy standpoint, there is rarely, if ever, a good time to impose trade restraints.

But international considerations must be weighed alongside domestic imperatives. Despite the decline in the total number of domestic shoe firms, thirty-seven states had shoe manufacturing factories. The leading

---

[16]   Memorandum for the Special Representative for Trade Negotiations, "Import Relief Determination under Section 202 (b) of the Trade Act," *Federal Register*, March 16, 1976.

The President rejected the USITC's proposed quota remedy for two reasons. First, he considered it too inflexible in view of the rapid expansions and contractions of the specialty steel market. Second, the USITC remedy did not take into account special factors affecting certain foreign supplying countries.

[17]   One adviser warned: "Italian labor would point to American protectionism as an excuse for Italy to erect protectionist measures to reduce its unemployment. The Italian problem is further complicated by the fact that Italy is the largest exporter of shoes to the U.S. ($320 million last year), and the Communists would seize on any U.S. import action against shoes – however liberal – to argue that the U.S. was harming Italy during a time of economic crisis. Economic pressures for protectionism exist in France and Spain as well."

producers of nonrubber footwear were Pennsylvania, New York, Massachusetts, Missouri, Tennessee, Maine, and New Hampshire. In each of these states, except Tennessee, production and employment had dropped substantially since 1968.[18] Moreover, by the first week in April, ninety-four senators and congressmen had contacted the White House with recommendations and expressions of interest in the President's decision.

Finally, the economy still suffered from the twin problems of inflation and unemployment. Estimating the effects of potential actions either on inflation or unemployment is difficult. However, the best estimates were that U.S. consumers could pay as much as $750 million more for shoes if a tariff-rate quota based on 1974 levels (one of the USITC recommendations) went into effect.[19]

THE DECISION-MAKING PROCESS

William Seidman sent the massive USITC report to the Office of the Special Representative for Trade Negotiations the day after he received it. Seidman asked Ambassador Dent to review the status of the specialty steel and footwear escape clause cases at the next Economic Policy Board meeting with the President on February 25. That discussion did not include detailed options for the two cases but focused on the timing of the decisions and several background factors. Dent told the President that interagency groups would consider the footwear issue and present it to him for his decision sometime during the first two weeks of April.

During February and March the subcabinet-level Trade Policy Staff Committee and the Trade Policy Review Group reviewed the USITC footwear report and the President's options. At the same time, Ambassador Dent and other administration officials met with industry and labor representatives and interested parties in the Congress to hear their views and assess the intensity of their feelings.[20]

---

[18] Massachusetts, New Hampshire, and Maine had lost nearly half their production during the period 1968–1975.

[19] Shoes account for 1.5 percent of the consumer price index.

[20] On February 27, Treasury Secretary Simon and Seidman left on a two week trip to the Middle East and Western Europe, meeting with leading governmental officials throughout the Middle East and in Spain, Italy, and the Federal Republic of Germany. On their return, Simon and Seidman reported to the President that Spanish, Italian, and West German officials feared the United States was turning protectionist and had expressed particular concern over the specialty steel and shoe escape clause cases. However, the timing and content of the Simon–Seidman meeting with the President suggests that it had little, if any, effect on the President's decision. Simon and Seidman did not return to Washington until March 11. The President made a tentative decision in the speciality steel case on March 12 that Seidman conveyed to Ambassador Dent and other leading economic officials. The

On March 12, 1976, Seidman sent Dent a memorandum requesting that he prepare a monthly status report for the EPB Executive Committee on trade policy issues, the first report to "outline those issues likely to arise during the coming six months including trade restrictive actions such as USITC findings, countervailing duties, and antidumping cases."[21]

Ambassador Dent presented his report to the EPB Executive Committee on March 22. The discussion focused on a broad range of trade matters – the automobile antidumping case, renewal of the waiver provision of the Jackson–Vanik amendment, the basis for reporting monthly trade statistics, possible administration-sponsored public hearings on foreign trade policy, and, of course, the footwear import case. The Executive Committee agreed to send the President the status report to help place his upcoming footwear decision in context.[22]

On April 1, the Trade Policy Committee, chaired by the STR, discussed the shoe import issue and agreed to present four options to the President: (1) adjustment assistance with a determination that import relief was not in the national economic interest; (2) adjustment assistance combined with a tariff-rate quota based on recent trade patterns;[23] (3) a stringent tariff-rate quota based on recession import levels (1974) with a prohibitive over-quota rate; and (4) announcement of intent to negotiate orderly marketing agreements (OMA's) with five principal supplying countries, with quotas applied on or before July 19, 1976, if the negotiations were unsuccessful.

The representatives of the nine departments and agencies in attendance outlined their views and expressed their preferences among the options. At the conclusion of the meeting, Ambassador Dent indicated that he, as chairman of the Trade Policy Committee, would draft an options memorandum reflecting the discussion for the President.

On April 5, Dent sent his memorandum to Seidman who, as Executive Director of the EPB, coordinated economic policy decision making for the President. Seidman and his staff, after reviewing the Dent memoran-

---

President's decision to seek orderly marketing agreements with the major specialty steel supplying countries was publicly announced on March 16. Seidman and Simon each sent the President a detailed memorandum before their meeting with him on March 17, including accounts of Spanish, Italian, and West German views on trade policy matters. However, the March 17 meeting focused on the Middle East situation, and only briefly noted European concern over a possible U.S. drift toward protectionism.

[21]   Seidman memorandum to Ambassador Frederick B. Dent, "Trade Policy Status Report," March 12, 1976.

[22]   The detailed report not only discussed the entire range of trade issues that the administration would face during the next six months, but it also provided several tables categorizing the pending import relief cases by type and country. Seidman sent the report to the President on March 23.

[23]   The second option was a modified version of STR's original proposal.

dum, did three things routine under such circumstances. First, they sent the memorandum and a request for comments to those White House offices and agencies in the Executive Office of the President (not already recorded on the memorandum) with an interest in the issue or whose views would be important to the President. These offices included the National Security Council, the Domestic Council, the Office of Management and Budget, the White House Office of Congressional Liaison, the White House Counsel's Office, and Counsellor to the President John Marsh. Second, they checked to confirm that the departments and agencies were identified with the option each supported.[24] Third, Seidman and his staff contacted three or four departments and agencies to check certain facts and arguments used in the memorandum or on matters where they felt the presentation might be strengthened.

Several departments and agencies promptly asked that the STR memorandum not go to the President until they could state their own case. They saw STR as a major advocate on the issue. It was STR that had originally suggested the footwear industry seek relief under the escape clause provisions. Moreover, STR strongly favored option number two (adjustment assistance combined with a tariff-rate quota). Although the memorandum contained analysis and arguments in support of each option, all the departments and agencies listed as supporting option number one (simply adjustment assistance) told Seidman's office that they wanted their own say. Also, the agencies supplied additional information to help develop a balanced assessment for the President.

The Economic Policy Board's standard operating procedures permitted departments and agencies to submit in a memorandum any additional views they wished on an issue; these memorandums were included in the materials sent to the President. During the week of April 5, Secretaries Simon and Kissinger, CEA Chairman Greenspan, Secretary Butz, and Brent Scowcroft, Assistant to the President for National Security Affairs, sent memorandums on the shoe import issue for the President to Seidman's office. Meanwhile, Seidman and his staff prepared a cover memorandum outlining the issues requiring the President's decision, the alternatives under consideration, and the advantages and disadvantages associated with each of these alternatives. The Dent, Simon and Kissinger, Greenspan, Butz, and Scowcroft "advocacy" memorandums were

---

[24] STR did not circulate the STR memorandum to the Trade Policy Committee agencies in contrast to the Economic Policy Board practice of providing a copy of options memorandums for the President to the heads of those departments and agencies who were recorded as supporting one of the options. Not surprisingly, the practice of not circulating "final" memorandums, based on a desire to prevent leaks, intensified the suspicions of those who feared that the memorandum, written by a competing advocate, did not fully or faithfully represent their views.

referred to in the cover memorandum and attached to it with a memorandum prepared by the White House Office of Congressional Liaison
detailing the ninety-four senators and congressmen who had contacted
the White House, all favoring some form of relief for the footwear industry.

The entire package – thirty-eight pages long – was submitted to the
President on April 12 as part of the briefing paper for his April 13 meeting with the EPB Executive Committee. Seidman's office also circulated
the entire package to the sixteen departments, agencies, and offices recorded as taking a position on the issue. The sixteen agencies were evenly
split in their recommendations between option one (providing no import
relief) and option two (a tariff-rate quota based on recent trade patterns). The recommendations of the American Footwear Industries Association and the footwear union, which supported options three (a tariff-rate quota based on recession import levels) and four (OMA's, with a
stringent quota if negotiations failed), respectively, were also recorded.
Seidman, who oversaw the process, drafted the final options decision
memorandum, and formally transmitted the package to the President,
was not recorded as supporting any of the options.

The heads of all the departments and agencies with an interest in the
issue were also invited to attend the April 13 meeting with the President.[25] The footwear import discussion, the first agenda item, lasted for
over an hour with the give-and-take typical of EPB meetings with the
President.

The President began the meeting by commenting that he had read the
entire package and had noted the division among his advisers. Eleven
advisers participated actively in the following discussion on the precise
parameters of alternative remedies, the nature of the administration's
commitment to the Congress and to the industry, the prospects for the
domestic industry and the impact of various options on the industry, and
the impact of the decision on overall foreign and trade policy objectives
and specific bilateral relationships.

After calling on each of the principal advocates for their views, the
President raised a series of questions – the costs of adjustment assistance,
the effect of the plummeting lira on Italian shoe exports, the most recent

---

[25] The meeting with the President included the Vice President, William Simon (Trea-
sury), Alan Greenspan and Burton Malkiel (CEA), Elliot Richardson (Commerce), James
T. Lynn (OMB), William Seidman (WH), W. J. Usery, Jr. (Labor), Frederick B. Dent (STR),
Charles W. Robinson (State), James M. Cannon (Domestic Council), John O. Marsh, Jr.
(WH), Brent Scowcroft and William Hyland (NSC), Frank Zarb (FEA), and Roger Porter
(WH).

Secretary of Agriculture Earl Butz was invited to attend the meeting but was out of the
country.

figures for the first months of 1976, the status of the specialty steel orderly marketing agreement negotiations, and the prospects for negotiating orderly marketing agreements on shoes. At the conclusion of the discussion the President indicated that he felt he "had a reasonable grasp of
the issue," that he wanted to think it over some more, and that he would
have a decision within a couple of days, leaving adequate time to prepare
the necessary documents and to notify industry representatives, the Congress, and foreign governments before a public announcement.

At no time during the course of the meeting did the President hint at
his own views or suggest which way he was leaning. As far as can be
determined, he did not discuss the issue privately with any of the principals after the meeting. Two days later, the President informed Seidman
of his decision, which Seidman formally communicated to appropriate
departments and agencies in an Economic Policy Decision Memorandum
(EPDM) on April 16.

The President determined that import relief for the footwear industry
was not in the national economic interest of the United States. He instructed the Secretary of Commerce and the Secretary of Labor to give
expeditious consideration to any petitions for adjustment assistance by
the footwear industry filed with them and authorized the secretaries to
file supplementary budget requests for adjustment assistance funds, if
necessary. Finally, he directed the Special Representative for Trade Negotiations to monitor U.S. footwear trade, including levels and quantities
of imports and domestic production and employment. He requested that,
if significant changes occurred, they be reported to him with appropriate
recommendations.

IMPLEMENTATION

On April 19 the EPB Executive Committee requested the Departments of
Commerce and Labor to report on their plans for providing expedited
adjustment assistance for the U.S. footwear industry, which they did at
the April 26 executive committee meeting.

Five months later, on September 22, 1976, the Executive Committee
again discussed the need to review several factors relating to the shoe
industry, including: (1) domestic production, shipments, employment,
investment, and imports; (2) the status of adjustment assistance petitions; and (3) the status of the administration's monitoring efforts. The
group formed an interagency task force for the review, including representatives from Treasury, State, Commerce, Labor, STR, CIEP, and the
USITC.[26]

---

[26] EPB executive committee minutes, September 22, 1976.

On October 12, 1976, the task force reported a softening in domestic production, a higher import penetration ratio, and continuing concern about the adjustment assistance program's effectiveness. The Executive Committee agreed that the Special Representative for Trade Negotiations should endorse reopening the shoe escape clause case and request that the USITC expedite its investigation. There were strong indications that the Senate Finance Committee was about to request a new USITC investigation. The Executive Committee also requested the task force to study possible changes in the adjustment assistance program.[27]

EVALUATION

Evaluating the process: characteristics

The decision-making process in the footwear import case exhibited two general characteristics: First, it was advocacy oriented; second, it was structured around principles of due process.

The advocacy orientation was reflected both in the memorandums prepared for the President and in the discussion. No adviser, except for Seidman, was disinterested in the outcome; all were advocates. Moreover, among agencies the advocacy was evenly split between two major alternatives. Eight advisers favored option one and eight favored option two. The President did not look to or receive his advice from a neutral, objective, and presidentially oriented staff. He was advised by individuals who pressed particular interests and objectives that were mutually exclusive, and thus were in competition with one another.

The competition, however, was characterized by due process. No important or interested party was excluded. Everyone received the same documents and heard the oral agruments. Each had the opportunity to counter, question, or dispute the claims and views expressed by others. The President received the advocacy memorandums in a single package, and held a collective discussion with his advisers. The process favored no individual advocate. No one was able to submit a private memorandum or have a private hearing with the President.

The perception that one advocate had an unfair advantage – some feared the STR memorandum might be the paper on which the President based his decision – prompted a spate of competing memorandums. The final memorandum, seen by all parties, was prepared by an honest broker. All interested parties had their say, but the President was not merely presented with a stack of individual memorandums.

The footwear issue was handled somewhat differently than the nor-

[27]   EPB executive committee minutes, October 12, 1976.

mal presentation of issues to the President by the EPB. Because the Trade Policy Committee had statutory responsibilities, the EPB did not exclusively oversee the process from the outset. Normally, few, if any, "advocacy" memorandums accompanied EPB options papers for the President because interested departments and agencies participated in the preparation of the options papers.

Typically, a draft originally prepared by a department, an interagency group, or by Seidman's staff was circulated to EPB members for their review and comments, and then the comments were incorporated into the final memorandum. If necessary, a meeting was held to settle any differences over facts and arguments in the memorandum.

All information, alternatives, and written views were sent to the President at the same time and *before* the crucial meeting with him. Thus, all of the competing interests had equal opportunity to state their case. Moreover, having read the papers before the meeting, the President could raise questions he wanted discussed by his advisers more knowledgeably than if the decision were made on the basis of oral presentations alone, or if he received the written materials after the meeting.

Finally, Seidman's role as honest broker was crucial to achieving the high degree of due process. It is significant that no one challenged his coordinating the preparation of written materials or his organizing and controlling attendance at the meeting, not even the STR whose recommendation was not adopted. It was important, of course, that Seidman was not himself an advocate on the issue. Seidman not only had the de jure responsibility for overseeing the process by virtue of his and the EPB's presidential mandate, but he also exercised de facto authority, which rested in part on his strategic position in the White House. But it also was strengthened because departments and agencies accepted his authority and felt the process he presided over was fair.

Evaluating the process: strengths

The footwear import decision demonstrated a number of strengths in the way advice to the President was organized. The issue was identified early; the President knew as early as February 25 that he would need to make a decision, received a March 23 background memorandum, and had an options memorandum on April 12, eight days before his final decision was required. The process precisely defined the problem and clarified what issues required resolution. In the end, it mobilized the best information and analysis available. During the two weeks following the April 1 Trade Policy Committee meeting, Treasury, the Council of Economic Advisers, and others marshaled some of their best resources to support their arguments with additional facts. By the April 13 meeting, there was agreement on the factual information and analysis presented to the President.

The President's range of realistic options was due less to the advisory process than to the structure of the issue. The Trade Act of 1974 prescribes the remedies available in escape clause cases. No great imagination or creativity was required to identify alternative courses of action.[28]

The papers and discussion provided a reasonably full evaluation of the anticipated consequences of each option and clearly identified the trade-offs between the two major competing alternatives. One participant summarized the EPB's role as follows:

> The Economic Policy Board functioned as an umbrella organization in bringing together the reports from the Trade Policy Committee and from various departments including Agriculture, State, Commerce, Labor, and the CEA. The meeting with the President on the issue was really quite good. It was very clear what positions were and the President was able to get the information that he needed in order to make a decision. In this case, even though it [the EPB] did not come to a decision, what it did that was terribly helpful was to get the information together in a reasonable form so that the President could make a decision.

The process also provided for prompt and effective implementation of the decision, a relatively easy matter in this instance since it basically involved preparing necessary documents for the President's signature. However, the EPB also reviewed the plans of the Departments of Commerce and Labor for providing expedited adjustment assistance and tried to assess the results and revise policy accordingly. Establishing an interagency task force in September 1976 to review the status of the shoe industry and to evaluate the adjustment assistance program resulted in supporting a new USITC investigation. Had Ford won the November 1976 election, the interagency study might have led to changes in the adjustment assistance program's structure or administration.

In summary, the process let all interested departments and agencies participate. It insured that a single interest or objective did not dominate. Finally, the decision was made with a full understanding of its relationship to related issues.

Evaluating the process: weaknesses

The process also exhibited three limitations. One was political insensitivity. The process provided for consideration of all major interests and

---

[28] A year later, the Carter administration, in considering the same question, presented the President with essentially the same array of options. See David S. Broder, "The Case of the Missing Shoe-Import Option," *Washington Post* (July 23, 1977).

values affected by the issue. However, foreign policy and economic policy objectives received more attention in both the memorandums and the discussion than did the likely domestic political reaction. The pattern of advice was far more substantively than politically oriented. The President may well have weighed domestic political considerations on his own, but they received little attention in his discussions with his advisers. His decision not to provide relief to the shoe industry cost him dearly in domestic political capital. Whether he, or his advisers, adequately appreciated and accepted that cost at the time is not clear.

An equally serious limitation was the lack of support among the President's advisers for a crucial option: seeking orderly marketing agreements with the principal supplying countries. This was the "solution" to the specialty steel escape clause case decided a month earlier; Jimmy Carter selected this option when he decided the shoe import case a year later.

In April 1976, two reasons were given for the unattractiveness of the OMA option. First, in light of the USITC's various remedy findings, no country had indicated a willingness to negotiate agreements. Second, the domestic industry, believing that negotiating OMAs would delay and dilute relief, was pushing for a stringent tariff-rate quota. Yet, presumably, the industry would have preferred orderly marketing agreements to no relief at all. Likewise, if the administration had committed itself publicly to imposing quotas if the negotiations failed, the supplying countries might well have been more willing to negotiate seriously. In short, a potentially viable option received inadequate consideration because it had no advocate. Since the President's advisers were clearly divided between two options, it would have been difficult for him to select a third alternative that had no effective spokesman arguing its merits.

A third possible weakness of the process was that the discussion operated within the constraint of a free trade philosophy. While the degree of commitment to a free trade philosophy varied from adviser to adviser, it set the bounds for the discussion. Thus, those who favored relief for the footwear industry pressed the threat to the administration's credibility in the Congress if it appeared to disregard commitments made during the passage of the Trade Act of 1974.

The constraint of a prevailing ideology – and the limitations it imposes – points toward an important principle of presidential decision making. A shared economic philosophy is more a reflection of the individuals selected to fill major administration positions than of the way advising the President is organized. In the end, people count as much as process.

7

The Economic Policy Board: an evaluation

$\mathcal{T}$he Economic Policy Board was a piece of machinery for decision making. It was not the only apparatus conceivable, nor was it the only organizational arrangement for presidential decision making that has existed. Before assessing how well the EPB performed certain basic advisory functions, it is well to briefly review its essential characteristics.

THE ECONOMIC POLICY BOARD: DISTINGUISHING CHARACTERISTICS

The Economic Policy Board was clearly a form of multiple advocacy. It was the product of personalities, dissatisfaction with existing arrangements, and an economic crisis. Most new administrations attempt some institutional innovations to distinguish themselves from previous administrations. The creation of the Economic Policy Board represented in part the quest for a new image of openness and candor, in part an effort to rejuvenate morale in departments and agencies dissatisfied with White House attempts to dominate them. Moreover, the serious economic conditions in the autumn of 1974 encouraged a willingness to reorganize. The absence of a dominant single figure in the economic policy community contributed to a collegial approach. Finally, the EPB sprang from a desire, common to new administrations, to reorganize the existing array of specialized, overlapping, and uncoordinated committees and councils that had proliferated during the previous administration.

The two and a quarter years following the EPB's creation on September 30, 1974, witnessed several institutional innovations, a refining of procedures, and a maturing of its operation. Despite its short life, the Economic Policy Board was one of the most comprehensive, sustained,

174

and systematic attempts to organize advice to the President over a broad policy area.

Above all, it was an open system in which all departments and agencies with a legitimate interest in an issue were included in the EPB's consideration of the matter. Significantly, in scores of interviews with participants and departmental staffers, not a single official felt his department or agency had been excluded from the EPB's deliberations. The weekly agenda was distributed, not only to the fifteen department and agency heads who were members of the full Board, but to an additional sixteen agency heads and officials with a continuing interest in issues regularly considered by the Board. Twenty-nine departments and agencies made presentations at executive committee meetings and twenty-seven departments and agencies prepared papers for EPB consideration. The Executive Director and his staff also personally contacted key individuals who were not members of the Executive Committee and invited them to attend when an issue affecting their department or agency was scheduled for consideration. One cabinet secretary who was a member of the full Board but not a member of the Executive Committee observed:

> I never had any feeling that I couldn't call up and say, "Bill [Seidman], I want to get this issue on and I want to get it on fast," and get results . . . It is easier to deal in a little group, and executive groups tend not to like to get the whole big group together. But we certainly were getting all the lists of projected meetings. I wouldn't have felt embarrassed to walk in just because I was individually interested in an issue and sit there and listen to it.

An executive committee member who had served in previous administrations noted:

> My impression is that the involvement of people in the processes of economic decision making was broader and fairer in this administration than any other I know about. I felt that a very conscious effort was made to insure that anybody who wanted to be heard or to be present or ought to be informed that a meeting was being held, was invited.

Another executive committee member, who had also served in the previous administration, reflected: "It was the first time in anybody's memory where you had everyone, including those on the periphery of economic issues, involved in the discussions."

The EPB also served as a sorter, a sifter, and a resolver. For a large number of issues, it was a forum for resolving some questions; on other issues, it organized the pattern of advice and developed the analysis of the problem before presenting it for a presidential decision. One partici-

pant with a quarter century of experience in the executive branch contrasted the EPB with earlier arrangements:

> There are several different modes in White House organization.
> One involves a presidential style in which the President says:
> "Don't bring me disagreements and interagency problems. You
> guys solve them." One example of this was Eisenhower. The result
> was lowest common denominator solutions. We had the NSC and
> the Operations Coordination Board, the Psychological Strategy
> Board, and a whole number of other things. We worked through
> papers and they were ground down until when we finished up they
> were nothing.
>
> The other style involves the President saying: "Don't try to re-
> solve things among the agencies. Bring me your problems." This
> was essentially the Lyndon Johnson approach. And then you have
> no incentive to resolve issues among the agencies. The premium is
> on getting to the President. That's where it's going to be resolved.
> So you take the most extreme position and then fall back at the
> very end.
>
> The EPB to me represented a middle course. First, there was an
> effort to resolve things at the agency level, but there was a court of
> last resort at the same time. You had to calculate that there were
> only so many times that you were going to get to the President. But
> there were certain things important enough that you were not
> going to sacrifice your position to reach an agreement.
>
> I am convinced that you need an institution or forum where you
> can discuss issues and try to resolve them. You need an honest bro-
> ker. And you need one other thing, a top guy, the President, who is
> available and accessible from time to time and prepared to make a
> decision.
>
> The Tin Agreement illustrates what I mean by how the EPB
> worked. In our interagency meetings we resolved some of the is-
> sues, but the basic issue of do we join the Tin Agreement or not
> join the agreement was unresolved until we took it to the President.
> We laid out the case and ultimately the President made the decision.

The EPB system was advocacy oriented, and exposed the President to
competing arguments and viewpoints from the advocates themselves in
a group discussion that permitted exchange and argument among the
advocates before the President.

The Assistant to the President for Economic Affairs was the EPB's
Executive Director and exercised operational control, working from a
White House base. William Seidman not only enjoyed the President's

confidence and support, but was viewed both as a peer and as an honest broker by his colleagues on the Board. As one executive committee member put it: "I think the fact that Bill Seidman is himself an extremely fair-minded individual and was willing to perform his role in a highly self-effacing manner contributed significantly to the success of the EPB." Another member added: "He [Seidman] was not without his views, but he was fair and neutral." And a third reflected: "The fact that Bill Seidman had no ambition other than to do a good job for the President and be the honest broker is what made the thing work on a day-to-day basis." Seidman, with no department or agency responsibilities, devoted his full time and energies to overseeing the EPB decision-making process and to structuring and balancing debates.[1]

The EPB process emphasized careful weighing of all views and considerations, the fruit of its philosophy that a competition of ideas and viewpoints was the best method of developing policy. The competition was regulated by an honest broker to insure that the process was orderly, systematic, and balanced. Thus, the EPB was a managed process. While the Executive Director and his staff did not act as intermediaries, their role extended beyond simply insuring due process for all participants. They also acted, on occasion, to promote a genuine competition, identifying points of view that were not adequately represented or that required qualification, augmenting resources so that a more balanced presentation resulted.

The President's role was similar to that of a magistrate: He considered the analysis and arguments made by his advisers, sought clarification where necessary, weighed the evidence presented, and then decided what action, if any, to take. One should, however, take care not to press the magistrate analogy too far. In some instances the President's decision supported an option recommended by one or more of the advocates, but in others he approved a new course of action fashioned after participating in the exchange with his advisers. Whatever the final outcome, the process was designed first and foremost to provide alternatives and arguments for the President's judgment — not to reach a consensus.

---

[1] In this sense, as in other ways, the EPB represented a multiple advocacy process. Alexander George has argued that multiple advocacy is a management-oriented theory in contrast to partisan mutual adjustment or unregulated bureaucratic politics. Alexander George, "The Case for Multiple Advocacy in Making Foreign Policy," p. 761.

"The theory of multiple advocacy poses sharply defined requirements for executive management of the policy-making system. . . Strong, alert management must frequently be exercised in order to create and maintain the basis for structured, balanced debate among policy advocates. As such, multiple advocacy goes beyond what is usually meant by 'adversary proceedings' or use of a 'devil's advocate.'" Alexander George, "Multiple Advocacy," in U.S. Commission on the Organization of the Government for the Conduct of Foreign Policy, *Appendices* (Washington, D.C.: GPO, June 1975), Vol. 2, p. 95.

The EPB staff attached to the Office of the Assistant to the President for Economic Affairs was small, independent of agency ties, and committed to the role of an honest broker. In addition to serving as the Board's secretariat, the EPB staff sought out issues, strove to highlight important interagency differences, and, from time to time, challenged departmental options and analyses. But the smallness of the staff and the conscious decision to concentrate on managing the decision-making process meant that the EPB relied on department and agency resources for most of the analysis and expertise.

The composition of the EPB Executive Committee and consistent participation by its members meant high continuity among the President's economic policy advisers. The Secretary of the Treasury, the Chairman of the Council of Economic Advisers, the Director of the Office of Management and Budget, the Assistant to the President for Economic Affairs, and later the Secretaries of Labor, Commerce, and State were personally involved in the major economic policy issues that reached the presidential level.[2] The group's composition varied somewhat depending on the issue under consideration and included other cabinet-level officials as appropriate. However, a stable core of advisers shared responsibility for collectively advising the President over the broad range of economic policy issues.[3]

By comparison with previous economic policy councils and committees, the Economic Policy Board was extraordinarily active, meeting 520 times and considering 1,539 agenda items during the two and one-quarter years of its existence.[4] Likewise, the EPB operated formally in comparison with previous high-level economic policy committees and coun-

---

[2]   The Secretary of State, who had only a very marginal interest in many domestic economic policy issues, was an exception. His participation was generally limited to foreign economic policy questions.

[3]   One senior official observed:

The EPB really did get good attendance. You got people from each of the relevant agencies coming each time. My experience with the Domestic Council was that it was more ad hoc. You would have a particular issue and a certain group was called; another issue and another group was called; . . . Very often I would find that, even when we were discussing the same issue, attendance would vary and sometimes you would have one interested agency and sometimes you wouldn't. In that sense the Domestic Council in general struck me that everything was handled in a more ad hoc fashion. The EPB was regular not only in terms of attendance but times for meetings. It was also regular in that there were regular meetings with the President.

[4]   Thus, the EPB held an average of nearly five meetings a week while the Troika and other economic policy councils established during the Truman, Eisenhower, Kennedy, Johnson, and Nixon administrations generally met once a week or once every other week and often even less frequently. See Arthur Okun, "The Formulation of National Economic Policy," *Perspectives in Defense Management* (December 1968): 9–12; Walter Heller, *New*

cils: advance agendas, papers distributed before meetings, minutes, options papers on issues for presidential decision, decision memorandums for implementing presidential decisions, and quarterly work plans.

The EPB Executive Committee established twenty permanent and ad hoc subcabinet-level committees and task forces, quarterly domestic and international policy reviews, and special sessions, in addition to the regular, daily executive committee meetings and weekly meetings with the President.

EPB members as a group had regular and frequent access to the President. On many issues the EPB not only prepared an options paper for the President's decision but also met with him for an open discussion. On other issues, when the President's schedule precluded a meeting or when the interested parties agreed that a meeting was not required, the President made his decision from an EPB options paper. The EPB Executive Committee met with the President nearly a hundred times and sent him scores of memorandums in addition to the papers reviewed with him at formal meetings. The EPB quickly established itself as the conduit through which the President made virtually all of his decisions on economic policy matters.

The scope of the EPB's policy concerns and involvement extended to both domestic and international economic policy. As the EPB matured, its members developed a sense of collective responsibility for a wide range of issues transcending their departmental or agency concerns.

In addition, the EPB also performed other functions: exchanging information among the administration's leading economic officials, resolving disputes between member departments and agencies, producing and clearing presidential speeches and messages, coordinating administration presentations to congressional committees, and serving as the place where the major White House policy councils responsible for advising the President met and coordinated their activities.

Finally, the EPB was exclusively the President's instrument. It had but one master. While the cabinet members who comprised it regularly testified before congressional committees on issues considered by the Board, the Executive Director, as Assistant to the President for Economic Affairs, was not confirmed by the Senate and did not testify before congressional committees. Unlike many elements of the Executive Office of the President, the EPB did not prepare reports for the Congress. Its mission, its allegiance, and its constituency were directed toward assisting a single individual – the President.

Dimensions of Political Economy (Cambridge: Harvard University Press, 1966); Hugh S. Norton, *The Role of the Economist in Government: A Study of Economic Advice Since 1920* (Berkeley, California: McCutchan, 1969).

PERFORMANCE OF
BASIC ADVISORY FUNCTIONS

Differences in presidential temperament and style powerfully influence the process by which presidents make decisions. A president who is uncomfortable around certain individuals or with certain procedures is unlikely to use them consistently in making his decisions. But to conclude that how comfortable the President feels is the single criterion of a decision-making system's merit is neither intelligent nor helpful.

Certain objectives and standards are generally applicable in evaluating any presidential advisory system. They concern how well the system performs several basic advisory functions including:

1. Identifying issues and opportunities meriting presidential consideration;[5]
2. Precisely and accurately defining problems and clarifying what issues require resolution or decisions;
3. Helping the President focus his attention and time on major, not minor, issues and preserving his choices on major issues through insuring that decisions at lower levels do not preempt his scope for action;
4. Mobilizing the best information and analysis available and agreeing on an appropriate and accurate body of relevant factual information and analysis for the President;
5. Insuring adequate consideration of all major interests and values affected by the issue;[6]
6. Developing a full range of realistic options or alternative courses of action;

---

[5] A common complaint about government in general and the White House in particular is that it primarily reacts to problems rather than anticipating them. The capacity of an advisory system to anticipate issues that will require presidential attention can contribute to thorough, careful, and timely consideration of those issues. The importance of this "forward looking capability" is reflected in the observation of one Washington veteran, whose governmental service spanned three decades, that most options papers for the President are prepared with "indecent haste" because most decisions are made under severe time constraints resulting from the reactive nature of much policy making.

[6] Edward K. Hamilton, in summarizing the principal lessons of the past decade in foreign policy making, argues:

> Where there is reasonable consensus that the United States has been successful in achieving its objectives, the result has owed much to efforts to widen and deepen the scope of relevant concerns taken into account in the decision process. The most obvious failures, on the other hand, have generally reflected a narrow conception of the objectives sought and a correspondingly narrow organizational channel of significant involvement. [Hamilton, p. 7.]

7. Evaluating the anticipated consequences of each option and clearly identifying trade-offs (costs and benefits) between competing alternatives;[7]
8. Providing a means for promptly and effectively implementing presidential decisions;
9. Assessing results and revising policy in light of that assessment.[8]

How well did the Economic Policy Board perform these basic functions?

Early warning and identification of issues

Precisely assessing the contribution the Economic Policy Board made in the early identification of issues is difficult because it is rarely clear where or when an issue would have been identified in the absence of the EPB. One negative measure of early warning effectiveness is the number of issues that emerge suddenly and, in the words of one senior civil servant, "send everyone scrambling." Are issues identified with sufficient time to gather and analyze all relevant information systematically? When crucial information surfaces after the decision is made – information that would have altered the decision – frequently it is because there was inadequate warning and time for thorough analysis. Some crises, like the Cambodian seizure of the U.S. vessel the *Mayaguez*, by their very nature do not permit early identification. But most day-to-day economic policy issues

[7] This would include considering the relative ease or difficulty of administering or implementing each option.

[8] This list is somewhat similar to the descriptions of the steps in presidential decision making found in Sorensen, pp. 18–19, and Allison and Szanton, pp. 232–233. See also Richardson, pp. 69–70; Alexander L. George, "Towards a More Soundly Based Foreign Policy: Making Better Use of Information," in U.S. Commission on the Organization of the Government for the Conduct of Foreign Policy, *Appendices* (Washington, D.C.: GPO, June 1975), Vol. 2, p. 10; and Hamilton, in *Ibid.*, Vol. 3, p. 11.

Francis Bator has summarized his views on the most important criteria for evaluating presidential advisory systems:

> The main test of organization is whether, in a strategic situation, the President is given a full and fair crack, in time, at the choices the way they really are. Does the Government confront him with a good map of reality; a hard specification of the choices open to him, and the contingent consequences and uncertainties, long and short term, of deciding in favor of option 1 or option 2 or option X? And does the execution truly reflect the President's will and intention after he has been confronted by such a map of reality and after he has been exposed, face-to-face on important matters, to the sharply stated views of his own principal barons within the executive branch and appropriate barons from the Hill and elsewhere?" [Bator Hearings, p. 112.]

do not suddenly appear full blown. Generally some information is available if policy makers are alert.

A second measure is how rapidly information on a potential problem is brought to the attention of the President and his principal advisers. Cumbersome standard operating procedures may significantly delay reporting important pieces of information. The way in which a White House policy body organizes the flow of information among the key participants can affect the speed with which problems are identified and receive high-level attention.

Two features of the EPB's structure and operation enhanced its capacity to quickly identify emerging issues. First, the Executive Committee established and used subcabinet-level interagency subcommittees and task forces to monitor various sectors of the economy.[9] These groups reported regularly to the Executive Committee and summaries of their reports were sent to the President. Moreover, the dozen or so committee chairmen prepared three-month and six-month work plans identifying issues they felt would need executive committee attention. The network of subcabinet-level groups, with regular access to the cabinet-level Executive Committee, was important in pinpointing problems early and greatly facilitated the vertical flow of information to the administration's leading economic officials.

Second, the daily executive committee meeting facilitated the horizontal flow of information among senior economic officials. The frequent executive committee meetings meant an issue could receive prompt attention once it was identified. At the daily meeting members passed on bits and pieces of information informally and could check questions with their colleagues. Frequently, the informal discussion before and after meetings identified an issue that merited preparing a paper for executive committee consideration.

As the EPB matured, fewer and fewer issues requiring cabinet-level or presidential attention slipped through the EPB network without relatively early detection. One participant, with high-level experience in the Executive Office of the President during the 1960s and 1970s, contrasted the EPB's ability to anticipate issues with his earlier experience:

> During the 1960's there was no committee or council that regularly brought the key players together to discuss economic policy issues in the way that the EPB does. As a result, then, we were constantly discovering issues hitting our desks requiring immediate attention. It was more frenetic and random. Now, with the EPB, except on rare occasions, there is ample lead time on an issue to prepare a

⁹ See Chapter 3, "EPB Organization," pp. 69–73

reasonably thoughtful analysis of the problem. There are fewer surprises; it is a much more orderly process.

While inadequate inventory statistics temporarily masked the precipitous drop in economic activity in the autumn of 1974, the daily meetings of the EPB Executive Committee, the weekly meetings with the President, and the attention devoted to assessing the state of the economy made rethinking macroeconomic policy a visible issue in time for the President to shape his 1975 State of the Union tax proposals in a noncrisis decision-making atmosphere.

Likewise, the EPB Executive Committee and the Food Deputies Group raised the issue of grain sales to the Soviet Union early in July 1975, focusing attention on the problem before events limited options. Similarly, information and alternatives on the footwear import decision reached the President early enough to place the decision in context with other trade policy issues pending during the first half of 1976. In short, the Economic Policy Board's network throughout the executive branch successfully identified and raised issues for high-level consideration with adequate time for thorough, deliberate decision making.

Defining issues

While the EPB identified issues easily, defining what decisions needed to be made and by whom was sometimes laborious and took large amounts of scarce executive time. One reason why was Seidman's basic approach to determining what issues the Board should consider. Anxious to cultivate a feeling of openness and due process, Seidman and his staff made little effort to keep the Executive Committee agenda down, particularly during the early months.

However, though many minor issues cluttered the agenda, the EPB was a major clearinghouse, clarifying what issues deserved further executive committee consideration, what issues OMB should handle through the budget process, what issues other policy councils (the NSC, the Domestic Council, and the Energy Resources Council) should assume lead responsibility for, and what issues a department or subcabinet-level group should address.

Focusing presidential attention on major issues

The EPB Executive Committee was the principal forum for sorting and refining which economic policy issues merited presidential attention. In the early months, when there was any doubt about whether to raise an issue with the President, invariably the EPB did so. While the new President and his team grew accustomed to each other, the EPB took his time for some issues that were only minor. As the EPB matured, gained the President's confidence, and learned which issues truly merited the President's time, the Board was more selective in the issues it took to the Oval Office.

The difference is illustrated in the contrast between the 1975 State of the Union tax proposals during the EPB's first months and the grain export issue during the late summer and fall of that year. In the case of the tax cuts, virtually every issue, from major questions concerning whether to propose a tax reduction to minor details concerning specific cuts, was taken to the President. Moreover, some issues came up repeatedly as various details changed.

The EPB spent relatively more time evaluating and refining issues for the President's consideration when it handled grain export policy in the autumn of 1975. Discussions with the President focused on the broad outlines of overall policy, not on fine details, although the Executive Committee regularly informed him on its deliberations. Several major economic policy issues crowded the President's agenda during August, September, and October 1975 – grain exports, the New York City financial situation, extension or modification of the expiring temporary tax reductions, a proposal for federal financing of energy resource development, the U.S. response to the New Economic Order, and preparations for the Rambouillet international economic summit conference. During this period the EPB Executive Committee, having matured with experience, not only organized advice to the President on these issues, but preserved his time by identifying which decisions merited his attention.

Mobilizing information and analysis

The quality of information and analysis the President receives on an issue is often directly related to the time available for preparation. Rushed deadlines generally result in relying on fewer sources and in less rechecking. Thus, the earlier a policy council can anticipate an issue and start preparing a data base, the more likely the President will get solid information and analysis. Moreover, those working on a study inevitably include the information they consider important and emphasize particular facts reflecting their perspective. In general, the wider the participation, the less likely the analysis produced will reflect a narrow perspective.

Another influence on quality is the basic analytical skills of those preparing materials for the President. The capacity to compute the effects of alternative tax reductions, the ability to analyze the price impact of given levels of grain exports, and the ability to forecast the cost to consumers of alternative trade barriers require certain skills and often specialized expertise. Despite many highly qualified and able economists throughout the executive branch, some observers of high-level economic policy making have claimed that "incredibly important decisions were being made with incredibly insufficient information by incredibly unanalytical people." [10]

Two practices characterized the way the EPB gathered information and analyzed issues. First, Seidman and his staff consistently sought to include all interested departments, agencies, and offices – which usually meant that a large number of individuals and groups helped develop the analysis on an issue. Second, Seidman deliberately involved staffs that would be natural checks on one another – Treasury and State; CEA, the CIA, and Agriculture; Commerce and Labor; OMB and most of the rest of the executive branch.

The EPB's capacity to mobilize information and produce high-quality analysis improved as the group matured, as sources of expertise were identified, and as staffs became accustomed to working together. The 1975 State of the Union tax proposals were based on the best analysis and forecasts that the Treasury, the CEA, and OMB could produce. [11] The information and analysis developed from early June to mid-October 1975 on U.S. and Soviet production, the demand for grain, and the price effects of various levels of U.S. grain exports provided a solid foundation for decision making. In the 1976 footwear escape clause case, the analyses developed by several advocates – STR, Treasury, State, and the CEA – contributed to a balanced and reasonably comprehensive picture of both the domestic shoe industry and the international footwear trade situation.

The quality of the EPB's information and analysis varied somewhat from issue to issue, as one might expect, and assessing quality requires highly subjective judgments. Yet, it is significant that virtually all of the major EPB participants as well as many staff-level officials, including many whose governmental careers spanned several administrations, expressed a uniformly high regard for the quality of the information and analysis produced by the EPB process. Indeed, in interviews, many identified the EPB's capacity to mobilize information and produce high-quality analysis as one of its principal strengths. A senior official with experience in previous administrations observed:

> I think that perhaps its most important strength was that it provided a mechanism for reaching into various departments and find-

[10] See William R. Allen, "Economics, Economists, and Economic Policy: Modern American Experiences," *History of Political Economy* 9 (1977): 79.

[11] During 1975 and 1976 the Troika forecasting record measured against the record of the principal private forecasters – Data Resources, Inc., Chase Econometrics, Wharton, etc. – was excellent.

ing staff expertise on the issues. I was most involved in tax matters and there of course you got into the Treasury as you would have with the old Troika arrangements, but I think the more important thing was that you could always get well informed staff members involved in the decisions from Commerce or from Labor and they could give you a better view than Treasury could of what would be the effect of a tax policy on their specific constituency. Or in discussions of structural unemployment where in the old Troika arrangements the staff work would primarily be done by the CEA staff who would then, on their own, try to find the expertise in the Labor Department and sometimes not get perfect cooperation. Here you communicated in the first instance with the Secretary of Labor who immediately could get the expertise.

Not that they didn't under other arrangements, but it is just a very different matter to have a CEA staffer call you up and request you to come to a meeting and to have the message come down from your cabinet secretary that he wants you to be at a certain place at a certain time to do such and such. He knows about it and has been involved in it.

A cabinet member reflected:

It [the EPB] is not really comparable to other interdepartmental bodies I have served on. In many respects I think it was a model for interdepartmental communication, cooperation, resolution of issues, etc. These basically were its strengths, that is, the opportunity it afforded for getting on the table the views and positions of the concerned departments and agencies, formulating issues requiring presidential decision, marshalling the pros and cons, developing relevant data, making sure it got done. . . . The work product was clear, balanced, and useful to the President and this contributed enormously to the success of the enterprise.

A senior White House staffer observed:

I think in terms of the papers I would give them pretty good marks. I can't think off hand of an example of something that came up where he [the President] got blindsided. The key test is whether or not after he has made a decision that something comes up that nobody had thought of. If that happens the staff system has not served him well. Also, can anybody legitimately claim that the papers prepared by the staff of the Economic Policy Board in any way warped or presented in a more favorable light option A instead of option B? I can't think of an instance in which that happened. I would in fact give the papers very high marks.

Still another official observed:

> Sometimes the papers prepared by individual departments and agencies the first time around were just awful. But as issues developed, the papers improved because of discussion and cross fertilization. Generally I would say that by the time the group got close to the end point of putting an issue to the President the paper quality was very good.

Range of interests and values considered

The EPB's emphasis on insuring participation by all interested departments and agencies contributed to the breadth of values and objectives considered. The formulation of grain export policy included consideration of agricultural policy, foreign policy, macroeconomic policy, and maritime policy interests. The papers and discussions on the footwear escape clause case considered domestic employment, consumer prices, specific bilateral relations between the U.S. and key exporting countries, the overall U.S. trade policy posture, the prospects for recovery for the domestic shoe industry, the nature of previous commitments to the Congress, the relationship of the footwear escape clause case to other pending trade cases, the actions that other nations would likely take in response to the President's decision, the domestic political impact, the impact of the President's decision on relations with the Congress, the budgetary impact of an expanded adjustment assistance effort, and the prospects for negotiating orderly marketing agreements.

Interviews with the participants revealed that EPB members and their staffs felt included in issues where their interests were at stake and that they felt no department or agency had dominated the process. As one member reflected: "It was generally a good discussion. Neither the papers nor the meetings were dominated by a single agency. In general I felt the papers were high quality and were balanced." Involving all interested agencies does not guarantee that all important interests, objectives, and values will receive adequate consideration. As the grain export and footwear import decisions revealed, the EPB process underemphasized domestic political considerations. What the EPB process did insure was that important interests and considerations were not excluded from the discussion.

Range of realistic options advanced

On many issues, even individuals with major differences can agree on the range of realistic options; turning the issue over to "imaginative" people is unlikely to produce significantly different alternatives. When faced with the question of whether to sign or to veto a bill, the alternatives are usually reasonably straightforward. Obviously, the tone and content of a signing statement or veto message allow considerable creativity and can be used to good strategic effect. But the fundamental decision between signing or vetoing remains.

The Trade Act of 1974 and previous experience with similar trade issues effectively prescribed the President's alternatives on the footwear escape clause case. The 1975 grain export policy's central issues — whether or not to suspend grain sales to the Soviet Union, whether to extend the suspension to Poland, and the basic structure of a long-term agreement — were reasonably straightforward in terms of realistic alternatives. Even on the 1975 tax cut proposals, the fundamental decisions concerned whether to, how much, when, what form, and for how long. It is unlikely that a tax reduction proposal would contain a wholly new approach that no one had thought of before, and the late 1974 early 1975 case proved no exception.

Thus, it is somewhat fanciful to think that bringing in "creative, bold, and imaginative people" will produce different and innovative solutions to every public policy problem. Some policy questions, such as welfare reform or national health care, may be more susceptible to new, innovative solutions. But policy debates are rarely based on one group having thought of alternatives about which another, less imaginative group, is unaware. It is generally differences in values, objectives, priorities, and interests that differentiate their positions.

The EPB did not function like a think tank or a brain trust. However, the EPB process consisted of more than merely collecting the views and proposals of departments and agencies on current economic problems. It was a dynamic process, fashioning alternatives through the interaction of individuals representing different agencies and viewpoints. For example, the position originally taken by STR on the footwear issue was modified as a result of the interagency discussion. The proposal for a long-term grain agreement emerged from a series of interagency meetings in which the individuals participating saw themselves not merely as representatives of a department or agency with a viewpoint to defend but also as members of a larger entity with responsibility for coming up with an effective solution to the problem.

The degree of agency identification varied from individual to individual and issue to issue. But importantly, fairly early, EPB members began viewing themselves as part of a group with its own identity, and not merely a forum for defending a departmental brief.

One characteristic that mitigated against departments individually pressing a large number of narrow options was the EPB's tendency to limit the number of alternatives presented to the President on an issue. There was no formal rule, but more than three alternatives was the exception rather than the norm. Sometimes two alternatives were presented. One assistant secretary decribed the process: "I think he [the President] got a full range of practical options. Sometimes we may have narrowed his scope by packaging them too narrowly. But we probably could more adequately decide than he could because he did not have the same time to work on it."

The way in which the discussions were conducted also contributed to the way in which alternatives were formulated. Generally, a department or an interagency group prepared the first draft of a paper. It knew the Executive Committee would review their paper and so they tried to present a range of options that the entire group would consider feasible. If the EPB had posed a question and asked for agency responses, it would undoubtedly have received more narrow and more parochial views. As a result of the process, the alternatives generated by the EPB reflected a nondepartmental approach to problems and were different than the options an individual department or agency would have given the President. As one subcabinet official reflected:

> Whether it performed well depended on whether there had been good staff work done before the meeting. . . . I think that in the case of agricultural policy issues we generally had a pretty good system for making sure that the options were well delineated before we got to the EPB meeting itself.
>
> I felt that the EPB mechanism forced staff work which led to a more rational decision whereas if there had not been an EPB meeting we might have ended up with a decision which we in a certain department would have liked but I am not sure it would have been a decision that was good for the administration or good for the country as a whole.

STRENGTHS

This evaluation of how the EPB performed several basic advisory functions has emphasized its systematic and comprehensive approach to policy development. Two general strengths characterized the process. First, the EPB enhanced the quality of the process by which decisions were made, and policy was formulated. Second, the EPB's operating procedures strengthened the President's influence and presence throughout the executive branch and, consequently, the likelihood that the departments and agencies responsible for implementing his decisions would support them. The first strength involves advice, the second execution.[12]

Decision making and policy formulation

The Economic Policy Board provided the President with a broad range of views and alternatives on economic policy issues through a process that insured the representation of many perspectives and interests, mobilized the resources of all interested agencies, provided a forum for competing views and alternatives, and critically examined specific proposals.[13] One member with considerable governmental experience observed:

> The EPB was a very substantial step forward over what we had before, particularly in getting competing viewpoints on a more consistent basis. That doesn't mean that there weren't occasions under the prior setup when there was an opportunity for competing viewpoints to be heard, but it was on a sporadic, catch-as-catch-can basis, a lot more than it was with the EPB.

Examining the 1975 State of the Union tax proposals, the grain export issue, and the footwear import escape clause case reveals that no single interest, individual, or agency dominated the EPB decision-making process. The EPB sought a systematic and balanced presentation of views to the President. One active participant reflected:

[12] Interestingly, these two strengths are similar to what I. M. Destler has called "choice" and "persistence" – "the President deciding" and "the President leading." As Destler points out, Presidents need advice aimed at insuring the "most fully informed Presidential choices, from among the widest range of reasonable policy alternatives. . . Yet Presidents need advice and support not just in deciding what they want, but in making their choices effective. They need help in implementation."

While Destler argues that these two objectives present the President with "a basic dilemma" of "choice versus persistence," the EPB, in the view of its participants, largely succeeded in fulfilling both. The dilemma for Destler arises in part from his definition of choice: keeping all options open; issues can be raised and reraised at any time. As he points out, "to carry a system of 'open options' to its logical conclusion is to forego effectiveness of execution almost entirely."

But the EPB experience suggests that it is possible for a presidential advisory system to systematically consider a wide range of options while maintaining a sense of continuity and persistence in pursuing fundamental policy objectives. Interestingly, Destler's organizational preference is for a system reasonably close to the type of arrangement into which the EPB ultimately developed – a departmentally (line) based system balanced by a White House assistant and staff to check and prod. I. M. Destler, "National Security Advice to U.S. Presidents: Some Lessons from Thirty Years," pp. 164–165, 167–171.

[13] William R. Allen found in his interviews with scores of former economic policy officials agreement that one way of improving policy analysis within the government was "to increase appropriate competition among the analysts." See Allen, p. 85.

I suppose it was inevitable that much of the work was done under pressure. But despite that, it was pretty good. I thought the system worked well. Overall, do I have something better to suggest? No. I believe that it was as good an operation and as effective a coordinating instrument as I have seen in my thirty years in government.

Importantly, the participants viewed the EPB as a place where they would receive due process. Departments and agencies saw and heard each other's arguments. Everyone, with rare exceptions, had equal access to the President through memos and meetings. Department and agency heads received all the papers that went to the President. A common complaint of those in departments and agencies in almost every administration is that those exercising operational control at the White House place their own advocacy memorandum on top of the documents going to the President. That was not a problem with the EPB. As one State Department official observed:

> I must say that I never had any problem with the papers. In retrospect it seems like the voting always looked like it was stacked against us. However, the papers did represent our view properly.
>
> In comparison with the problems of STR [Office of the Special Representative for Trade Negotiations], the EPB was a shining example. With STR we never got a chance to see the papers before they were sent forward and the bootlegged copies that we got hold of did not represent our position fairly. We did get an opportunity to look at and influence the EPB papers.

In short, those involved felt that the process was not only comprehensive and systematic, but fair. In the words of one cabinet member:

> Everyone had the feeling that they were getting a fair shake, that the work product was clear, balanced, and useful to the President, and this contributed enormously to the success of the enterprise.

In making decisions and formulating policy, the EPB provided a means for seeing that policies on related issues were reasonably consistent. Several participants observed that the EPB not only organized decision making on particular problems, but it organized well a wide range of issues. One added:

> I think the role of the EPB in systematizing economic policy making as far as I could judge was genuinely effective. And I think the EPB may well have made a significant contribution to what seems to me a relative success on the part of the administration once it got over the zigging and zagging of the early months in its economic policy.

By assigning responsibility for a broad policy area to his economic advisers collegially, Gerald Ford communicated to his leading officials a sense of shared responsibility for economic policy, transcending their specific line assignments. Consequently, the 1975 State of the Union tax proposals were integrated with the energy proposals. The grain agreement negotiations were coordinated with the maritime negotiations and with foreign policy interests, macroeconomic policy, and agricultural policy concerns. The footwear import decision was integrated with other trade policy issues and with foreign policy and macroeconomic policy concerns. The shared responsibility of the core advisers strengthened the interconnections between related issues. As one active participant reflected: "By going to the EPB you had a better recognition that you were only part of a bigger picture that was taking place all the time."

The Economic Policy Board also made a modest contribution to policy formulation by focusing on long-range studies that cut across departmental lines. One cabinet official felt that one of the two most important advantages of the Economic Policy Board was "the opportunity it afforded to look at some longer-range problems rather than exclusively be involved in firefighting." During 1975 and 1976 the Economic Policy Board undertook a number of such studies dealing with capital formation, productivity, product liability, services and the multilateral trade negotiations, the taxation of international investment, and an evaluation of the federal statistical system. Since long-range studies were not the EPB's main activity, they had the advantage of not being compartmentalized, isolated, or divorced from the regular activities of day-to-day policy makers.

Moreover, the study task force chairmen reported regularly to the Executive Committee, thus maintaining the attention and commitment of senior officials and providing the motivation of an action-forcing event for those engaged in the study. As one former executive office official observed:

> A lot depends on the very high-level people and what they encourage. . . . What it takes is a man who has some vision longer than next week's affairs and who is willing to deprive some of the resources that theoretically are needed for day-to-day activities in order to man or staff some resource base for the longer range and then to give him some head.[14]

[14] John H. Jackson, former General Counsel in the Office of the Special Representative for Trade Negotiations, cited in *Ibid.*, p. 53.

It is often difficult to get senior officials. pressed with daily demands on their resources, to commit staff time to long-range research and studies. As one staffer in a previous administration told William Allen: "Once in a while one of our bosses will sort of encourage

The EPB did not have a great deal of time for long-range planning and issues. Like their predecessors, Ford administration economic officials faced a steady succession of near-term problems. But the EPB's quarterly reviews and major studies succeeded in shifting some resources and thinking to longer-range problems.[15]

Implementation and presidential influence

Once a decision was made through the EPB process it generally enjoyed broad support throughout the executive branch. Department and agency officials had participated in developing options papers and had made their case directly to the President; naturally they felt more committed to presidential decisions. One cabinet member observed that departments:

> ... were more likely to support, understand, and follow through on what was decided with less likelihood that there would be some slip-up between the decision and the execution. Because the participatory process was fair, it minimized the risk that a dissenter would undercut or try to block or obstruct the execution of the decision.
>
> I think this is an approach that contributes to the control of leaks because leaks more often than not come from somebody who was pretty sure he was right but whose view did not prevail and who was not present when it was decided that his view should not prevail. Had he been there, in most instances, he would have recognized that there really was a good case to be made for the result in fact reached. And once you have heard that, it becomes much, much harder to cling to the idea that you were uniquely right and that the public interest requires vindication by somehow going public, even if anonymously.

The EPB's guarantees of due process removed a common justification for attempting to reopen or reverse a decision – namely, that had one's

us a little bit in this [research]. But they forget about it next week when they need something – it all goes out the window, and this is the way it goes on throughout the year, so in the end you don't really get anywhere." *Ibid.*, p. 55.

By making a collective commitment of resources for considering long-range issues cutting across departmental lines, the EPB helped address this problem.

[15] A series of interviews with senior economic analysts and economic policy advisers conducted by William R. Allen during the early 1970s revealed wide consensus by economists in the executive branch that the working day and pattern of assignments was very "chopped up" and that one was constantly "shifting gears from topic to topic, person to person, many, many times a day." Moreover, there was wide agreement that there was little time for long-range thinking because one was always "just overwhelmed with operational stuff." *Ibid.*, pp. 75–76.

arguments been heard, they would have been heeded. The very act of participation bound EPB members to support the outcome in a way they would not have felt had they been denied a voice. One participant reflected:

> It is much more difficult to oppose a presidential decision, even if one's opposition is quiet, subtle, or simply takes the form of noticeably tepid support, if you have had the opportunity to fully argue your case. No one expects to win every battle. But everyone wants to have a voice in those matters that concern them most. The fact that we were never cut out of the process on issues that were important to us made a difference in the kind of support we gave the President's decisions even though they did not always come out the way we would have liked them to.

Moreover, the frequency of meetings, the sense of shared responsibility for policy, and the systematic distribution of minutes and Economic Policy Decision Memorandums (EPDMs) helped communicate not only what administration policy was but also the perception of an administration generally united on economic policy matters. One departmental secretary observed that "what the group did was make everyone conversant on virtually all of the problems and the direction we were going so, for the most part, we were all pretty well speaking with one voice." A senior executive office official noted:

> The EPB was a very good device for communicating what the policy line was. Just knowing that, a cabinet secretary would be unlikely to "stray from the reservation."
> I think one of its most important strengths was that it was a superb coordinating mechanism in the sense of keeping everybody informed as to what the important issues were and what the positions on those issues were.

For the cabinet secretary who must daily explain and defend administration policy, knowing the rationale and background of specific decisions can be as important as knowing the details of a program. As one cabinet secretary put it:

> The EPB has been invaluable to me both as a departmental secretary and as a cabinet officer. Just the meeting and discussing and understanding why decisions are made the way they are each day. You are in a better position when you are making speeches, when you are talking to different groups that ask why this decision was made.
> In light of the frustrations that I had witnessed in the past when

I used to talk with the departmental secretary when I was an assistant secretary and I would ask: "What are we doing this for?" And he would say: "Well, I don't know. I will try to find out." And he did not have any input into decisions. I really don't have any major complaint with the EPB for not being responsive to any request that I had. . . . On most issues they have been willing to listen. That is not to say that I didn't disagree with a lot of decisions. Certainly I have. But I would rate the EPB excellent in comparison with the past.

Knowing what was decided, who decided it, on what basis the decision was made, and who had participated in the decision-making process made a real difference. The due process that characterized the EPB's deliberations also contributed to the legitimacy of the decisions that emerged. As one participant noted: "I never felt that those decisions that went through the EPB were made arbitrarily or capriciously. It was a deliberate and thorough system. . . . For the most part the President was very well informed on a subject by the time he had to make a decision. We knew that he had listened to our views."

The openness of the EPB process also contributed to the intangible but important element of morale. For cabinet officers, frequent visits to the White House and regular meetings with the President strengthen their position within their department and with their constituency. A cabinet officer perceived as lacking clout at the White House is often considered weak by those whose support and cooperation he needs. But the cabinet officer who has frequent access to the President and some influence at the White House is viewed as a great asset by those within his department who want a strong advocate for their proposals and problems. One cabinet secretary remarked:

We felt that we had an adequate opportunity to get our input into the decision-making process. . . . The EPB made us feel a part of what was going on.

I thought that the regular daily meeting was very important. I felt kind of out of everything if I missed two or three EPB meetings in a row because I was out of town. It's not far from this address to the White House, but if you are not over there fairly regularly, it can be a hell of a long way, even though you are a senior official. Even besides the actual EPB meeting, being at the White House serves a real purpose for a cabinet officer.

I recommended very strongly to my successor that he try to stay a part of the Economic Policy Board. You feel like a dunce going over to see George Meany or Leonard Woodcock or Fitzsimmons and they could tell you what went on over at the White House. If you know and have been a part of it, it makes a difference. Most of the decisions that were made in the White House either in some way had flowed through the EPB or you had heard about them as a result of being part of the EPB. And so you weren't caught by surprise.

Moreover, for subcabinet officials and senior career civil servants, knowing that their work would be considered by several cabinet-level officials and frequently by the President had a tonic effect on morale. One long-time Washingtonian observed:

> I think it is very good for staff morale to have input into particular decision processes. This is the point I keep making again and again about the importance of the orders coming through the Secretary. Staffs also like the opportunity to be able to show their expertise and there is an enormous amount of it in the government hidden away here and there. The EPB was very important in bringing people together and building morale. The interactions among the staffs on a regular basis was a good thing for everyone involved.

One of the daily executive committee meeting's most important ancillary effects was its influence on the perspective of the participants. Bringing departmental and agency heads together regularly as a group of peers to discuss a broad range of issues altered the way they, and their principal subordinates, viewed problems. The EPB provided a respite from the cabinet members' daily diet of congressional hearings, sessions with subordinates, meetings with constituency groups, and public appearances urging support for administration programs. The EPB sessions brought the cabinet officer into contact with his peers in an atmosphere where he did not necessarily have to defend or sell a policy but could consider the direction policy should move. As one cabinet secretary explained, the EPB provided him with a more balanced outlook and a better understanding of overall policy objectives:

> If a Secretary of Labor is being as responsive as he should, he has a tough job. He can't live if he can't at least get along with the organized labor movement. He has got to live with the congressmen and the senators, and the labor movement is going to run the congressmen and senators, and they will put pressure on the Secretary of Labor. So it takes balance and understanding to carry this job out.
>
> And I could see myself in the dog house to no end this past year if I had not been part of the Economic Policy Board, and was attuned and could express why we were doing some of the things that we were doing. To try to be responsive here to the pressures

you get from different angles, the EPB helped me see things from a broader perspective. The single most important thing in helping me do a good job as Secretary of Labor was having been a part of the Economic Policy Board.

The collegial atmosphere benefitted from considering issues broader than any single department's responsibility and from the absence of a dominant figure. No single member of the EPB Executive Committee – Simon, Ash, Lynn, Greenspan, Dunlop, Richardson, Seidman, Burns – consistently dominated the group or prevailed with the President.

WEAKNESSES, LIMITATIONS, AND COSTS

Any advisory system or decision-making process, either structurally or operationally, has certain weaknesses, limitations, and costs. The Economic Policy Board's insiders were remarkably uniform in their assessments of its strengths, less agreed in their assessments of its limitations. However, most of the specific criticisms and costs identified involved two general concerns: (1) the breadth and comprehensiveness of the EPB's pattern of advice; and (2) the effectiveness and efficiency of its operation.

Patterns of advice

While there was wide agreement that the EPB systematically organized a large number of substantive inputs, several observers felt that it lacked adequate political sensitivity. Political considerations is one of those convenient phrases that holds different meanings for different people. In considering how much "political sensitivity" exists in a decision-making process, it is useful to differentiate between two kinds of extragovernmental inputs.

First are the views and attitudes held by key people in groups an issue affects, for example, leading business and labor leaders. Here, the Ford White House made a genuine effort to invite and consider the views of outside groups. The White House Office of Public Liaison invited the leaders and representatives of scores of groups and associations to the White House for meetings with senior White House officials, both to explain current administration policy and to hear the concerns of these leaders. William Seidman and his staff spent a great deal of time talking with and listening to extragovernmental economists, businessmen, bankers, and labor leaders. The Ford White House worked hard to change the image Nixon's White House had of being isolated and insulated. Leaders seeking a White House hearing on an issue found the doors open, not shut.

The second type of extragovernmental input is less personal and direct but often even more influential – assessing the political benefits and costs of various alternatives to specific groups, regions, states, and sometimes the country as a whole based on polls, soundings, and political feel. Here the EPB process and the Ford White House fell short.

Similarly, integrating congressional sentiment on an issue revealed an uneven performance. Frequently, a department or agency would report discussions with interested committee and subcommittee members. The Republican and bipartisan leadership meetings let the President sense the intensity of congressional sentiment on many issues. The Assistant to the President for Legislative Affairs, Max Friedersdorf, was invited to attend EPB meetings with the President. But input from the small White House congressional liaison staff, daily facing incredible demands on its time and resources, came sporadically and frequently late in the process. Moreover, the fact that a Republican President was dealing with a Democratic Congress sometimes openly, sometimes subtly, reduced the incentives for close consultation.

In short, the domestic political consequences of many decisions received little systematic attention in the EPB process. One White House staffer observed:

> One problem that I saw with the EPB from where I sat was that it tended to talk too much to itself. It did not have in it, and I think it needed in it, more of a political component, and should have had that factored in earlier on. It sometimes operated at the President's political expense.
>
> I think an institution was created with a set of norms that were first-rate for the analysis of economic activities and programs but without a full perception of policy as a political phenomenon as well as an economic one.

Domestic political considerations *were* discussed from time to time at executive committee meetings and occasionally in EPB meetings with the President. But because it was designed to advise the President on the economic merits of his options, some members felt uncomfortable providing him with political advice. Most, though not all, executive committee members felt they were not particularly well qualified to make political judgments, while other sources were better qualified. One senior White House staffer explained:

> I don't think a president needs or wants political advice from his economists or political advice from his foreign policy advisers, any more than he wants economic advice from his congressional relations expert or national security advice from his press secretary.

The subject matter is far too complicated and far too complex, requiring in some cases years of experience to even know what you are talking about. It is a very risky business to hire somebody and give him an economic assignment and expect him to give you political advice.

The best thing, it seems to me, is to make certain that the process does not fuzz up the two concerns. The worst thing you could do is to give the President what he thinks is economic advice which has got a heavy electoral political input in it without telling him that is what you have done. And the danger of arguing that you have got to have more political advice in the economic policy process before he makes his decision is that you begin to fuzz up complex technical arguments with the question of how the folks in Peoria are going to vote if you do that.[16]

This reluctance is understandable, but in fact no systematic arrangements existed to give the President political advice on economic policy issues. The President had several sources for his domestic political advice: Donald Rumsfeld, Richard Cheney, Robert Hartmann, and John Marsh on his White House staff, and a kitchen cabinet known as the transition team, composed of old friends and confidants, that he met with periodically. But their political advice was intermittent, not consistent or continuous. They provided much advice on some issues, such as the New York City financial situation or major tax cut initiatives, but very little on others, such as the shoe import escape clause case and the grain export issue.

Those on the White House staff responsible for providing political advice were consistently invited to attend EPB meetings with the President; and they received papers for the meetings in advance. But they rarely, if ever, attended the daily executive committee meetings or special sessions, usually because their other responsibilities were so time-consuming; their involvement with economic issues invariably came late in

---

[16]   A similar view was expressed by Paul McCracken, former chairman of the Council of Economic Advisers:

> It is essential also that advisers retain and remember their professional credentials. If the advice they dispense is some indeterminate mixture of their economic analysis and their judgment about the political scene, they are apt to serve poorly both economic analysis and political decisions. The President will get his political inputs elsewhere and he himself is presumably a quite expert practitioner of the profession or he would never have made it to the White House.

See Paul W. McCracken, *Reflections on Economic Advising: A Paper and Interview*, International Institute for Economic Research, Original Paper 1, March 1976 (Ottawa, Illinois: Green Hill, 1976).

the process. Generally they were not major participants in the EPB discussions with the President and seldom gave the President political advice on economic policy issues on other occasions. As one explained:

> I don't think that there was a lot of input from White House political advisers on economic policy questions. The President, given his own extensive background in politics at the national level, of the people in the building who were best qualified to think about problems from the political standpoint, he exceeded the capacity of the rest of us. For example, we didn't do any significant polling separate and apart from the campaign, back in 1974 and 1975.
>
> We didn't have the money for it. We didn't have any way to finance it. We might conceivably have used some of that kind of information in designing policy, but we never did it.
>
> In terms of having separate meetings where we talked politics or the politics of an economic decision – no, not really. I can't give you a specific example. Now, it is not inconceivable that Marsh or myself would have said: "We ought to be sensitive to the political implications of going this route." But in terms of any sort of rigorous, continuous thing, we didn't do it.[17]

One aftermath of Watergate was the feeling that purely political considerations were somewhat suspect, that statesmanship should prevail over politics, that the public good rather than special interests should guide public policy. A cabinet member reflected:

> One of the ironical and negative products of the post-Watergate atmosphere was a self-conscious constraint in dealing with the political implications of the issues under discussion. There was, I think, throughout the Ford White House a tendency to draw an artificial line between the merits and the politics of issues under discussion. This disregards the proposition that the Presidency is and ought to be a political office. Its very accountability to the people under the Constitution is a political accountability.
>
> The line should rather be between the use of improper political influence or improper political means. But to recognize that you are always dealing in a political context and that any factor that affects the political impact of the decision is legitimate tended to be diminished by a sort of leeriness in talking in those terms.
>
> I found myself often the only one who would even mention a

---

[17]　The papers prepared through the EPB process similarly emphasized the economic and substantive costs and benefits associated with alternatives. One participant, an economist by training, who thought the papers "were very balanced and accurately reflected the views of departments and agencies," reflected: "In retrospect, although I did not think it at the time, I think the papers maybe didn't have enough political content of a sophisticated sort."

political implication of something and I didn't feel any inhibition about it. It is not the fact that it is political that makes it improper. It's these other things as to which it is important, of course, to maintain high and sensitive standards.

This feeling was reinforced by those who argued that statesmanship also promised the greatest political dividends. They argued that, if the President consistently refused to placate special interests, voters would respond to a leader whom they felt had the public interest as his primary goal.

The EPB's underemphasis on domestic political consequences did not mean that political considerations played no role in the President's decisions. Over a quarter of a century in Washington had developed and refined Gerald Ford's political instincts, and he did not make his decisions on economic policy issues in a political vacuum. But the atmosphere in which he made them and the EPB's pattern of advice consistently emphasized nonpolitical considerations. Would a different pattern of advice, one that emphasized political considerations as well as economic analysis, have resulted in any different presidential decisions? The answer is not clear. What is clear is that the EPB process, which systematically organized substantive advice and views, did not include and was not supplemented by an equally systematic, consistent assessment of political considerations.

Some members felt a second problem with the EPB's advice was that it operated within the framework of a single ideology. As one participant described it: "The EPB was very much dominated by a certain ideology, a very conservative ideology, but not by a specific person or individual."[18]

Theoretically, to the extent that the President's advice comes from those who share a common viewpoint or ideology, he is likely to receive a needlessly limited set of alternatives. Alan Greenspan, William Simon, and Arthur Burns shared a basic commitment to what was frequently referred to as "the old time religion" in economic policy. Moreover, James Lynn, Roy Ash, Earl Butz, Rogers Morton, Elliot Richardson, and John Dunlop all shared not only a strong commitment to the market as a means of efficiently allocating resources, but also skepticism in varying degrees about further governmental intervention in the economy. There were some ideological differences among the President's economic advisers, but these differences did not consistently pit the same individuals or groups against each other. Some were allies on one issue and opponents on another.

While the ideological differences between Gerald Ford's economic ad-

---

[18] He added: "In fact, the curious thing to me about the Ford administration was that in the economic policy making area I did not identify any giant emerge of the status of a Shultz or a Connally. Maybe the EPB had something to do with that."

visers were narrow on many issues, strong differences remained, flowing from their institutional positions representing different constituencies. Others involved matters of judgment rather than matters of ideology. One participant, when asked about the prevalence of a single ideology, responded:

> I don't think it is a fair criticism. I think he [the President] got a very broad range of advice. Obviously we were essentially a conservative Republican administration and the President had a fairly deeply ingrained set of personal views about economic policy, developed over twenty-eight years of public life. He was not a liberal Democrat. He was not inclined to waste much time on Walter Heller's view of how the economy ought to be run. But I think it would be fair to say that on most of the big issues we had a fairly broad range of viewpoints presented to him.
>
> And, if you looked at the makeup of the Economic Policy Board and the people who were involved in the process, you had people like Simon, quite conservative especially on fiscal matters and a strong advocate of tax reform in a way that many people like myself disagreed with, including Greenspan; Greenspan, essentially very conservative on economic policy; Arthur Burns, conservative certainly where monetary policy was concerned but more of an interventionist in terms of things like incomes policy; Carla Hills was a very aggressive advocate for more federal spending for housing, not a view that tracked with the views of some of the other people on the Board; John Dunlop, Bill Usery, and the normal conflict between people concerned about consumers and prices on the one hand and farm income on the other hand.
>
> There was broad enough diversity in the views that were considered that I just don't believe that the criticism is valid. And the other thing that I would say is that the President was by no means unaware of the other school of thought. He was very widely read. The sessions that the Economic Policy Board used to sponsor with outside economists who oftentimes articulated a different viewpoint were helpful to the President. I come back to the ultimate test. Was there a body of information or knowledge or options on a particular issue that had he had available to him would have led to a different decision? I don't think so. And I don't think unless you can make that argument, you can validate the criticism that the range of opinion available to him when he made his decisions was limited.

To the extent that a shared ideology existed, it minimized divisiveness even though members' views differed. The fact that differences were not principally ideological, and that there were not consistent splits among the members, helped maintain group cohesion without submerging differences of opinion and analysis.

But balancing these advantages was a subtle pressure for members to conform. A general commitment to free trade dominated the discussion of footwear imports. Those who favored providing relief for the domestic industry referred to previous administration commitments to the Congress and the potential political costs of failing to aid the industry. But all the while they articulated their commitment to free trade.[19]

Still the tone of EPB meetings with the President did not constrain members who disagreed with a dominant view, at least in terms of their relationship with the President. As one senior White House staffer observed:

I think that the combination of the meetings, the paper flow and the President's style, his willingness to listen to debates and arguments and never to reduce an individual's access because he had disagreed with him on his last decision, really made the system function fairly smoothly. I think that is key. I know from my own experience that you were always free to argue and debate and take the other side, sometimes to disagree very strongly, and he would make his decision and you were perfectly free to go back in two hours later and do it all over again on some other issue if you felt strongly about it. And his personality was such that that never seemed to bother him. He never let disagreements over policy or arguments in any way lead him to change the degree of access that a particular individual had to him.

There is inevitably a trade-off between group cohesion with its more harmonious working relationships and group norms that inhibit a free

---

[19] William Allen, in his interviews with scores of government economists, found that many pressures tend to mold a common orientation and that departments and agencies are apt to go along with what is considered right policy because they don't want to lose their effectiveness on other issues. As one put it: "There's a limited number of spears you can afford to shatter." See Allen, pp. 62, 66. Alexander L. George has noted:

Recent emphasis on the hazards of high group cohesion has led to the delineation of two different patterns of group conformity: firstly, the long familiar pattern of group pressure on individual members which leads them to hesitate to express doubts and misgivings regarding the dominant view being expressed out of fear of recrimination, anxiety about presenting a disloyal self-image, or fear of eviction from the group; and secondly, a less obvious pattern, labelled Groupthink by Professor Irving Janis, in which conformity springs from strong group cohesion brought about, or accentuated by a threatening, stressful environment.

["Towards a More Soundly Based Foreign Policy: Making Better Use of Information," pp. 12–13.]

expression of views. The Economic Policy Board struck something of a balance.

A third concern related to the EPB's pattern of advice involved the amount of time and effort devoted to strategic thinking. In retrospect, some members of the Executive Committee felt that while the EPB handled a wide range of issues, many interrelated, it did not demonstrate a capacity for strategic thinking. All parties were represented, issues were resolved, some interrelationships between issues were identified, the trade-offs between competing alternatives were clarified, and major issues were taken to the President. But, despite the EPB's acknowledged ability to handle a large volume of business and produce decisions quickly, it gave little sustained attention to an overall strategic plan.

EPB meetings repeatedly discussed the need to reduce the rate of growth in federal spending, the need to shift national resources toward investment in productive capacity to insure adequate jobs for a growing labor force, and the need to reduce the level and degree of government intervention in the economy. Yet, some felt the discussions devoted insufficient attention to integrating these themes into a comprehensive economic program. As one cabinet member reflected:

> As to its limitations, I think the problem may be really not inherent in the design of the EPB or even the staffing of the EPB or its membership. It is rather attributable to the style of the particular president under whom it served. President Ford, perhaps as the result of his long experience as a minority leader, tends in my view to take problems one at a time, treating them essentially as if they were of coordinative importance.
>
> Putting it the other way around, I think a significant limitation of his presidency was its lack of a visible strategic pattern or conceptual framework to which particular issues could be related and seen in terms of their relative importance, priority, and so on. The result was that while in many instances the EPB could identify upcoming problems and get on top of them, it lacked the benefit of a coherent planning intelligence which maintained more or less steadily in perspective a broad overview of what it was that the administration was trying to accomplish and what were the kind of things that needed to be approached on a long lead time basis.
>
> So it is conceivable that the EPB could be even more valuable to a president and an executive style that did think in more comprehensive, strategic terms and with a clear sense of relevant priorities.

Effectiveness and efficiency

A second general limitation concerns how effective and how efficient the EPB was operationally. Once again the evidence is mixed, and members' assessments varied on: (1) how effectively the EPB systematized policy through a single channel – or, put another way, how frequently did someone circumvent the EPB by end runs to the Oval Office? (2) how efficiently the EPB focused scarce executive time and talent on major issues – or, put another way, did the process waste cabinet and presidential time on trivial issues? (3) how efficiently the EPB handled an issue – or, put another way, did its collegial structure and formal procedures impose significant time delays?

Circumventing the EPB.   While the Economic Policy Board was the President's main channel for advice on economic policy issues, it was not the only one. The President met monthly or bimonthly with Arthur F. Burns, Chairman of the Board of Governors of the Federal Reserve System. The President also discussed the economy with Alan Greenspan, who frequently briefed the President individually on the details and meaning of changes in particular economic statistics. From time to time the President met with cabinet officers individually. But as one senior White House staffer explained, these meetings were "rarely in terms of making a policy decision, frequently in terms of information and advice as to what was going on in the economy, data as it was about to come out. Sometimes Alan would simply call me and give me those numbers and some very brief analysis which I would pass on to the President . . . but their meetings were not in terms of a policy debate about should we do this or should we do that."

However, there were attempts, a few successful, to circumvent the EPB. One participant candidly described the milieu in which the EPB operated:

> Any institution like the EPB will always be under attack. There is always a power struggle in the White House and the EPB represented a "power base." There will be those with a preference for more secretive and less open systems who will attack it. By the same token, those strongest cabinet officers who would rather see the President directly and don't believe that discussion with others will benefit their view will at the very least maintain an end run capability if they can.

One type of end run tries to get a presidential decision through another channel completely. This often involves organizing an ad hoc group to advise the President on an issue outside the established procedures. The President's $28 billion tax reduction proposal in October 1975 was the single dramatic example of this form of end run on an economic policy issue during the Ford administration. During July, August, and September 1975, White House Chief of Staff Donald Rumsfeld and his deputy Richard Cheney met frequently with CEA Chairman Alan Greenspan, OMB Director Jim Lynn, and his deputy Paul O'Neill to discuss possible tax reduction initiatives and budget strategies.

The number of participants was small because they wanted to keep it confidential. They parcelled out the staff work in bits and pieces to different CEA and OMB staffers with explicit instructions not to consult with officials outside the Executive Office of the President – especially not with the Treasury Department – in developing estimates and projections for fear of leaks. Ultimately, in late September and early October, after the fundamental decision to propose a major tax reduction and spending restraint initiative was made, the EPB was involved in refining the details of the tax proposal.

This method of operating succeeded in its objective; the surprise initiative did not leak. However morale suffered and the President did not receive alternative views. One senior official revealed:

> The EPB has been effective, quite effective in most cases, in systematizing policy making. The notorious end run was that dollar for dollar tax cut thing by Greenspan and/or Lynn. . . It cost us the election.
>
> I got a call at home Sunday night from Jim Lynn saying that the President had decided this and so I had no participation in it. . . Had I been a little more settled in office myself I would have gone to the President and resigned because here was the most important domestic policy decision that was going to be made that year and affecting future years and we had had no knowledge whatsoever of it. In retrospect it might have been prudent for me to have just said: "There is no way that I can be effective after this." In effect the end runners . . . had dictated the course of action which imprisoned us. It was a terrible mistake.

A second form of end run involves individual attempts to "propagandize" the President outside (preferably before) the meeting concluding the regular decision making process. The proposal to form an Energy Resources Finance Corporation is the leading example of this form during the Ford administration. The ability to end run the system in this instance was strengthened by the fact that the proposal fell within the jurisdictions of both the Economic Policy Board and the Energy Resources Council. Moreover, it had a major promoter outside the EPB – Vice President Nelson Rockefeller.

The final meetings in which the President approved the proposal were regular Economic and Energy meetings. However, unlike the normal EPB process, individual participants spent considerable time with the President outside the meetings seeking to persuade him to their viewpoint. One observed:

The Energy Independence Authority was Nelson's baby, bless his heart. And he was in there using the regular meeting he had every week to pump the heck out of it. I can understand him doing that. And then the President would have meetings with [Federal Energy Administrator Frank] Zarb about it. I could see that coming, so frankly I went in and had fifteen to twenty minutes with him to express my own view. So it was all done seriatim instead of by an agreed paper. I think the paper was of much less importance than the circular chairs where we all went in and saw the President.

I thought that was a terrible thing, because it was a terrible waste of the President's time. It is also unfair to the players because you don't know what kind of misrepresentations are being made while each player is in there. You can have quite innocent misrepresentations. Individual one-on-ones tend to get that way not because people are evil or want to deliberately misrepresent but because if you are an advocate it is just too easy to forget to make another argument that may tend to work against your position. We are all human. I do it myself.[20]

Some EPB members and subcabinet-level officials perceived end runs as a more serious problem than others did, but almost no one felt that the EPB process was regularly or even frequently circumvented. When pressed for examples, most identified the $28 billion tax reduction initiative and the Energy Resources Finance Corporation proposal. Some suggested a direct correlation between an issue's importance and an end run's likelihood. But most considered the EPB a marked improvement from past procedures.

I think it represented from everything I could see a great improvement over what we had before. On the other hand, it will work or not work depending on what kind of signal you get from the President as to how much he is going to insist that it work. To the extent that any president will entertain end runs or make decisions on the basis of the latest and what he thinks may be the best advice from one of the players, you can have all of the fine coordinative work that you want, and it won't work. Now I think that President Ford was quite good on that. Infallible? No.

[20]   This same official also noted another end run, again on an energy policy matter.

Another end run was the second time that the President came in to buy an even longer phase-in on the deregulation of oil. I wasn't even consulted on that one and I thought the decision was a terrible mistake. It may or may not have been, but I had the feeling that had we really institutionalized that decision and gone in straight up, by combining the ERC and the EPB the decision might have been different. I am not saying that the decision would have been different. But I sure as heck would have felt a lot more comfortable with it.

The basic point is that compared to prior ways that things were done, I would say it was far less of business being done that way than I had seen in the past.

The participants interviewed agreed unanimously that successful end runs depend on the President's willingness to tolerate them: "By and large, end runs were pretty difficult for most of the actors in the system. The few they were not difficult for frequently ran into a stone wall when they tried it. That's because the President was disciplined enough to stop them."
Another official pointed out:

> There is no way to preventing end runs if cabinet officers are determined to do that unless the President shuts them off. The best way to prevent end runs is to have a system that makes them unnecessary. If there is a feeling that there is a good, viable process, that in itself will diminish them, if not completely eliminate them. I am really not aware of any outstanding cases.
>
> I think in fact that it worked pretty well. There were many more end runs before the EPB certainly.

Still another official observed:

> President Nixon apparently preferred to have more written pieces of paper on which to base decisions. President Ford has a tendency to welcome more open discussion. During the latter two years everyone felt that he had a right to participate in the discussion with the President and with the other senior members of the EPB. Whereas in the earlier years, if a decision was not going to be worked out through an interagency group, there was a tendency to try to run around the end and go to someone on the senior staff that would get a viewpoint made to the President.
>
> I think a lot depends on the attitude of the President. In the case of agricultural policy, I don't think there was much end running. In almost all circumstances when we were making a decision that was more a broad political question than an economic question, Secretary Butz made a point to advise Mr. Seidman that he was working on an end around. Usually, in almost every case, it was brought back to the EPB anyway. And then the President would have a meeting where Secretary Butz would be there with the other members of the EPB and would have an opportunity to give his view. I thought that worked nicely.

The Economic Policy Board was clearly more powerful and preeminent within those areas of its undisputed domain than on those issues where its interests were shared by another major policy community – for example, the foreign policy community or the energy policy community. Over time, the EPB's relationship with the foreign policy establishment became progressively more harmonious (see Chapter 2). Nevertheless, the EPB was substantially less effective on those issues with strong foreign policy content than on issues more firmly within its jurisdiction. Tensions between the Treasury and State Departments on Third World issues continued through 1975 and much of 1976. Likewise, the negotiation of the U.S.–U.S.S.R. grain agreement showed that while the EPB played the major role on suspending sales and the grain agreement questions, the State Department operated virtually unchecked on linking an oil agreement with the grain agreement. The EPB was never able to weigh in effectively on this issue; nor was the President in a position to really decide it.

Similarly, the EPB only partially corralled the issue of whether the administration should propose an Energy Resources Finance Corporation. Ultimately, the final decision to propose creating such a corporation was made at an economic and energy meeting with the President, attended by all the major administration players with a legitimate interest in the issue, and on the basis of a paper prepared through the EPB process. But this meeting had been preceded by numerous one-on-one meetings between the President and various advocates that likely were more decisive in his approval of the initiative than was the large formal meeting.

That the EPB had greater difficulty in managing policy development on foreign economic and energy related issues is hardly surprising. A coordinating body will obviously have more problems at the boundaries of its sphere of jurisdiction, particularly when there is a strong administration figure like Kissinger involved. The EPB was no exception. At times, the economic and foreign policy communities worked well together. Joint committees and joint options papers from the EPB (Seidman) and the NSC (Kissinger or Scowcroft) to the President effectively governed the decision-making process on several commodities policy issues, the problem of questionable corporate payments abroad, and the preparations for the international economic summit conferences. But collaborative efforts were naturally most frequent when they could be helpful to one another. Those in the economic policy community anxious to suspend grain sales to the Soviet Union because of their fear of future inflation were delighted that Kissinger also urged a suspension on sales for diplomatic purposes. The desire to restrain USDA meshed with the desire to exert leverage on the Soviets. But Kissinger was understandably less anxious to involve major economic policy actors when he felt their interests might run counter to his preferred course of action, and thus he tried to personally control the negotiating strategy relative to a parallel Soviet oil agreement.

Inevitably some tension will exist between policy councils and communities when their interests diverge. The tension that existed between the State Department and the President's principal economic advisers may be related to the fact that Gerald Ford developed foreign policy and economic policy in dramatically different ways: the former by delegation to a powerful individual who played a very close hand; the latter by a broad, open, participatory process. Providing for joint working groups and exchanging information can reduce the isolation of a policy council. But ultimately, the interplay and integration between the key advisers and advisory bodies in his administration rests with the President.

Trivial issues.   A more frequent criticism by EPB participants was that the process tended to take cabinet-level time – and occasionally the President's – on trivial issues. During the EPB's formative period, Seidman consciously included almost any issue that a department or agency head wanted on the agenda; it kept morale high and established his credentials as an honest broker.

A trivial issue to one member, of course, may be crucial to another; however, most objective observers agreed that some were minor in comparison with others. In assessing the time costs of these issues, it is useful to know that of the 1,151 agenda items considered at the regular executive committee meetings, 488 of them, or 42 percent, were disposed of in five minutes or less. Moreover, as the EPB matured, the Executive Committee considered relatively fewer agenda items at its daily meetings and a smaller number of issues went to the President for his decision.[21] Had the EPB continued in a second Ford administration, its greater selectivity of issues would probably have continued.

Collegial bodies and time delays.   Any process involving relatively more people and using recognized procedures will take more time and involve more delays than a less systematic process involving fewer people. Simply the mechanics of securing agreement on a relevant and appropriate set of facts, analysis, and alternatives can be time consuming, particularly if many interests are involved. On some decisions that the President insisted go through the EPB process, his final decision was somewhat delayed.

However, three factors tended to minimize the costs of time delays. First, departments and agencies, recognizing the EPB as their channel to the President, built EPB consideration into their planning. Moreover, the

[21]   See Tables 1 and 3 in Chapter 3.

EPB monitoring system identified issues far enough in advance to eliminate most pressures for a quick decision.

Second, because the EPB met daily, it could when necessary generate high-level attention quickly and sustain it until the issue was ready to go to the President or was resolved in some other way.

Third, since Seidman was based in the White House, was an Assistant to the President, and was closely identified with the President, his requests for departmental resources were almost invariably honored. Not least, interviews with the participants confirm that while the EPB process occasionally involved time delays, they were the exception rather than the rule.

Policy implementation and departmental leadership

A third general limitation concerns the EPB's impact on policy implementation and strong leadership by individual cabinet members. When the President does not embrace the advice offered by a cabinet officer with primary administrative responsibility in the area, that official's credibility is weakened, to some extent, with the Congress. The EPB system, by giving all points of view a relatively equal voice, tended to weaken the ability of senior executives responsible for particular policy areas to "deliver" on commitments to their constituencies.

The suspension on grain sales to the Soviet Union in the summer of 1975 undercut Secretary Butz and thereby made it difficult for him to carry the administration's banner very well in the farm community. Much of Butz's difficulty arose from the public perception that others were making agricultural policy and that the decision-making process was tilted against him. But in addition, much of the problem was that Butz was losing on substance – large grain sales were going unmade, and exports were being restrained despite Butz's firm public identification with the contrary policy. This undercut his credibility, just as the decision against relief for the domestic shoe industry inevitably weakened the Special Trade Representative in future congressional negotiations.

The EPB contributed to an understanding among administration officials of the rationale behind presidential decisions, and it fostered a sense of participation and due process that strengthened the legitimacy of the decisions made. But these are hardly all that matter to officials responsible for policy implementation. They also have stakes in winning, in being seen as effective in getting their way on administration policy within their spheres; otherwise, their credibility with all those they need to influence is weakened. The EPB process constrained and balanced departmental parochialism, but it also weakened many cabinet members' ties to and leadership of their own constituencies by strengthening those advisors with broader economic policy responsibilities. Decision making through a multiple advocacy system like the EPB emphasizes presidential choice and direction of policy; but sometimes the price is the weakening of other centers of strength and support throughout the executive branch.

In considering the strengths and weaknesses of using a collegial body to advise the President, one is struck that the EPB's limitations were different than those frequently attributed to permanent interagency groups. While the EPB's operation was far from perfect – sometimes discussions were rambling and superficial, sometimes trivial issues consumed scarce executive time, sometimes concerns about leaks inhibited discussion – serious work did happen, and the discussions encouraged a perspective broader than narrow departmental interests. Executive committee members resisted the tendency toward expanding attendance by both periodic cut-backs as well as "principals only" executive sessions.[22]

Neither did the EPB breed a special staff isolated from ongoing operations. Indeed, by conscious decision, the size of the staff was kept extremely modest. Reasonable security regarding EPB papers and discussions was maintained, and, despite some members' anxiety about security, few leaks occurred. Finally, on most issues, real bargaining and dispute resolution took place within the EPB framework.

Balancing weaknesses against strengths and considering both the subjective assessments of leading administration officials and more objective measures, the EPB was a success. Gerald Ford described it as "the most important institutional innovation of my administration." Indeed, the EPB not only had the reputation of being the most effective policy council in the Ford period, but also the most sustained, comprehensive, and successful collegial attempt ever to advise a president on economic policy matters. This raises the question: What can we learn from the Economic Policy Board experience that might be generally applicable? What organizational principles for structuring multiple advocacy entities does it suggest?

[22] Since meetings were held in the West Wing of the White House, individuals from departments and agencies, with the exception of a cabinet secretary, had to be formally cleared into the White House complex by Seidman's office, which helped control attendance.

8

Organizing the White House for presidential decision making

 $\mathcal{T}$ he growth and increased complexity of government, the interrelatedness of many important issues, the competing demands for scarce resources, and high expectations for presidential performance have contributed to renewed interest in organization, particularly in how the White House is organized. This study is primarily concerned with organizational arrangements, procedures, and process. There are two dangers with such an emphasis.

First, concentrating on the process by which decisions are made and advice is organized may overemphasize the importance of procedures and underemphasize the importance of people. Neither governmental life nor presidential decision making are mechanical; moreover, any organizational arrangements depend in crucial ways on individual personalities and informal networks and relationships.[1] In general, the less structured

[1] Those who work in government very long soon recognize the point of a well known passage in Tolstoi's *War and Peace*.

> When Boris entered the room, Prince Andrey was listening to an old general, wearing his decorations, who was reporting something to Prince Andrey, with an expression of soldierly servility on his purple face. "Alright. Please wait!" he said to the general, speaking in Russian with the French accent which he used when he spoke with contempt. The moment he noticed Boris he stopped listening to the general who trotted imploringly after him and begged to be heard, while Prince Andrey turned to Boris with a cheerful smile and a nod of the head. Boris now clearly understood – what he had already guessed – that side by side with the system of discipline and subordination which were laid down in the Army Regulations, there existed a different and a more real system – the system which compelled a tightly laced general with a purple face to wait respectfully for his turn while a mere captain like Prince Andrey chatted with a mere second lieutenant like Boris. Boris decided at once that he would be guided not by the official system but by this other unwritten system." [Part III, Chapter 9.]

See Chester L. Cooper, "Some Perspectives on the Art of Decision-Making in National Security: An Introduction," in Keith C. Clark and Laurence J. Legere, *The President and*

the organizational pattern – for example, adhocracy – the more important are informal networks and processes. But, even under more formal
organizational arrangements, individual relationships can play a major,
sometimes decisive role.[2]

The second danger is assuming that structure is decisive, that if one
could just get things organized properly, then good decisions would au-
tomatically follow. But the fact that good organizational arrangements
cannot *guarantee* wise decisions should not obscure the contribution certain organizational arrangements can make to the likelihood of quality
decisions. One may be able to limit arbitrary, capricious, and uninformed
decisions even if one cannot guarantee good judgment.[3]

STRUCTURAL PRINCIPLES
FOR MULTIPLE ADVOCACY

Multiple advocacy characterized the Economic Policy Board's structure
and operation. Moreover, it was a collegial enterprise, a committee effort, without most of the operational limitations normally attributed to
interagency cabinet committees. Those who viewed it most closely, including several with governmental experience spanning a number of administrations, considered the EPB highly successful, particularly compared with similar groups in the past.

Multiple advocacy in theory, as Alexander George has argued, and in
practice, as the EPB illustrates, is a potentially successful arrangement

the *Management of National Security* (New York: Praeger, 1969), pp. 8–9; and Hamilton,
p. 7.

　　[2] Francis M. Bator emphasized the importance of informal arrangements in his testimony before the House Subcommittee on Foreign Economic Policy: "Formal structure matters less than semiformal and informal process, and, in particular, the positioning of the
right sorts of people, with the right connections in a few critical jobs." Bator Hearings, p.
108.

　　[3] This view is shared by Alexander L. George:

> The way in which policy-making procedures are organized – whether via multiple
> advocacy or according to some other procedural model – often may make little
> difference so far as the substance and quality of decisions is concerned. It would be
> naive and misleading to suggest that any particular policy-making model can guar-
> antee "good" decisions in every or even most instances. Rather, the case for multiple
> advocacy must rest on the more modest expectation that it will help prevent some
> very bad decisions and should generally improve the quality of information process-
> ing and appraisal.
>
> In any case, multiple advocacy need not work perfectly in order to be valuable.
> In some cases even a modest amount of multiple advocacy may suffice to highlight
> considerations that would otherwise be neglected or improperly appraised. [Alex-
> ander L. George, "Multiple Advocacy," pp. 98, 99.]

for systematically advising the President if certain conditions are met. What organizational principles can one distill from the EPB experience as guidelines in organizing multiple advocacy entities?

(1) *A White House policy council's effectiveness depends on its having the President's imprimatur.* The President must demonstrate by the way he makes decisions that he relies on the policy council. Departments and agencies must perceive it as the President's vehicle.

The most important sign of authority is regular access to the President through papers and meetings. It must have the assurance that others are not covering its papers with secret memorandums and recommendations. Moreover, the President must not permit end runs by departments or individuals but instead must insist that executive-branch officials channel their advice and proposals to him through the responsible policy council.

Without the President's imprimatur, officials are unlikely to take a policy council seriously, attend its meetings, devote their best resources to it, or comply with its decisions. To the extent that such officials perceive a council as having power and access, they will respect and use it. As one cabinet secretary noted: "I felt that the EPB was a place where there was somebody with clout. That makes a difference."

(2) *The policy council must meet and operate at the cabinet level.* A White House interagency body with primary responsibility for advising the President must operate at the cabinet level so that the participants can speak authoritatively for their department or agency. No subcabinet-level group is likely to have regular access to the President and can be overridden on major issues by one or more cabinet officers who disagree enough to take the matter to the President.[4] Moreover, genuine cabinet-level participation means that the policy council will probably get a department's or agency's best resources.

(3) *An honest broker should control the policy council's operations.*

---

[4]   One assistant secretary with experience in several administrations suggested that any permanent interagency group to advise the President must involve cabinet secretaries because "it wouldn't do much good to drop lower because these people don't have authority." However, he added that "the staff work has to be done by the assistant secretaries, the deputy assistant secretaries, and the upper echelons of the civil service; that's where the real expertise in the administration lies."

Another senior official who had worked for several years in subcabinet level posts reflected:

> There is no question the cabinet members must be involved. It is necessary to involve people at lower levels as well. But you have to involve the cabinet secretary because if you don't, you will quickly find yourself in the position of having worked endless hours putting things together, thinking you have everybody on board, and the cabinet secretary walks in and says "that doesn't represent my views." So you need it to operate at the cabinet level for cooption purposes.

Successful multiple advocacy entities do not run themselves. Someone must be in charge – calling meetings, setting agendas, developing papers. This individual must be genuinely perceived as an honest broker by the participating departments and agencies. This is a key distinguishing characteristic of a successful multiple advocacy system. If the process reflects the views of interested departments and agencies fairly, if they feel they receive due process, then they will use the council as a primary forum for considering major policy issues.[5]

Successful brokerage at the presidential level requires certain attributes of temperament and ability as well as certain structural arrangements. The honest broker should not have other responsibilities that would prevent him from devoting sufficient time to managing the policy development process. Operating a policy council, if it is done well, takes time. While the members of a council must be prepared to commit time and resources to it, they all have other demanding responsibilities, including managing their own department or agency and testifying repeatedly before congressional committees. Managing the policy process cannot be their primary concern. Likewise, the honest broker must be free from any institutional tie that would compromise his position or represent a conflict of interest.

The broker must be intelligent and capable enough to be accepted as a peer by the other members. He must have all of the skills of an effective advocate, yet consciously eschew that role and genuinely accept the role of honest broker. This is in large part a matter of temperament and personality. The honest broker is less visible, less public than the advocate. Such individuals must feel comfortable with a measure of detachment. Intellectually, the honest broker finds satisfaction in pulling the strands of a problem together or in laying out a complex issue for someone else's judgment. The advocate, by temperament, presses hard for his convictions and seeks to advance the interests of the institution and the constituency he represents.

The honest broker's effectiveness also requires that he enjoy the President's confidence. The other participants must perceive him as close to the President. To the extent that officials in departments and agencies perceive an individual and the council that he manages as having access to the President, they will participate in its activities and contribute to its development of policy.

[5] One cabinet secretary reflected:

> Each cabinet officer has his own point of view. I don't think you should both oversee the process and be one of the principal people making your arguments. The person running the operation should be as neutral as he possibly can be, and not someone with a parochial or institutional interest. He must be sure that everyone's ideas are pulled out.

Finally, the successful honest broker must be willing to function as an advocate if the discussion is not sufficiently balanced and the President needs to hear an underrepresented point of view. He needs to reach for advocacy as an instrument of brokerage rather than undertaking brokerage because he is told to do so.

(4) *The policy council staff should be small and consist of generalists.* White House policy councils often develop large staffs for a variety of reasons. A relatively large staff can exercise greater quality control while a small staff may simply become a paper shuffler. Moreover, a larger staff has resources to develop alternatives neglected by individual departments, provide more information and analysis, if necessary, and undertake long-term studies. Thus, those who favor giving the policy council's manager a relatively large staff argue that without an independent staff the quality of the council's work will suffer.

Yet, granting that an independent staff has important capabilities, serious risks come with size. The individual members of large staffs quickly specialize, partly along lines of interest and expertise, and partly because it is more efficient. Greater specialization moves people toward advocacy since the more one knows about a subject area, the more likely one will develop views, often strong views, about what should be done on particular problems. When staff members begin taking positions in interagency meetings and are perceived as advocates by other participants, they undermine the notion of the Executive Director as honest broker.[6]

Moreover, the larger the staff, the greater the tendency to generate information and analysis internally rather than seeking it from departments and agencies. One senior official in the Executive Office of the President reflected on what a staff should do and the size of the staff necessary to perform those functions:

> I think it ought to perform a facilitating function. It ought to move papers. It ought to take care of schedules. It ought to work at trying to put a concept into a framework that will help the President in deciding. But it needs to be very careful in the process of developing that concept framework that it doesn't take over and preordain the outcome.
>
> I think the staff needs to be small because if it gets to be more than two or three people it begins to have the potential for getting

---

[6] One senior official compared the relatively small EPB staff to the relatively large CIEP staff:

The EPB had the advantage of flexibility. It wasn't terribly structured like CIEP. It was a rather flexible instrument. It was headed by an honest broker. It didn't have a superstructure of its own which would have turned it into yet another entity, like CIEP. CIEP could not play a coordinating role because it was a player itself.

fed up with the participants and simply going off and doing its own thing because it knows better than the participants.[7]

A small staff has the added advantage of not being viewed as a competitor by member departments and agencies. Senior officials and their staffs in line departments and key Executive Office agencies such as the CEA and OMB have tremendous pressures on their time and resources. They will commit their time and resources to the extent that they feel the process is fair and worthwhile. This atmosphere is most likely to exist if the process is well-managed, and if department and agency officials do not feel they are competing with another staff in the White House.[8]

Finally, a large, independent staff attached to the manager makes it possible for him to end run the system himself. As Graham Allison observed in his study for the Murphy Commission: Won't the "holder of the ring" more often than not decide to "play the game himself," as did "Bundy on Vietnam" and "Kissinger on everything?"[9] It is especially tempting to bypass the system on major or sensitive issues. On balance then, the advantages of a small staff of generalists outweigh the benefits of a relatively large staff independent of member departments or agencies.

(5) *The policy council should have responsibility for advising the President over a broad policy area, such as economic policy or national security policy.* Assigning responsibility for a broad policy area to a single entity helps insure coordinated policies. A more fragmented decision-making process, with several departments or interdepartmental task forces reporting separately to the President, places the burden of integrating policies almost entirely on the President. The number of entities reporting directly to the President and the scope of their mandates influence how much policy integration occurs and who does whatever integrating is done.

[7] It is interesting to compare the EPB, which maintained a small staff, with the National Security Council which, as I. M. Destler has argued, "provided the umbrella for the emergence of a Presidential foreign policy staff." Indeed, Destler claims that this is what the NSC "has most importantly become." Destler, "National Security Advice to U.S. Presidents: Some Lessons from Thirty Years," p. 146.

[8] In scores of interviews with Economic Policy Board participants, there was unanimity on the importance of keeping any EPB staff small and noncompetitive – from two or three to five or six professionals. There was also consensus that one should rely heavily on assistant secretary–level task forces and that the small staff attached to the executive director should "utilize to a great extent staffs outside the White House."

[9] Graham Allison, "Overview of Findings and Recommendations from Defense and Arms Control Cases," U.S. Commission on the Organization of the Government for the Conduct of Foreign Policy, *Appendices*, Vol. 4, p. 38. The language is in reference to a White House staffing proposal advanced by Francis Bator.

Assigning responsibility for a broad area also helps insure that the policies will be comprehensive. Fragmenting responsibility among several departments or groups weakens accountability. When everyone is responsible, no one is responsible. A single coordinating entity also provides a place for focusing on long-term issues that cut across departmental lines.

A group of senior officials responsible for advising the President on a wide range of decisions is likely, over time, to develop a broad perspective, to think about issues in the context of their collective responsibilities. In effect the President is saying to these officials: "Draw yourselves out of your narrow confines. I want you to help advise me on this broad range of problems."

(6) *The policy council's deliberations should include all departments and agencies with a legitimate interest in an issue.* The legitimacy of a process depends on its reputation for fairness. Participation is perhaps the most basic measure of fairness. Participants in developing an interagency paper may feel that the final product is inadequate, but they usually feel less aggrieved than if they had been excluded from the process entirely. No multiple advocacy entity can function successfully for long if important parties are excluded consistently from its deliberations on those issues where they feel their interests are at stake.

(7) *The size of the core group or executive committee of the council should be kept reasonably small.* Large groups are notoriously unwieldy, time consuming, and cumbersome. Small groups are generally more efficient and flexible than large ones. It is easier to expand the size of a core group to address a particular problem than to reduce the size of a large group to consider an issue quickly.

The numerical threshold separating small and large groups is difficult to pinpoint. The EPB began with a five-member executive committee drawn primarily from the Executive Office of the President and later expanded to include three additional departmental secretaries. The fifteen-member full board rarely met. Interestingly, none of the participants, when interviewed, felt that the additional three members had made the Executive Committee too large or unwieldy, though several suggested that further additions would be unwise. When asked who they would include if they were starting the Executive Committee from scratch, they generally favored a seven-member body including four departmental secretaries (Treasury, State, Labor, and Commerce), the heads of two Executive Office units (CEA and OMB), and an Assistant to the President for Economic Affairs. There was little support for a Troika-type arrangement (Treasury, CEA, and OMB). As one OMB official put it: "It is too narrow without State and Labor and Commerce."

(8) *The policy council should be established by executive order and should function as a nonstatutory body.* The President needs and wants sound, balanced, thoughtful, and candid advice. He is more likely to receive such advice consistently if he and the senior officials close to him have systematic ongoing arrangements for identifying problems, analyzing information, and examining alternatives. The advice is more likely to be candid if it is confidential, whether in papers or meetings, a powerful justification for executive privilege. While the flow of information, analysis, and advice to the President needs to be organized, the process need not be highly visible. Indeed, the quality and candor of the process may well require that the arrangements are not very visible.

The Brownlow Committee's recommendation of presidential assistants with "a passion for anonymity" remains sound advice. There is no reason inherent in the honest broker's duties why he should testify before congressional committees, be responsible in any way to the Congress, or become a public spokesman for the President's decisions. In short, a cabinet-level interagency council responsible for advising the President should have an exclusive allegiance to the President and respond to a single master.

Moreover, any policy council established by statute acquires its own budget. An independent appropriation, even a modest one, inevitably encourages spending what is available and developing a need for more. On the other hand, the White House staff can easily accommodate a small handful of professionals assigned to the policy manager. Since a policy council's director acts as an extension of the President, the White House staff is the appropriate place for him. Policy councils do not need a statutory base, and there are many good reasons for them not to acquire one.[10]

These structural principles, suggested by the Economic Policy Board experience, provide the foundation for a presidential decision-making process based on multiple advocacy from a broad range of executive branch officials, a system that functioned successfully over a sustained period of time. Moreover, these principles and the EPB experience can

---

[10]   The National Security Council was established by statute in 1947 with no requirement that the director of the staff be confirmed by the Senate or testify before the Congress. The Domestic Council was established by Reorganization Plan No. 2 of 1970, also with no requirement that the executive director be confirmed by the Senate or testify before the Congress. The Council on International Economic Policy, established by statute after the President's legislative reorganization authority had expired, included a provision in the legislation which required the executive director to be confirmed by the Senate and to testify before congressional committees. All three policy councils had their own budget and appropriation separate from the White House staff and all three developed relatively large staffs.

contribute to thinking about organizing the White House for presidential decision making.

WHITE HOUSE ORGANIZATION: THE QUEST FOR INTEGRATION

Both presidents and scholars have supported the concept of more fully integrating departments and agencies in the presidential decision-making process. Newly elected presidents during the preinauguration days almost invariably proclaim their commitment to openness in their decision making and to an enlarged role for cabinet department and agency heads.

In November 1968, just one week following the election, the *New York Times* reported:

> Richard M. Nixon intends at this time not to allow his personal White House staff to dominate the functions or control the direction of the major agencies and bureaus of the Government.
>
> Sensitive to the possibility of empire building within his own small cadre of assistants, he plans instead to organize his White House staff in a way that will encourage and not inhibit direct communication between his Cabinet officers and the President.
>
> He is said to be firm in his view that his Cabinet officers should have the major responsibility for policy-making under the President and should be guaranteed regular access to the White House.[11]

Eight years later, James Reston wrote about the plans for President-elect Jimmy Carter:

> Unlike Richard Nixon, he is giving priority to his Cabinet over his White House staff, and insisting the Cabinet members, who are closer to the nongovernmental institutions of the nation than White House aides, work together as a Presidential council in the formulation of national policy.[12]

The *National Journal* reported:

> Said an aide, "Carter hopes to use his Cabinet members in formulating and implementing policy, so it is only natural that we first know who they are and how they are likely to operate. Then a

[11] Robert B. Semple, Jr., "Nixon Rules Out Agency Control by Staff Aides," *New York Times* (November 14, 1968), p. 1.

[12] James Reston, "Half-Speed Ahead," *New York Times* (December 15, 1976), p. A25.

White House staff can be put together to conform with their needs and working methods."[13]

With similar emphasis, several scholars have urged the establishment of cabinet-level interdepartmental entities – some new in scope and composition, some modifications of existing arrangements. Graham Allison and Peter Szanton, calling for the broader use of cabinet members in presidential decision making, have proposed "that the National Security Council be abolished and that an executive committee of the cabinet become the chief forum for high-level review and decision on all major policy issues that combine substantial 'foreign,' 'domestic,' and 'economic,' implications."[14] Maxwell D. Taylor has proposed an enlargement along similar lines of the membership and functions of the National Security Council.[15]

Bayless Manning has called for the creation of a cabinet-level International and Domestic Affairs Council to deal with "intermestic" issues, while retaining the National Security Council to deal with "security" issues.[16] Stephen Hess has argued that "the Cabinet must become the focal point of the White House machinery" and envisions a system with an indeterminate number of subgroups of the Cabinet preparing policy papers and proposing options with "issues of major importance . . . debated by the Cabinet."[17]

---

[13]　Dom Bonafede, "The Carter White House – The Shape Is There, But No Specifics," *National Journal* 8 (December 25, 1976): 1799.

During the transition period, two other leading Washington journalists sensed some tensions in the newly elected President's thinking about how he would relate to his cabinet. Hedrick Smith of the *New York Times* wrote: "A dilemma arises from his inclination to be a strong, activist President – with the consequent flow of power to his White House staff – and his contrary assertion that he intends to delegate authority to strong, independent, autonomous Cabinet officers whom he wants to be his main policy advisers." Hedrick Smith, "Which White House Style for Carter?" *New York Times* (December 26, 1976).

Edward Walsh of the *Washington Post* wrote: "He campaigned as the Washington outsider promising to bring a horde of new faces with new ideas to the nation's capital. He said he would not try to run the government from the White House, but would rely on a strong and independent Cabinet to carry out his policies." Later in the article Walsh quoted Carter as saying: "I think you all will have noticed that we have a wide variety of backgrounds and political philosophy within the department leaders themselves, he said, but I will be the primary focal point for the evolution of policy for the next administration." Edward Walsh, "Carter May Be One-Man Show: A Subordinated Cabinet," *Washington Post* (December 27, 1976), pp. A1, A7.

[14]　Allison and Szanton, p. 259.

[15]　Maxwell D. Taylor, "The Exposed Flank of National Security," *Orbis* 18 (Winter 1975): 1011–1022.

[16]　Bayless Manning, "The Congress, The Executive, and Intermestic Affairs: Three Proposals," *Foreign Affairs* 57 (January 1977):306–324.

[17]　Hess, pp. 214–215.

Robert H. Johnson has suggested eliminating the National Security Council, and other parallel bodies, and replacing them with less formal cabinet-level councils to address particular problems, supported by a unified "Cabinet staff."[18] Finally, Adam Yarmolinsky, suggesting that "the National Security Council may in fact have outlived its usefulness," has proposed creating a Council on Interdependence "equivalent to the traditional concept of the Cabinet," but with its own staff and "an independent existence, as a forum for the resolution of differences among the principal officers of the executive branch." The National Security Council staff, a subunit of the larger Council on Interdependence staff, would be the new staff's "crisis arm."[19]

All these proposals share a concern over the interrelatedness of issues and a desire for greater involvement by the heads of departments and agencies in White House decision making. While the specific proposals vary, they share a common theme – an interest in integrating international and domestic considerations by combining specialized councils and committees into a single entity.[20]

These suggested organizational arrangements (and the proposal advanced below) acknowledge that a systematic decision-making process involving all relevant interests will help mobilize the best information and analysis available, implement decisions successfully, and develop coherent and comprehensive policies.

However, three structural questions underlie any proposal to organize the White House for presidential decision making. First, how many channels for policy advice should report to the President? Second, what policy areas should they cover and what should be their composition? And third, what relationship should they have with one another?

ORGANIZING FOR PRESIDENTIAL DECISION MAKING: A PROPOSAL

There is a natural tendency for the President to permit and even encourage the proliferation of entities reporting directly to him. Creating a new

[18]   Robert H. Johnson, *Managing Interdependence: Restructuring the U.S. Government* (Washington, D.C.: Overseas Development Council Paper #23, NIEO Series, February 1977).

[19]   Adam Yarmolinsky, *Organizing for Interdependence: The Role of Government*, a paper prepared for the National Commission on Coping with Interdependence (New York: Aspen Institute for Humanistic Studies, 1976).

[20]   The Manning proposal of an International and Domestic Affairs Council would not eliminate the National Security Council but would result in two major White House policy-making entities.

council or cabinet-level committee reporting directly to the President demonstrates presidential concern and action both to the participants and to the public. It may also help assuage the bruised feelings of a specific constituency – the March 1976 creation of the Agricultural Policy Committee chaired by the Secretary of Agriculture was a symbolic action calculated to improve the President's sagging popularity in the farm community. Most presidents view such groups – or their civilian equivalent, presidential commissions of prominent private citizens – as inexpensive ways of building political support and demonstrating some movement in addressing a problem. Political considerations often influence White House organizational decisions. Furthermore, presidents comfortable with an ad hoc decision-making style tend to create many formal or informal groups reporting directly to them.

While political considerations may encourage the proliferation of entities reporting to the President, organizational purists resist such developments on several grounds. The more entities reporting directly to the President, the more specialized and narrow their outlook and mandates are likely to be. Furthermore, the more likely it is that some issues will fall through the proverbial crack since it will be difficult to pinpoint responsibility. Not least, creating numerous specialized committees invites jurisdictional battles, inevitably duplicates effort, and contributes to a feeling of uncertainty regarding who is responsible for what.

The more interrelated the problems facing the President, argue organizational purists, the more compelling the case to reduce the number of groups reporting independently to him. The more groups reporting to him, the more he must assume responsibility for fitting the pieces together. If the integration of his administration's policies concerns him, he will find himself constantly wanting to know how various problems relate to one another: how alternative energy policies would affect environmental pollution, the rate of economic growth, and inflation. Presidents who use adhocracy generally are either less concerned about policy consistency or are confident they can do a great deal of the integrating themselves.

A president interested in identifying the interrelationships among issues will want those advising him to share his concern for integration and coherence. If a group reporting to him has responsibility for a broad range of related issues, they have an incentive to draw his attention to the interrelationships between the issues. The budget process within the executive branch, designed to produce a unified federal budget, is a good example of how the President needs those advising him (in this case the Office of Management and Budget) to help identify the interrelationships and trade-offs involved.

One major consideration in organizing the White House, then, is policy integration. The argument to this point suggests that, in the interest of coherence, the fewer decision-making channels to the President, the better. Carried to its logical extreme, the quest for integration would result in a single entity – and this is the central concept behind the proposals of several eminent scholars.

But a second series of factors also merits consideration. How much public policy work can a single entity efficiently handle? How broad an area of public policy can it assume responsibility for and still function effectively?

The empirical evidence of the EPB's experience is helpful here. Any single group can consider only a finite number of issues. There are limits, even if the group is prepared to meet daily at the cabinet level. If the group is to discuss and refine issues before taking them to the President, then it cannot hope to advise the President over the entire spectrum of public policy. During the two and a quarter years of its existence, the EPB averaged nearly five meetings a week. The EPB typically reviewed an issue three or four times before it was ready to go to the President, not only preparing information for his consideration but differentiating between major and minor questions. The Economic Policy Board, which was extraordinarily active, perhaps represents the upper limit of business a single entity can successfully transact.

There are other good reasons for questioning the wisdom of a single channel to the President for considering major issues. The broader the policy area a council has responsibility for, the fewer officials who will have a genuine interest in most of the issues under consideration. Secretaries of State generally have little interest and few, if any, institutional stakes in urban mass transit alternatives. Likewise, the Secretary of Housing and Urban Development is generally not intimately concerned about U.S. policy in the Far East or in foreign aid programs. Cabinet members' specialized interests are one reason for the eclipse of the full cabinet as an institution. Cabinet members' time is precious and they are reluctant to spend it on problems that do not involve them. They attend cabinet meetings principally because the President is there.

If the cabinet, or some similar entity, served as the single high-level channel of formal advice to the President, and if its members attended only those meetings where issues genuinely affecting their department were scheduled for consideration, then the composition of the group would constantly change from meeting to meeting. One consequence would likely be little group sense of responsibility.

Furthermore, transmitting policy advice and recommendations to the President through a single institutional mechanism, whether the cabinet, an executive committee of the cabinet, an enlarged National Security Council, or a Council on Interdependence, would encourage developing a large support staff. Many of the proposals urging the establishment of a single overarching institution explicitly envision and encourage developing such a staff. But the history of large staffs attached to White House policy councils show them frequently assuming a major role in developing policy alternatives and intermediating between department and agency officials and the President. Thus, the quest for policy integration suggests merit in limiting the number of groups reporting directly to the President, while the desire to use interdepartmental entities effectively suggests the need for more than one.

The second structural question concerns what policy areas these policy councils should cover. There are many possible ways of slicing the public policy pie. In thinking about specific areas, two additional objectives merit consideration. First, one should avoid divisions that are likely to produce consistent overlaps and jurisdictional battles. Second, the more closely a policy council's work is tied to a regular work flow, the more easily its members will develop a sense of collective responsibility. Moreover, to the extent that existing institutions have worked well, they should be used.

The Bureau of the Budget, now the Office of Management and Budget, has served the President well for half a century in preparing a unified federal budget. Allocating scarce resources among persistent claimants involves literally thousands of decisions annually, and those decisions are not well handled by a committee. The budget process that has evolved within the executive branch is generally considered fair, efficient, and effective. National security issues and diplomatic relations are another regular stream of decisions that every president faces. Economic policy decisions constitute a third regular flow. A fourth group of decisions concern social policy issues: what to do about crime and law enforcement, health care, Indians, and the welfare system. Many of these issues have important economic and budgetary implications, and those in the economic policy community and OMB should be involved as participants in the discussions. But these issues are not primarily economic. Moreover, the budget process is essentially conservative; OMB is placed in the inevitable position of saying no. Budgetary considerations are important and essential, but the budget process is not the best forum for considering new policy initiatives. They will come primarily through other policy channels.

It is simply asking too much of a single entity to handle everything that is not addressed in the budget or does not relate to national security. If the Economic Policy Board, which had responsibility for all foreign and domestic economic policy, had also assumed responsibility for all other domestic or social policy questions, it would have collapsed of its own weight. In short, four principal channels of advice to the President – the budget process and three cabinet-level interdepartmental councils responsible for national security, economic policy, and social policy – is a reasonable division of labor, given the objectives of keeping the number of entities with direct reporting relationships to the President to a minimum while not placing excessive burdens on any single institution.

There are two other conceivable additions: energy and international economic policy. But neither is a compelling case. Energy policy does not present a steady stream of decisions for presidential consideration in the way that national security, economic policy, and social policy do. Furthermore, energy policy is critically intertwined with economic policy because the mutual impacts are so great; the appropriate membership of the two entities would be strikingly similar.

Every administration from Truman to Nixon, at one time or another, established separate committees or councils to deal with domestic and international economic policy. None of the divisions was generally considered successful, and there is a growing consensus that the line between domestic and international economic policy has blurred to where it is unwise to consider them in isolation. Again, international economic policy does not produce a steady stream of presidential decisions; about 20 percent of the EPB's work was on primarily international issues. Moreover, combining responsibility for domestic and international economic policy issues did not overload the EPB system.

The fourfold division proposed – the budget, national security, economic policy, and social policy – would provide direct, regular access to the President for each department. Every cabinet member should have membership on at least one of these policy councils. A few cabinet members, such as the Secretary of State, whose department has strong interests in both national security and economic matters, would have membership on two councils. To prevent unnecessary jurisdictional conflicts and to insure that budgetary interests are considered throughout the policy formulation process, the Director of OMB should be a member of the Economic Policy Council and the Social Policy Council, and meet with the National Security Council when issues involving major budgetary considerations are under discussion.

Three senior White House assistants – an Assistant to the President for National Security Affairs, an Assistant to the President for Economic Affairs, and an Assistant to the President for Domestic Affairs – would manage the three councils as brokers, not advocates. Periodically, perhaps weekly, these three senior presidential assistants, the OMB Director, and the President, or his chief of staff, would settle any jurisdictional questions and how others not members of a particular council could contribute to its consideration of an issue if they wished.

The system would work best if the size of the councils were flexible for dealing with specific issues, but each council would have a core group of officials to provide continuity. This core group would likely develop, as the EPB did, a sense of collective responsibility for the policy area as a whole. Such a system, if those participating were prepared to make it work, would provide the President with an organizational foundation for systematic, comprehensive, and coherent policy development. The President deserves no less.

APPENDIX

Three organizational models: adhocracy, centralized management, and multiple advocacy

*P*residents receive advice in many different ways and from many different sources – White House staffers, cabinet and subcabinet officials, senators and congressmen, presidential commissions and task forces, business and labor leaders, friends and family. Some presidents – Lyndon Johnson, for example – have leaned heavily on sources of advice outside the executive branch. Johnson's outside expert task forces generated many of the ideas for his Great Society programs and, particularly during the early years of his presidency, he consulted frequently with members of both houses of Congress.[1] But reliance on sources outside the executive branch is the exception rather than the rule for most presidents. Stephen Hess, after reviewing the range of outside sources of advice to presidents, concluded:

> Outside advisers, singly or collectively, . . . can serve certain useful purposes, but they are only tangentially connected to the continuing problems of running the government. While the art is to know which outside advice system is most useful for which purposes, ultimately Presidents will conclude that such systems are supplemental and that they must receive major advice from White House staff, heads of agencies, or some combination of the two.[2]

This essay is principally concerned with how advice to the President is organized within the executive branch. Most scholars attribute to Dwight D. Eisenhower a highly ordered decision-making style and to Franklin D. Roosevelt a more loosely structured and competitive decision-making style. Moreover, each president inevitably adopts a variety of approaches in making policy decisions[3] and may change his decision-making approach during the course of his admin-

---

[1] See Norman C. Thomas and Harold L. Wolman, "The Presidency and Policy Formulation: The Task Force Device," *Public Administration Review* 29 (September–October 1969): 459–471.

[2] Stephen Hess, *Organizing the Presidency* (Washington, D.C.: Brookings Institution, 1976), pp. 169–173.

[3] See Norman C. Thomas, "Presidential Advice and Information: Policy and Program Formulation," *Law and Contemporary Problems* 35 (Summer 1970): 540–572; Richard T. Johnson, *Managing the White House: An Intimate Study of the Presidency* (New York:

istration.[4] This essay does not attempt to link decision-making approaches with individual presidents. Rather, its central concern is examining how useful various decision-making approaches are in providing policy advice to the President.

The President, in responding to the increasing interrelatedness of policy issues, the diffusion of power in the executive branch, and the expectation of coherent, comprehensive policies, must reconcile his decision-making approach with multiple objectives. Presumably all presidents want reliable information and careful analysis, all necessary but not extraneous data, information and advice in an understandable form, a full range of realistic alternatives, and clearly identified trade-offs – advantages and disadvantages – between various policy alternatives. Presidents also want a process that differentiates major issues from minor issues so they can spend their time most efficiently on major issues. The process should make the best use of scarce executive talent, respond quickly and effectively to crises, and generate creative approaches to problems.

In developing his decision-making process, the President must also consider how it will influence his capacity to provide leadership to the executive branch and whether the process itself will help insure the implementation of his decisions. For many presidents, how others view the decision-making process is important because of its influence on his public image and professional reputation. Franklin D. Roosevelt refused to delegate large chunks of responsibility to any individual, at least in part because he wanted to create and maintain the image of a strong leader firmly in command. The qualities of speed and surprise may also contribute to a president's leadership image. A systematic and deliberate process may convey the appearance of the President as a prisoner of his machinery.[5]

Presidents are also sensitive to the milieu in which they operate. The pressure

Harper & Row, 1974); Stephen Hess, *Organizing the Presidency*. For an interesting discussion of formal and informal approaches in national security decision making, see Keith C. Clark and Laurence J. Legere, pp. 25–28, 217–218.

[4] Clark Clifford, in referring to the study of advising the President as a subject difficult "to come to grips with," observed:

> The reason it is so difficult to lay down any kind of formula is that the differences and idiosyncracies of presidents are manifested oftentimes most dramatically in the manner they choose to select and organize their advisers. . . . After he's been there awhile, he'll place his own stamp of character and personality upon the manner in which he runs it. [Barron, p. 9.]

Some students of the Nixon presidency claim that it sought increasing centralization of White House operational control. See Richard P. Nathan, *The Plot that Failed: Nixon and the Administrative Presidency* (New York: Wiley, 1975); Heclo, p. 13.

[5] Early journalistic assessments of the Carter economic policy-making machinery emphasized his personal role as President in shaping the pattern of advice. One article concluded that by failing to use his own interagency machinery (the Economic Policy Group) and developing policy individually with different advisers on different issues, President Carter was his own economic policy architect. Juan Cameron, "Jimmy Carter Gets Mixed Marks in Economics I," *Fortune* (June 1977): 98–104. Similar assessments are found in Robert J. Samuelson, "On Matters Economic, It's Carter Who Calls the Shots," *National Journal* 9 (April 9, 1977): 549–550; and "Who Runs Policy? Nobody, really – except the man in the Oval Office," *Time* 111 (November 21, 1977): 70–77.

to know what they are doing and thinking is great. No detail is too small to engage the interest of some member of the White House press corps. Decisions about national security strategy, devaluations, or delicate diplomatic initiatives, for example, raise inevitable questions about timing, access to information, and the danger of leaks. In making these types of decisions, presidents frequently limit the number of persons from whom they receive advice to preserve confidentiality. Most presidential policy decisions, however, do not a priori require strict confidentiality, and presidents have much latitude in organizing the advice they receive.

But a president cannot maximize simultaneously the multiple objectives he may have in devising organizational arrangements and a decision-making process. He cannot, for example, increase the likelihood of confidentiality by making decisions with the advice of relatively few people and at the same time have the advantages of a more open process — participation by those who will implement his decision, and the greater likelihood that important considerations will not be overlooked. Thus, each president must weigh carefully his objectives, and sometimes change them from issue to issue.

The President has numerous organizational options ranging from institutionalizing a devil's advocate to fostering an unregulated pluralistic system such as partisan mutual adjustment.[6] However, since the establishment of the Executive Office of the President and an enlarged White House staff, presidents have generally pursued one of three general approaches to organizing advice from their immediate staff and from executive departments and agencies. These three basic models have many variations and the same president may use different approaches for different policy areas. These three models clearly do not exhaust either the reasonable possibilities or the advisory systems that presidents have actually employed. For example, both Presidents Ford and Truman handled foreign and national security policy primarily through delegation to, and heavy reliance upon, the Secretary of State. Likewise, Richard Nixon delegated much responsibility on economic policy issues to Treasury Secretary John Connally and later to his successor George Shultz.

Examining these three organizational approaches will identify their strengths and limitations, and the objectives they are most helpful in achieving. In describing and discussing organizational models, it is well to remember Alexander George's perceptive observation that "the reality of a policy making system is always more opaque and inconsistent than the theoretical model which rationalizes it."[7]

ADHOCRACY

One organizational approach presidents commonly use is adhocracy.[8] As the term suggests, adhocracy minimizes reliance on regularized and systematic pat-

---

[6]   See Alexander L. George, "The Case for Multiple Advocacy in Making Foreign Policy," *American Political Science Review* 66 (September 1972): 751; and "The Devil's Advocate: Uses and Limitations," in U.S. Commission on the Organization of the Government for the Conduct of Foreign Policy, *Appendices*, Vol. 2, pp. 83–85.

[7]   George, "The Case for Multiple Advocacy in Making Foreign Policy," p. 752.

[8]   At a 1975 conference on Presidents and Their Advisers at Princeton University, Edgar

terns of providing advice and instead relies heavily on the President to distribute assignments and select whom he listens to and when. The President thus determines the thrust of his advisers' activities. Frequently he will rely on an "expert" to address an issue or develop an initiative. That individual may and frequently does consult with other officials in developing a proposal, but he alone is responsible for organizing the advice the President will receive on the issue.

Adhocracy has two different forms. Transition adhocracy frequently typifies decision making during the early months of an administration when the President and his appointees are learning about each other and are first grappling with the problems of governing rather than campaigning. When a president first enters office he inevitably relies on individuals rather than institutions, particularly on people whom he either knows well or considers expert. A classic case of transition adhocracy occurred in developing President Carter's national energy plan announced on April 20, 1977. Rather than using an interagency forum such as the statutory Energy Resources Council, the President assigned his White House energy adviser, James R. Schlesinger, to develop the program. Schlesinger consulted with some of his administration colleagues on various parts of the program, but not nearly as much as they considered desirable or wise.[9]

Transition adhocracy is in large part the product of newness. Many individuals are new to their jobs and adjusting to a new environment. Any new administration begins in relative chaos. Even the Eisenhower and Nixon administrations, which ultimately adopted very formal internal procedures, required a settling-in time.

Traditional adhocracy, on the other hand, may characterize a president's decision-making process at any time in his administration. It may involve giving different advisers competing assignments to develop an initiative or program. Whether explicitly competitive or not, adhocracy involves few regularized channels. A different but limited constellation of officials addresses virtually every major problem. Moreover, the distribution of assignments and responsibilities generally leaves jurisdictional boundaries unclear and frequently results in jurisdictional battles.

Adhocracy may involve giving responsibility to an interagency group rather than to an individual, but that group's assignment is usually confined to a specific task, such as developing a position on the minimum wage or preparing alternatives for welfare reform. The group is ad hoc in the sense that its mandate is for a specified duration and the scope of its responsibilities is restricted to a single issue. Thus, a president who chooses adhocracy organizes his policy advice by assigning responsibility for developing a position or initiative on an issue to an individual or a group. As issues arise, or as initiatives are contemplated, groups are formed to address them. As decisions are made, groups are disbanded.

R. Fiedler, former Assistant Secretary of the Treasury and Deputy Director of the Cost of Living Council, observed that while "little is known about the quality and processes of presidential economic advisory systems," it was his view that much of it was "ad hoc and unstructured." Dom Bonafede, "White House Report/Scholars Tackle Problem of Presidential Advisory System," *National Journal* 7 (November 22, 1975): 1610.

⁹ See James M. Naughton, "Carter Shaped Energy Plan With Disregard for Politics," *New York Times* (April 24, 1977), pp. 1, 28.

However, much of the advice a president receives is not the result of studies he has commissioned or issues on which he has made assignments. Many issues come from individual cabinet officers seeking presidential support for a proposal or a program. A president whose organizational approach is consistent with adhocracy is more likely to settle many issues bilaterally with his cabinet officers than would a president with a more highly structured decision-making process.

Franklin D. Roosevelt's adhocracy resulted in almost interminable chaos. He dispensed conflicting assignments almost at random with no individual and little institutional machinery to pick up the pieces. Today, over three decades later, adhocracy as an approach to presidential decision making remains, but is less random and less chaotic than in Roosevelt's time. After an administration has passed through its shakedown period, some recognized forums for addressing problems emerge even in the absence of explicit presidential direction. Relatively entrenched pieces of presidential machinery – the Office of Management and Budget, the White House staff secretary's office, the National Security Council staff, and the domestic policy staff – often act like safety nets assuming responsibility for decisions or organizing advice for a presidential decision in the absence of the President's intervention or alternative organizational arrangements. In short, traditional adhocracy, while it does not rely on regular, systematic policy-making channels, no longer operates in a vacuum.

Frequently, as the President learns to avoid relying on a single source of information, adhocracy evolves into what might be called multiple bilateralism. The process is bilateral in that department heads or personal advisers individually raise issues with the President or the President personally assigns a problem to someone. It is multiple in that, before making his decision, the President personally creates multiple advocacy by seeking the advice of other interested parties. Under such an arrangement, the President receives multiple advice but only because he makes it happen. He guarantees due process rather than having someone else do it for him.

Adhocracy is attractive to many presidents for a variety of reasons. It communicates the image of a president personally in command. This partially explains why presidential task forces and committees proliferate under adhocracy. Creating a new body that reports directly to the President demonstrates his concern about the problem and conveys a sense of action.

The President can also control easily the number of advisers involved in a given issue, a real strength when maintaining confidentiality regarding a new initiative is considered important. Moreover, adhocracy is highly flexible. With no regularized and systematic procedures, it can respond quickly. Furthermore, its flexibility can help bring economic and political considerations together in a single process.

Flexibility, increased confidentiality, the ability to respond quickly, and the image of a president in command are its strengths; adhocracy, however, also entails certain costs to the Chief Executive. Its random character means issues are treated unevenly since the individual or group designated is responsible for mobilizing the best information, developing the best analysis, and identifying and thinking through all the viewpoints the President should consider before his decision.

Adhocracy's random way of assigning responsibilities makes comprehensive examination of a policy area difficult and unlikely. There is little order in how interdepartmental issues arise and are resolved. New initiatives and policies are generally studied piecemeal. Different individuals and groups are responsible for various pieces of policy in a given area. No one other than the President is responsible for insuring that important issues receive presidential consideration and that both immediate and long-term issues in broad areas of public policy are treated comprehensively. In this sense, adhocracy mirrors the fragmentation of power characteristic of the American political system.

Furthermore, even while adhocracy elevates a president's visibility, it places a heavy burden on his time. First, he must constantly consider the composition and timing of the assignments he makes. Rather than relying on standard procedures, adhocracy is a decision-making process in a constant state of flux. Issue interrelatedness means that the President himself must recognize and consider the ways in which one set of policy decisions affects a related set. For example, developing an energy program requires choices between alternatives that will affect domestic prices, aggregate economic growth, redistribution of income, and the quality of the environment. The greater his reliance on adhocracy, with different sets of advisers working on related problems, the more a president himself must perform the difficult task of assessing how different policies relate to each other. Since developing coherent and consistent policies requires considerable effort and planning, relying on adhocracy increases the likelihood of patchwork policies. Adhocracy does not have the advantage of grouping knowledgeable people in stable relationships.

Second, adhocracy usually involves many individual contacts between the President and his advisers. Multiple advocacy, in contrast, relies on the President's hearing competing viewpoints simultaneously and seeing the interchange between his advisers.

Third, since adhocracy does not differentiate between major and minor issues, a president will face the pressure to make more decisions than he would under a process that does much of the sorting for him. The President determines how involved he wants to be on an issue. With no systematic way of receiving advice on all the issues in a broad policy area, the President himself must identify the issues that merit his attention and insure that one of his most precious commodities, his time, is not dissipated on minor issues.

Adhocracy also frequently entails two other costs for the President. By focusing responsibility on a single individual, as in the case of the development of the Carter energy program, adhocracy sometimes excludes major administration figures from issues in which they have a legitimate interest. Even if interested departments, agencies, and presidential advisers have an opportunity to present their views, strong policy preferences on the part of the individual responsibile for organizing the advice will likely dominate the alternatives and supporting analysis presented.

Adhocracy's somewhat chaotic character also leaves the President vulnerable to special constituency pleading. In one-on-one sessions with the President, an adviser can argue strongly, and often convincingly, for his preferred policy, minimizing its risks and disadvantages. Presidents may counter such special pleading by consulting individually with others holding opposing views. Cabinet secretaries, presidential assistants, and other key advisers usually are articulate and persuasive. Several advisers who have worked under unregulated entrepreneurial advocacy observe that the President's decisions seem to them largely the result of who talked to him last.

In summary, the costs of adhocracy include the heavy demands it places on presidential time, the burden it places on the President for integrating various policies, the failure to differentiate between major and minor issues, the potential exclusion of major interests, the lack of provision for comprehensive examination of a policy area, and the scope it affords for one-on-one special pleading. The extent and seriousness of these costs varies from president to president and case to case. In some instances the disadvantages are minimal; in other instances they exact a high price.

CENTRALIZED MANAGEMENT

Centralized management is a second basic organizational model the President can use in patterning his policy advice. A prominent feature of a centralized management process is heavy reliance on the White House and Executive Office of the President staffs to filter the ideas, proposals, and recommendations of departments, agencies, and bureaus before they go to the President.

Reliance on staff entities within the Executive Office is grounded in a desire for analysis and recommendations from individuals who share the President's perspective. The staffs not only manage the flow of day-to-day communications between departments and the President but pull the strands of a policy problem together and provide an objective assessment of relevant information and alternatives. Its order and rationality appeal to decision makers wary of a more broadly based, competitive approach to organizing policy advice.[10]

A centralized management staff is generally large enough that staff members specialize in their own particular policy areas, developing contacts throughout the executive branch to help them monitor developments and acquire data. Relying on Executive Office staffs for an objective assessment of a problem does not preclude participation by departments and agencies, even significant participation. Still, the White House–based staff is generally the driving force. It usually prepares the final document submitted to the President, and is somewhat wary of consistent and full involvement by cabinet departments and agencies since part of its mission is to "transcend" the departmentalism and limited perspectives of executive branch agencies.

Sifting and distilling the wide variety of proposals and ideas transmitted to the President from within the government is an important role of a central management staff. Likewise, when two or more departments fundamentally disagree on an issue, the White House–based staff frequently handles the conflict and recommends a resolution to the President. It defines the important issues, the

[10]   See Alexander L. George, "The 'Formal Options' System," in U.S. Commission on the Organization of the Government for the Conduct of Foreign Policy, *Appendices* (Washington: GPO, June 1975), Vol. 2, pp. 86–88.

nsiderations, and the required decisions. As Alexander George has
t, a centralized management approach sees the President as a "unitary
cision maker," shielded from raw disagreements over policy.[11]
ne theory behind centralized management is to give the President ob-
ysis and advice, the practice is frequently different. Centralized management staff members can easily become advocates since they do not view themselves primarily as brokers between various interests in the executive branch.
Instead they see themselves as providing the President with their own best thinking and with their own assessment of problems from his point of view. Those
who head White House–based central management staffs generally know the
President and his thinking well and have frequent access to him. They have a
sense of how he views problems and which issues and factors he considers most
important. Thus, centralized management almost invariably concentrates power
in two or three individuals, since presidents comfortable with this management
strategy tend to consult with fewer individuals than do presidents more comfortable with adhocracy or multiple advocacy.

In short, a centralized management approach to policy formulation gives primary responsibility to the President's Executive Office and immediate staff. It
emphasizes careful, systematic examination of policy questions with control
vested in individuals familiar with the President and his views. Executive branch
departments and agencies may have substantial input but generally play a distinctly secondary role, since centralized management seeks to overcome what is
viewed as departmental parochialism and inertia.

Interestingly, presidents have rarely instituted a full-fledged centralized management system, although several have been suspicious of relying on departments
and agencies.[12] Indeed, Graham Allison and Peter Szanton claim that "at bottom,
the organizational strategy of each of the last four Presidents has been so to
strengthen the Executive Office of the President as to make it possible to do
without the departments, and then to look for counsel not to cabinet officers but
to White House assistants."[13]

One reason why presidents like centralized management is its potential for

[11] George, "The Case for Multiple Advocacy in Foreign Policy Making," p. 752.

[12] Presidents seem more inclined to use centralized management in dealing with national security and foreign policy issues than with economic issues. Indeed, no president
has systematically attempted to make economic policy through a centralized management
system. One likely reason is that the economic policy community within the executive
branch is more fragmented than the foreign policy establishment and therefore more difficult to dominate. Furthermore, the mere existence of the Council of Economic Advisers
would make it difficult to erect a centralized management economic policy staff of any size.
The CEA, since its establishment in 1946, has generally refused to assume a major role in
coordinating and managing the economic decision-making process, and instead has viewed
its mandate as advising the President from the standpoint of the professional economist.

[13] "Organizing for the Decade Ahead," in *Setting National Priorities: The Next Ten
Years*, edited by Henry Owen and Charles L. Schultze (Washington, D.C.: Brookings Insti-
tution, 1976), p. 256. A similar view is found in Thomas E. Cronin, "Presidents as Chief
Executives," in *The Presidency Reappraised*, edited by Rexford G. Tugwell and T. E. Cronin
(New York: Praeger, 1974), pp. 240–241.

Proceeding from a conviction that "the presidency is weak in policy analysis," William

Carey has urged the creation of "a strong policy development staff [in the White House] with the job of probing for policy directions and framing options for the President over time." In this recommendation, Carey was concurring with the conclusion of "an organization task force in the Johnson years (and suppressed by presidential fiat upon completion) . . . that there was an immediate and paramount need to create a new Office of Policy Development for the President . . . that the new unit should be part of the White House . . . [and] that the staffing of the new office would call for the highest order of professional abilities and the determined support of the President himself." William D. Carey, "Presidential Staffing in the Sixties and Seventies," *Public Administration Review* 29 (September–October 1969): 451–452.

Relying on a neutral, objective staff within the White House would have been a principal element in the strategy. As Carey explains:

> What is needed most acutely is a policy planning staff to be concerned with analysis of public investment priorities and the formulation of administration goals. Its aim would be to lift the presidency out of the rut of patching and piecing together fragments of policy, and to supply an independent White House initiative for long-range planning. [p. 457.]

Merely seeking to strengthen the capability of the Executive Office of the President does not necessarily mean that a president has adopted or is pursuing a central management strategy. Increased reliance on White House assistants characterized the Kennedy, Johnson, and Nixon presidencies. The Ford presidency, in many respects, reversed the trend by giving cabinet officers a greater role.

The Nixon–Kissinger National Security Council staff and the Nixon–Ehrlichman Domestic Council staff are frequently considered the most notable examples of a highly systematic centralized management approach to policy formulation. Both Nixon and Kissinger were anxious to shield the President from the State Department bureaucracy, which they considered unimaginative, resistant to change, and unwieldy in size and organization. Moreover, Nixon and Kissinger were attracted by the desire to develop a policy system that would insure secrecy and permit surprise.

Dissatisfaction with the general viewpoint and quality of executive branch personnel contributed to the creation of a Domestic Council staff under John Ehrlichman, Assistant to the President for Domestic Affairs, which was designed to parallel the Kissinger National Security Council staff in providing the President with an independent, presidentially oriented entity to advise him on domestic policy.

In some respects the Nixon–Kissinger NSC and the Nixon–Ehrlichman Domestic Council staffs combined features of both centralized management and multiple advocacy. In the early stages there was widespread and genuine participation by departments and agencies. White House–based staff members did not dominate the development of an agreed upon options paper, although they were frequently major participants. In the latter stages of the process, however, including preparing a cover memorandum and discussion with the President, the Kissinger and Erlichman systems more nearly resembled centralized management. These cover memorandums, drafted by the NSC or Domestic Council staffs, restated the options and/or advocated specific courses of action. The staffs took considerable care to keep the content of these cover memorandums from individuals in departments and agencies.

Representatives of departments and agencies were also excluded from discussion with the President on many issues. One assistant secretary stated that it was not uncommon to be unable to find out "whether the papers had gone to the President, when the papers were due to go to the President, or if the President had already made a decision and the White House was merely waiting to announce it." In short, at different times in their evolution, the Nixon–Kissinger NSC and the Nixon–Ehrlichman Domestic Council resembled what might appropriately be called "truncated multiple advocacy."

increasing their control over the policy-making process. A leading critic of centralized management noted:

> By instituting centralized control and direction of the search for and evaluation of options at the NSC level, Nixon has greatly enhanced presidential control over foreign policy decision making and weakened the ability of officials in departments and agencies to exercise independent judgment and influence over decisions.[14]

A relatively large, able, and energetic White House–based staff may also aid the President by raising issues for his attention and decision that might not necessarily reach the White House otherwise.[15] A centralized management staff can also help cope with the perennial presidential problem of "bureaucratic politics." Alexander George aptly describes the process:

> As in other types of complex organizations, subunits of the executive branch tend to engage in quasi resolution of conflict and to avoid uncertainty in relations with each other by means of "negotiating the internal environment" within the organization. Left to their own devices, those subunits which share responsibility for a particular policy area often adapt by restricting competition with each other. As a result, policy issues may not rise to the presidential level, or when they do, they often take the form of concealed compromises that reflect the special interest of actors at lower levels of the hierarchical system.[16]

A centralized management strategy also provides the President with a loyal and competent resource, dedicated to him alone, that will respond quickly. The level and pace of activity at the White House trains such staffs to produce results rapidly and efficiently. Presidents, seeing a seemingly inevitable procession of crises and possibilities for new initiatives, soon learn to value a relatively large and responsive staff.

When the President wants to prevent leaks or premature discussion, a centralized management system will at least increase his likelihood of controlling

---

[14]   George, "The Case for Multiple Advocacy in Making Foreign Policy," p. 753.

[15]   The Nixon–Kissinger NSC staff used National Security Study Memorandums (NSSMs) as a procedural means for raising issues for presidential consideration that might or might not otherwise receive presidential attention. I. M. Destler has argued that Nixon's decision to renounce the use of biological weapons illustrates this potential benefit of a study directed by a centralized management staff by contrasting the NSSM device with the situation Nixon inherited.

> Only the Army really wanted them [biological weapons] and, within the Army, mainly the branch specializing in them. But ... the issue never got to President Johnson for his review because neither the Secretary of Defense nor the Secretary of State was willing to pay the bureaucratic political price of recommending a change. Under the Nixon system, however, once the White House ordered a study, the staff could see to it that the "option" of renouncing biological weapons was presented as one alternative for NSC discussion and Presidential decision. [I. M. Destler, *Presidents, Bureaucrats, and Foreign Policy*, p. 133.]

[16]   George, "The Case for Multiple Advocacy in Making Foreign Policy," p. 753.

the timing and announcement of a new policy or initiative even though it does not guarantee confidentiality.

However, a centralized management strategy also involves substantial costs and risks for the President. First, the notion that these staffs are preferable rests on the premise that staff members are objective and view problems from the President's perspective. Yet the notion of staff objectivity is suspect for at least two reasons. As staffs specialize, and staff members become knowledgeable about a given policy area or problem, they usually develop strongly held views and opinions. Soon many become advocates, supporting specific positions in interagency discussions. Moreover, staff perceptions of what the President wants often undermine objectivity. On issues where presidential preferences do not exist or are not known, the temptation to anticipate them is negligible; but on issues where the President's leanings are known, few can resist the temptation to offer advice or structure a problem to correspond with the President's preferences.[17]

Second, despite the growth in the size of the White House staff and the Executive Office, the President's immediate staff resources are small compared to the whole executive branch. The White House staff cannot hope to duplicate the substantive expertise or the range of concerns on an issue that exist in the executive branch. A centralized management staff also cannot sensitively assess potential administrative difficulties with various alternatives or manage in any detail how a policy is implemented.

Third, excluding or downgrading key officials, and thereby the departments that they represent, can impair a president's long-term capacity to lead. As Theodore Sorensen observed regarding the relationship between the President and his advisers: "He [the President] rules, to a degree, not only with their advice but with their consent."[18] The credibility of a cabinet officer with his constituency;

---

[17] Allison and Szanton, in a somewhat similar vein, observe:

Staff is responsive to the President – that is its principal virtue, but also its worst defect. Staff is too responsive. It has no purpose but to serve its single superior. It brings to that service no counterpressure from statutory responsibilities, bureaucratic loyalties, professional identification, or congressional supervision. Staff members tend to become courtiers. This is true everywhere, but nowhere more so than in the White House. And the result is deepening presidential isolation and unrealism as the White House becomes, in Senator Charles Mathias' words, a presidential "house of mirrors" in which all views and ideas tend to reflect and reinforce his own." [Allison and Szanton, "Organizing for the Decade Ahead," p. 256.]

The quotation from Senator Mathias is from *Executive Privilege: The Withholding of Information by the Executive*, Hearings before the Subcommittee on Separation of Powers of the Senate Judiciary Committee, Ninety Second Congress, First Session (Washington: GPO, 1971), p. 17.

Samuel Orr, in a reasonably balanced assessment of the Nixon–Kissinger NSC system, concluded: "The kinds of analyses that are done, the way the choices are presented to the President and the NSC, and the shape of the resulting policies inevitably reflects the biases of the President and his leading officials, such as Kissinger." Samuel C. Orr, "Defense Report/National Security Council Network Gives White House Tight Rein Over SALT Strategy," *National Journal* 3 (April 24, 1971): 881.

[18] Sorensen, p. 81.

the diligence and attention given to implementing presidential decisions; the public and private support before the Congress and the public provided by his advisers; the image of having strong men in his administration: These are assets that a president should not dispense with lightly.

Fourth, excluding departments and agencies in developing presidential policies can produce presidential decisions that do not accurately reflect political realities. Departments and agencies are useful channels through which "outside actors" in the Congress and interest groups can make their views known. An open system with full participation by departments and agencies can usually give the President a reasonably accurate sense of how the Congress and the public would respond to various proposals. A more closed system is less likely to transmit nuances and sensitivities.[19]

Fifth, centralized management can place an enormous burden on the individual responsible for operating and overseeing the staff. If he becomes the President's principal adviser on most issues within a broad policy area, then inevitably the most pressing issues will force less urgent matters back. Even the most able mind can only focus on so many things at any given time. This disadvantage is critical when a number of sensitive issues arise simultaneously. If the staff director is unwilling to delegate and insists on immersing himself fully in the details and analysis of virtually every issue before it is sent to the President, then he becomes a bottleneck on issues and decisions. This is not a necessary feature of a centralized management system – he could delegate responsibility on some issues – but concentrating power in a single individual and in a single staff makes it a potential risk.[20]

Sixth, while most centralized management strategies will likely involve departmental participation in at least the early stages of policy development, the existence of a large, independent staff with easy access to the President almost inevitably means that the assistant to the President will lift some issues out of the process and handle them on his own with the President. This "Royal Court" pattern of policy making is more likely to occur when issues are highly sensitive, require quick decisions, or when the President and the central staff director have firm predispositions on them.[21]

---

[19]   Alexander George has made a similar criticism of the Nixon–Kissinger NSC staff system:

> . . . By weakening the struggle over foreign policy within the executive branch, the new NSC system also limits the opportunities "outside" actors have had to influence the making of policy by participating informally in the play of "bureaucratic politics" among the various actors in the executive branch. [George, "The Case for Multiple Advocacy in Making Foreign Policy," p. 756.]

This criticism applies with even greater force to economic and social policies where Congress and the public have traditionally accorded the President less deference in policy making than in foreign affairs.

[20]   An example was the Nixon–Kissinger NSC system, which relied heavily on Kissinger's personal attention to and analysis of problems before they were taken to the President. It consistently produced prolonged delays in dealing with some issues and inattention at the highest levels to other issues. George, "The 'Formal Options' System," p. 90.

[21]   This was a common observation of the Nixon–Kissinger NSC system. See Wilfred

In summary, a centralized management strategy entails certain costs for the President. Relying heavily on his immediate staff will inevitably undermine morale and initiative in departments and agencies. Moreover, the objectivity of a presidentially oriented staff may be an illusion if the staff ends up mirroring and reinforcing perceived presidential inclinations. It cannot mobilize the same resources nor reflect the range of concerns that exist in departments and agencies. Implementing a large number of issues requires the cooperation of departments and agencies who will withhold it if they feel alienated. Thus, centralized management widens the gulf between policy formulation and implementation, and the gulf between the President and his executive branch.

MULTIPLE ADVOCACY

Multiple advocacy, a third decision-making model available to the President, is an open system based on inclusion. Unlike centralized management, multiple advocacy is designed to expose the President to competing arguments and viewpoints made by the advocates themselves rather than having viewpoints filtered through a staff to the President. Moreover, these competing viewpoints are presented collectively to permit exchange and argument among the advocates.

Optimally, the final stages of decision making under a multiple advocacy process would include a meeting between the President and his advisers where they had an opportunity to present, and he had an opportunity to hear, their arguments orally. Such a meeting does not replace a document outlining the issues, options, and trade-offs; but when the participants know that they will have a chance to present their arguments personally, it facilitates producing agreement on an options paper. A multiple advocacy process does not depend on meeting with the central decision maker. If time, logistical obstacles, or the President's personal preference dictates making the decision from documents without a meeting, the multiple advocacy process can produce such a paper efficiently. This also applies to adhocracy and centralized management. All three models can theoretically function either as a paper system or as a process that includes meetings with the central decision maker.

In contrast to partisan mutual adjustment or unregulated bureaucratic politics, multiple advocacy relies on an honest broker to insure that interested parties are represented and that the debate is structured and balanced.[22] Multiple advocacy emphasizes carefully weighing all views and considerations. It is grounded in the concept that a competition of ideas and viewpoints is the best method of

L. Kohl, "The Nixon–Kissinger Foreign Policy System and U.S.–European Relations," *World Politics* 28 (October 1975): 1–43.

[22] George, "The Case for Multiple Advocacy in Making Foreign Policy," p. 761.

The theory of multiple advocacy poses sharply defined requirements for executive management of the policymaking system. . . . Strong, alert management must frequently be exercised in order to create and maintain the basis for structured, balanced debate among policy advocates. As such, multiple advocacy goes beyond what is usually meant by "adversary proceedings" or use of a "devil's advocate." [George, "Multiple Advocacy," p. 95.]

developing policy – not unregulated entrepreneurial advocacy but orderly, systematic, and balanced competition.

The President's role is to consider the analyses and arguments made by his advisers, seek clarification of unclear proposals or assessments, weigh the evidence presented, and then decide what action, if any, to take.[23]

The executive director's staff is generally small and, like him, assumes the role of an honest broker. Departments and agencies provide most of the substantive expertise and resources used in developing issues. The executive director and his staff are not intermediaries between departmental advocates and the President, but they do more than simply insure due process. They promote genuine competition of ideas, identifying viewpoints not adequately represented or that require qualification, and augmenting the resources of one side or the other so that a balanced presentation results.[24] In short, they insure due process *and* quality control.

Multiple advocacy is also characterized by continuity among those individuals who advise the President on issues relating to a broad policy area such as economic policy. The issues under consideration may range from tax reductions to unemployment programs, from anti-inflation measures to housing subsidies. The group may vary somewhat, depending on the issue. However, a stable core of advisers shares responsibility for collectively advising the President over the entire range of issues in the policy area.[25]

[23]   In some instances the President's decision may support an option recommended by one or more of the advocates, but in other cases he may participate in the exchange with his advisers, fashion a course of action, and then approve it.

[24]   See Alexander George's discussion of this characteristic in "Multiple Advocacy," pp. 95–96; and David K. Hall, "The 'Custodian Manager' of the Policymaking Process," in U.S. Commission on the Organization of the Government for the Conduct of Foreign Policy, *Appendices* (Washington, D.C.: GPO, June 1975): Vol. 2, pp. 100–101.

[25]   Alexander George has provided the most systematic published discussion of multiple advocacy in "The Case for Multiple Advocacy in Making Foreign Policy" and "Multiple Advocacy," already cited. George's principal interest is in foreign policy making, but there is no reason his analysis could not be extended to other policy areas.

The multiple advocacy model that I have outlined contains three important similarities to the George model and two differences in emphasis. We agree: (1) that multiple advocacy is a process designed to expose the central decision maker to competing arguments; (2) that multiple advocacy is a management-oriented theory in that it relies on an "honest broker" (Porter) or "custodian manager" (George) to regulate the process and insure that it is systematic, fair, and balanced; and (3) that the President's or the central decision maker's role is similar to that of a magistrate.

The differences in emphasis are: (1) I emphasize the importance of continuity among those individuals advising the President on a broad policy area, such as national security or economic policy, because continuity can help the President deal with the interrelatedness of issues. Moreover, it also helps differentiate multiple advocacy from certain forms of adhocracy. George is silent on the specific question of continuity among advisers. This difference is one of emphasis rather than substantial disagreement. (Correspondence from Alexander L. George, February 20, 1979.)

(2) George envisions an independent, "analytically-oriented" staff for the "custodian manager": "The executive who employs multiple advocacy will require a strong, indepen-

A genuine multiple advocacy process provides the President with several benefits. It provides that all points of view will be explored and contested. On any given issue, a number of aspects merit consideration. These will usually be reflected by the different perspectives of different governmental players. It is unwise to expect any single individual or staff to think through a problem from all perspectives – a liability of relying on a centralized staff to formulate options and discuss alternatives.[26] As Theodore Sorensen observed: "The interaction of many minds is usually more illuminating than the intuition of one. In a meeting representing different departments and diverse points of view, there is a greater likelihood of hearing alternatives, of exposing errors, and of challenging assumptions."[27] Similarly, Alexander George has argued that multiple advocacy "is more likely to secure a critical examination and weighing of them [ideology, beliefs, and alternatives] . . . than a highly centralized policy making system."[28]

Multiple advocacy is a process that mitigates against the suppression of conflicting views. Defining differences, rather than submerging them, highlights the trade-offs between competing values and objectives and helps insure that any compromises result from conscious deliberation rather than bureaucratic politics. Moreover, it is a process that guarantees against ex parte judgments.

Multiple advocacy can also improve the quality of alternatives developed and the arguments used to support them. As Joseph Bower has pointed out: "The personal commitment of a subject to an initial position motivates him to defend his choices by presenting all the information which supports his position . . . group search is stimulated in both extent and quality."[29]

A properly functioning multiple advocacy system bridges the gap between policy formulation and implementation. Political scientists frequently observe that, in the American political system, policy formulation receives more attention and effort than policy implementation. Indeed, for many years the conventional wisdom made an important distinction between policy and administration, a term largely synonomous with implementation. But in recent years, students of

dent, analytically-oriented staff such as that of the National Security Council." ("Multiple Advocacy," p. 98.) I envision a smaller staff, composed primarily of generalists. The National Security Council staff during at least the last three administrations has been independent, analytically oriented, *and highly specialized*. This relatively small staff would rely on mobilizing staff capabilities within departments and agencies, rather than competing with them. Our difference on this issue may reflect the difference between economic policy making, where there are a relatively large number of strong departmental and agency staffs (Treasury, State, Commerce, Labor, CEA, OMB) and foreign policy making where there are relatively fewer strong departmental and agency staffs (State, Defense, and the CIA) apart from the NSC staff.

[26] See Graham Allison and Morton H. Halperin, "Bureaucratic Politics: A Paradigm and Some Policy Implications," in *Theory and Policy in International Relations*, edited by Richard H. Ullman and Raymond Tanter (Princeton: Princeton University Press, 1972), p. 48.

[27] Sorensen, p. 59.

[28] George, "The Case for Multiple Advocacy in Making Foreign Policy," p. 752.

[29] Joseph L. Bower, "The Role of Conflict in Economic Decision Making Groups: Some Empirical Results," *Quarterly Journal of Economics* 79 (May 1965): 263–277.

policy implementation have increasingly concluded that much of what traditionally has been considered policy making occurs in the process of implementation.
If those responsible for implementing policies are to make decisions consistent
with the intentions of those who formulated the policies, then they must understand the rationale behind the policy. Insuring that those responsible for implementing policies have a voice in formulating those policies strengthens the likelihood of such understanding.[30]

Perhaps even more importantly, individuals responsible for implementing a
policy are less likely to undermine a decision with which they disagree if they
have had an opportunity to express their views than if they have been excluded.
Those excluded from developing a policy frequently contend, with some justification, that had they been permitted to raise certain questions and present their
case, a different decision might have resulted. Accordingly, they feel less obliged
to support the outcome of the process wholeheartedly. Participation binds the
participants to support the outcome; they do not feel that bond if they are denied
a voice in the deliberations.[31]

Much presidential decision making occurs in preparing and refining proposals
to submit to the Congress. If those proposals are to remain reasonably intact,
then the President needs the support of departments and agencies. Their energy
in advocacy and their willingness to generate support from interest groups depends on the strength of their attachment to the proposal. Their participation
from the outset, the feeling that this is partly their proposal, can significantly
influence their enthusiasm for the policy at later stages in the political process.

Not least, the quality of the President's decisions improves when he provides

---

[30]   Hugh Heclo describes the importance senior officials in the permanent government
attach to understanding what is behind decisions communicated from above:

> Since policies are often bundles of mutual understandings rather than clearly spelled-
> out directives, senior bureaucrats are in a strategic position to interpret the policy
> themes accurately or inaccurately to officials further down, who in turn are expected
> to relate their choices on specific issues to the overall intentions. One supergrade
> explained how interaction with political appointees could be a key factor in gaining
> a sense of what has gone into a decision and, hence, in guiding those below:
>
> "I don't want to run my hands over every little scar from the last battle, but we
> do need to know the general way something was decided. I'll be dealing in the same
> area again, and knowing that something was decided on its merits gives an indica-
> tion of what policy is meant to be. If it was decided on tactical, or personal, or party
> grounds, that's okay, but then I know that the next time someone asks it's all up for
> grabs." [*A Government of Strangers*, p. 179. See also p. 195.]

[31]   Alexander George notes: "This is consistent with research findings in other settings
which suggest that as long as the individual is satisfied that a proper degree of deference
has been granted to his point of view by organizational superiors, his hostility reaction will,
in all probability, be minimal if his superiors do not accept his judgment." George, "The
Devil's Advocate: Uses and Limitations," p. 85. Cf. Murray Horwitz, "Managing Hostility
in the Laboratory and the Refinery," in Robert L. Kahn and Elise Boulding (eds.), *Power
and Conflict in Organizations* (New York: Basic Books, 1964), pp. 79–82, cited by Louis
G. Gawthorp, *Bureaucratic Behavior in the Executive Branch* (New York: Free Press,
1969), p. 42.

for the participation of those responsible for ultimately implementing policies. Those responsible for implementing a program are sensitive to potential administrative difficulties that can prove crucial in evaluating various alternatives.

In short, multiple advocacy helps bridge the gap between policy formation and implementation in three ways. It provides the decision maker valuable information on the administrative implications of different alternatives, increases understanding of the rationale behind a program by those who must implement it, and strengthens support for presidential policies in departments and agencies.

Another merit of using multiple advocacy is that it mirrors most closely the configuration of forces existing in the political process as a whole. Departments and agencies in presenting their views are not seen as disloyal or untrustworthy because their perspective differs from the President's. Instead, they are viewed as reflecting real interests and perspectives that will inevitably emerge in subsequent stages of the political process – when congressional committees scrutinize the proposal and the permanent bureaucracy implements it. In this sense, multiple advocacy enhances the likelihood that the initial stages of policy development occur under conditions reflecting the political forces that will come into play before the process is completed. Such "outside" forces as congressional committees and interest groups can participate informally through their contacts with departmental personnel, not only influencing the information considered in developing the President's position but also influencing the reaction when a decision is announced. Multiple advocacy in these ways mobilizes the resources of the executive branch more systematically than does adhocracy and more completely than does centralized management.

Including departments and agencies in the presidential decision-making process not only enhances morale in the executive branch, but strengthens the President's influence in at least two ways. First, a president's influence in the executive branch is related to the influence and ability of his cabinet secretaries. A cabinet officer has a better professional reputation and more clout if he is perceived as having influence at the White House. Participating in presidential decision-making meetings is one of the most visible signs that a cabinet secretary has access to and the confidence of the President. It enables the cabinet secretary, and indirectly the President, to exercise more effective control of his department or agency.

Second, departments and agencies have a narrower and more parochial perspective than the President. A president expands his influence when he sensitizes his officials to a broader set of interests. By incorporating his cabinet officers and other top advisers into his decision-making process, the President provides an environment that causes them to see problems in a wider setting. Moreover, participating in making decisions equips them to support the policies ultimately adopted more effectively.

Properly managed multiple advocacy, then, has several advantages. It provides representation of all points of view; alternatives can compete on their merits. It helps bridge the gap between policy formulation and implementation. It creates a context for policy making that reflects the political forces it will later have to engage. And it strengthens the President's influence throughout the executive branch.

These advantages seem compelling; yet, like adhocracy and centralized management, multiple advocacy has limitations and costs. Its greatest limitation is the difficulty of successfully operating it. Disparities in resources, talent, and abilities among the advocates can distort the process. Theodore Sorensen, a veteran of many White House decision-making meetings, observed that "the most formidable debater is not necessarily the most informed, and the most reticent may sometimes be the wisest."[32] Thus, a genuine competition of ideas may be undermined by one or more advocates consistently dominating the process because of superior skills and resources.

Another difficulty is that there is no guarantee the advocates will represent all viable policy alternatives. Options advanced by individual departments may simply maximize a single objective. The goal is a useful and balanced array of alternatives, not lowest common denominator recommendations.[33] The executive director's role in promoting a healthy interaction among his colleagues is crucial here.

There is also the danger that a department or agency may withhold pertinent information or produce a biased analysis, and go unchallenged. It puts departmental representatives "in a position to influence, and in some cases to control, the degree of precision with which a problem is presented, discussed, and settled, despite the best efforts of the President's Special Assistant."[34]

When a single group of advisers is responsible for developing policy alternatives over a broad area, group norms stifling creativity and reflecting a single ideology may emerge. Theodore Sorensen described this limitation in some collegial bodies:

> Even the most distinguished and forthright adviser is usually reluctant to stand alone. If he fears his persistence in a meeting will earn him the disapprobation of his colleagues, a rebuff by the President, or (in the case of a "leak") the outrage of the Congress, press, or public, he may quickly seek the safety of greater numbers.[35]

[32]   Sorensen, p. 62.
[33]   For a discussion of the limitations of consensus-oriented committees, see Henry A. Kissinger, *The Necessity of Choice* (New York: Harper, 1960), pp. 344–347.
[34]   Hammond, p. 906.
[35]   Sorensen, p. 62. Bill Moyers reflected on the effect of small group interaction during his years in the White House:

> I think that one of the significant problems in the Kennedy and Johnson Administrations was that the men who handled national security affairs became too close, too personally fond of each other. They tended to conduct the affairs of state almost as if they were a gentlemen's club, and the great decisions were often made in that warm camaraderie of a small board of directors deciding what the club dues are going to be for the members next year. The reason this is a handicap is simply that when you're debating fundamental policies, the consequences of which are profound, you should press your debating opponents to the very limit of their reasoning faculties. If you are very close to them, if you are good friends with them, you are less inclined, in a debating sense, to drive your opponent to the wall and you very often permit a viewpoint to be expressed and to go unchallenged except in a peripheral way. [Hugh Sidey interviews Bill Moyers, "The White House Staff vs. the Cabinet," *The Washington Monthly* 1 (February 1969): 3.]

Multiple advocacy also has at least four limitations in addition to the difficulties inherent in operating it successfully. First, full participation takes an enormous amount of time – both in using scarce executive talent and in mobilizing the resources scattered throughout the executive branch. The more people who are consulted and included, the longer it will generally take to develop agreement on an analysis of the problem and a range of alternative solutions. A system that relies on systematically including a large number of participants in a recognized process does not produce policy advice rapidly.

Second, the risk of leaks on a sensitive issue is directly related to the number of individuals considering it. Multiple advocacy, operating on the principle of inclusion, continually runs that risk.

Third, since multiple advocacy emphasizes defining differences rather than generating consensus, it forces a large number of decisions to the top. The overload can become formidable if the major participants choose to appeal every disagreement to the President's desk. Multiple advocacy can involve the President in making a large number of decisions, but it also taxes his most precious commodity, his time.

Finally, multiple advocacy gives all points of view a relatively equal voice, and thus tends to weaken the ability of senior executives responsible for particular policy areas to "deliver" on commitments to their constituencies. When the President does not embrace the advice offered by a senior executive with administrative responsibility in the area, this weakens, to some extent, that official's credibility with the Congress.[36]

DIFFERENTIATING CHARACTERISTICS

Before concluding the discussion of adhocracy, centralized management, and multiple advocacy, an important caveat is in order. The three approaches or models are not mutually exclusive.[37] Since it is possible to combine elements, it is

---

[36] This is part of a broader dilemma identified by I. M. Destler, which he labels "choice vs. persistence." See "National Security Advice to U.S. Presidents: Lessons from Thirty Years," pp. 164–168.

[37] For example, Francis Bator has urged adoption of a system that combines elements of multiple advocacy and adhocracy. He argues that the White House staff should be small and function as a catalyst. A White House assistant "should keep his public, diplomatic, extra-executive branch operating role to a minimum and, in general, reduce his visibility. He should try to use the rest of the government rather than play solo." Moreover, "he should expose the President to a variety of conflicting views and face to face debate." Not least, Bator argues, "it is a mistake for the White House to try to supplant and to exclude Cabinet and sub-Cabinet officers, and the senior bureaucracy. They are there to be used. If used skillfully, by and large they will perform skillfully." Bator Hearings, pp. 108–109.

All of these themes are central to the multiple advocacy model. Yet Bator also recommends against high-level, broad-purpose standing committees of fixed membership, suggesting that they are likely to serve merely "a cosmetic or cheerleading function." He favors less structured arrangements – "overlapping aggregations of ad hoc task forces" and "informal networks of sub-Cabinet and Cabinet officers." (*Ibid.*, p. 113.)

Bator claims: "The key to efficient management lies in the timely formation of ad hoc

frequently difficult to identify a particular institutional arrangement exclusively with one of the three organizational approaches. Accordingly, it is useful to discuss at greater length three fundamental characteristics that differentiate adhocracy, centralized management, and multiple advocacy.

The first characteristic is continuity, the pattern of a relatively fixed group of officials responsible for advising the President on a broad range of issues such as national security, domestic social policy, or foreign and domestic economic policy. Continuity may range from formal (a specified group is designated to advise the President in a broad policy area and does so) to informal (a group or "club," to borrow Francis Bator's term) is brought together fairly consistently to consider a wide range of related issues.[38] There is little or no continuity in arrangements of ad hoc groups of differing membership that address separate but related issues.

One measure of continuity is whether the President's internal advisers (White House and executive branch officials) are familiar with a broad range of related problems. Does a reasonably consistent constellation of officials advise the President on a given range of problems, or does he typically receive advice from a different group of individuals depending on the issue? Continuity of advisers directly influences how often policy discussions include considering the impacts that an action to deal with problem A will have on problems B and C. Moreover, the greater the continuity among the President's advisers, the greater the likelihood that they will share the breadth of his perspective.

Continuity characterizes both an interdepartmental multiple advocacy entity responsible for advising the President over a broad policy area and a centralized management staff with a similar mandate. By definition, the essence of adhocracy is the freedom and flexibility of less systematic institutional arrangements.

A second distinguishing characteristic is the role of the individual responsible for organizing and coordinating the advice the President receives on an issue. The executive director of an interdepartmental committee, the head of a central management staff, and the individual assigned responsibility for "coming up with some ideas for dealing with this problem" may approach the task very differently.

One approach is that of the honest broker who views his principal role as that of mobilizing resources, identifying various alternatives, defining and clarifying differences between competing viewpoints, and insuring that all perspectives are adequately represented. His effectiveness depends in large part on whether he is perceived as neutral, fair, and objective by the other participants. He is not pri-

sub-Cabinet groups of often overlapping membership, each charged with forward planning and management of some specific cluster of issues." (*Ibid.*, p. 114.) Interestingly, the "ad hoc management style" that he advocates relies heavily not on the President, but primarily on the President's Special Assistant, for making assignments and establishing groups to address specific issues. Bator's prescription is closer to multiple advocacy than adhocracy and might appropriately be termed ad hoc multiple advocacy.

[38] Specifying precisely the amount of continuity that characterizes any given arrangement is often difficult. As Francis Bator, a proponent of ad hoc groups of often overlapping membership, observed: "I do not wish to overstate the distinction between formal standing committees and ad hoc groups. The choice is never clear-cut or exhaustive." *Ibid.*, p. 114.

marily interested in influencing the outcome in a specific direction, but in insuring that the process is balanced, representative, and fair.

The advocate represents a different orientation. He is not necessarily oblivious or hostile to other viewpoints. He may or may not include certain parties as part of the process. However, he considers his advocacy as legitimate and important and generally views himself as knowing the President's interests on the issue; most likely he received his assignment because the President had special confidence in his expertise. He is concerned with the substantive outcome and may use his control over the process to achieve his own policy preferences.

A successful multiple advocacy system requires an honest broker exercising operational control of the process. Centralized management is not dependent on an honest broker and the head of a central management staff is likely to be a key adviser to the President and, hence, an advocate. Adhocracy, theoretically, can operate with either honest brokers or advocates. An honest broker will produce results similar to those of multiple advocacy except for continuity of advisers, a system we might call ad hoc multiple advocacy. It is more likely, however, that ad hoc groups will operate under the direction of advocates.[39] Advocates and advisers with institutional ties and responsibilities are plentiful. Honest brokers, with no institutional ties and yet with the clout to bring together cabinet-level department and agency heads to work on a problem, are rare.

A third characteristic important in differentiating adhocracy, centralized management, and multiple advocacy is the participation pattern of White House assistants and staff, and representatives of departments and agencies, a pattern influenced by the President's style and preferences. Some measures of participation include:

1. Determining which issues will be addressed and ultimately considered by the President.[40]
2. Having opportunity to submit ideas, suggestions, or analysis on a problem, including being invited to attend interdepartmental meetings that initially discuss the problem and alternative solutions.
3. Being involved in drafting the initial document or options paper on the issue.

[39] For example, the Carter energy program was developed under the direction of James Schlesinger, an advocate. The Carter welfare reform proposals were developed under the direction of Secretary of Health, Education, and Welfare Joseph Califano, an advocate. The Carter tax reform proposals were developed under the direction of Secretary of the Treasury W. Michael Blumenthal, an advocate.

[40] In practice, there are several regular work flows – the multitude of decisions in preparing the annual Federal Budget, positions on key pieces of legislation, the disposition of enrolled bills, presidential determinations on escape clause trade cases – that require constant decisions at the White House.

Other decisions come from deliberate planning and initiative outside a regular work flow, for example, the decisions to develop a set of proposals on regulatory reform, on tax reform, on establishing a national health care program, or on a new public service jobs program. Setting the agenda of such issues and establishing priorities are important measures of participation and influence.

TABLE 9.

Adhocracy, centralized management, and multiple advocacy: differentiating characteristics

	Continuity[a]	Operational responsibility	Role of departments, agencies, and White House–based staff
Adhocracy	Relatively little emphasis on continuity. Reliance on ad hoc arrangements.	Can operate under the direction of either honest brokers or advocates. If under honest brokers, approximates the results of multiple advocacy, except for continuity. In practice, generally directed by advocates.	Degree of departmental participation depends heavily on the individual responsible for organizing the advice for the President. Varies widely from issue to issue.
Centralized Management	Emphasizes continuity through reliance on a single White House–based staff responsible for overall coordination and issue management.	Head of a central management staff is likely to be a personal adviser to the President and assume an advocacy role. Lack of reliance on departments and agencies reduces the need for the role of honest broker.	Designed to reduce dependence on departments and agencies and to emphasize role of White House and Executive Office staff in developing policy alternatives.

Multiple Advocacy	Emphasizes continuity through reliance on a single high-level interdepartmental mechanism responsible for overall coordination and management of issues for a broad policy area (e.g., national security, economic policy, social policy).	Notion of an honest broker exercising operational control of the process is essential to its successful functioning. If operational responsibility is exercised by an advocate, the other participants must view him as an honest broker.	Designed to maximize the use of departmental resources and expertise and to minimize reliance on substantive expertise from White House staff. Departments perceive themselves as included.

aContinuity refers to the pattern of a relatively fixed group of individuals responsible for advising the President on a broad range of problems; a continuity of individuals, not policy.

4. Commenting on and influencing the shape, form, and precise language used in the final paper sent to the President.
5. Having opportunity to submit additional comments and recommendations and having these comments included in the final document.
6. Having access to the final document sent to the President.
7. Participating in any meetings with the President on the issue.

Even with a president who prefers to make most decisions from documents rather than discussions with the protagonists, there is still a wide variation in the participation of the White House staff and departmental representatives.

Multiple advocacy maximizes the use of and participation by departments and agencies and minimizes the role played by the White House staff. Centralized management reduces dependence on departments and agencies and emphasizes the role of White House and Executive Office of the President staff in developing policy alternatives for the President.

Departmental participation under adhocracy depends on those in control of the ad hoc groups. In general, since the President will probably give responsibility to advocates, for the reasons already discussed, it is likely that they will not make as conscientious an effort to include all interested parties as an honest broker would. These three criteria for differentiating adhocracy, centralized management, and multiple advocacy are summarized in Table 9.

There is a place for multiple advocacy, adhocracy, and centralized management. The President should not opt exclusively for only one of these models; rather, he should be versatile and adaptive in making intelligent use of all three from time to time. Moreover, multiple advocacy, adhocracy, and centralized management are concepts, not blueprints. Different circumstances require different organizational responses. An executive should weigh carefully the strengths and limitations of alternative decision-making processes in fitting them to particular circumstances and available resources.

Bibliography

Allen, William R. "Economics, Economists, and Economic Policy: Modern American Experiences." *History of Political Economy* 9 (1977):48–88.

Allison, Graham. "Overview of Findings and Recommendations from Defense and Arms Control Cases." In U.S. Commission on the Organization of the Government for the Conduct of Foreign Policy. *Appendices.* Washington, D.C.: U.S. Government Printing Office, June 1975. Vol. 4, pp. 1–110.

— and Morton H. Halperin. "Bureaucratic Politics: A Paradigm and Some Policy Implications." In Richard H. Ullman and Raymond Tanter, *Theory and Policy in International Relations.* Princeton: Princeton University Press, 1972.

— and Peter Szanton. "Organizing for the Decade Ahead." In Henry Owen and Charles L. Schultze, *Setting National Priorities: The Next Ten Years.* Washington, D.C.: Brookings Institution, 1976.

Bailey, Stephen. "The President and His Political Executives." *The Annals of the American Academy of Political and Social Science* 307 (September 1956):24–36.

Balz, Daniel J. "Juice and Coffee and the GNP – The Men Who Meet in the Morning." *National Journal* 8 (April 3, 1976):426–433.

Barron, James T. "Advising the President." *Princeton Alumni Weekly* 76 (November 24, 1975):9–11.

Beer, Samuel H. "Political Overload and Federalism." *Polity* 10 (Fall 1977):5–17.

Bergsten, C. Fred, and William R. Cline. "Increasing International Economic Interdependence: The Implications for Research." *American Economic Review* 66 (May 1976):155–161.

Bonafede, Dom. "White House Report/Scholars Tackle Problem of Presidential Advisory System." *National Journal* 7 (November 22, 1975):1607–1610.

— "The Carter White House – The Shape Is There, But No Specifics." *National Journal* 8 (December 25, 1976):1799–1801.

Bower, Joseph L. "The Role of Conflict in Economic Decision Making Groups: Some Empirical Results." *Quarterly Journal of Economics* 79 (May 1965):263–277.

253

Broder, David S. "Ford Team Seeks Small, Open Staff." *Washington Post* (August 17, 1974).

"The Case of the Missing Shoe Import Option." *Washington Post* (July 23, 1977).

Bundy, McGeorge. *The Strength of Government*. Cambridge: Harvard University Press, 1968.

Cameron, Juan. "Jimmy Carter Gets Mixed Marks in Economics I." *Fortune 95* (June 1977):98–104.

Carey, William D. "Presidential Staffing in the Sixties and Seventies." *Public Administration Review* 29 (September–October 1969):450–458.

Clark, Keith C., and Laurence J. Legere. *The President and the Management of National Security*. New York: Praeger, 1969.

Cooper, Richard N. *The Economics of Interdependence: Economic Policy in the Atlantic Community*. New York: McGraw-Hill, 1968.

"Trade Policy is Foreign Policy." *Foreign Policy* 9 (Winter 1972–73):18–36.

Cronin, Thomas E. "Presidents as Chief Executives." In Rexford G. Tugwell and Thomas E. Cronin, *The Presidency Reappraised*. New York: Praeger, 1974.

De Rivera, Joseph. *The Psychological Dimension of Foreign Policy*. Columbus, Ohio: Merrill, 1968.

Destler, I. M. *Presidents, Bureaucrats, and Foreign Policy*. Princeton: Princeton University Press, 1972.

"National Security Advice to U.S. Presidents: Some Lessons from Thirty Years." *World Politics* 29 (January 1977):143–176.

Making Foreign Economic Policy. Washington, D.C.: Brookings Institution, 1980.

Economic Report of the President, 1974. Washington, D.C.: U.S. Government Printing Office, 1974. Also 1975 and 1976.

Executive Privilege: The Withholding of Information by the Executive. Hearings before the Subcommittee on Separation of Powers of the Senate Judiciary Committee, Ninety Second Congress, First Session. Washington, D.C.: U.S. Government Printing Office, 1971.

Farrell, Kenneth. "Public Policy, the Public Interest, and Agricultural Economics." *American Journal of Agricultural Economics* 58 (December 1976): 785–794.

Fenno, Richard F. *The President's Cabinet*. Cambridge: Harvard University Press, 1959.

Gawthorp, Louis G. *Bureaucratic Behavior in the Executive Branch*. New York: Free Press, 1969.

George Alexander L. "The Case for Multiple Advocacy in Making Foreign Policy." *American Political Science Review* 66 (September 1972):751–785.

"Towards a More Soundly Based Foreign Policy: Making Better Use of Information." In U.S. Commission on the Organization of the Government for the Conduct of Foreign Policy. *Appendices*. Washington, D.C.: U.S. Government Printing Office, June 1975. Vol. 2, pp. 7–16.

The Devil's Advocate: Uses and Limitations." In U.S. Commission on the Organization of the Government for the Conduct of Foreign Policy. *Append ices.* Washington, D.C.: U.S. Government Printing Office, June 1975. Vol. 2, pp. 83–85.

"The 'Formal Options' System." In U.S. Commission on the Organization of the Government for the Conduct of Foreign Policy. *Appendices.* Washington, D.C.: U.S. Government Printing Office, June 1975. Vol. 2, pp. 86–93.

"Multiple Advocacy." In U.S. Commission on the Organization of the Government for the Conduct of Foreign Policy. *Appendices.* Washington, D.C.: U.S. Government Printing Office, June 1975. Vol. 2, pp. 94–99.

"The Collegial Policymaking Group." In U.S. Commission on the Organization of the Government for the Conduct of Foreign Policy. *Appendices.* Washington, D.C.: U.S. Government Printing Office, June 1975. Vol. 2, pp. 120–123.

Gilmour, Robert S. "Central Legislative Clearance: A Revised Perspective." *Public Administration Review* 31 (March–April 1971):150–158.

Hall, David K. "The 'Custodian-Manager' of the Policymaking Process." In U.S. Commission on the Organization of the Government for the Conduct of Foreign Policy. *Appendices.* Washington, D.C.: U.S. Government Printing Office, June 1975. Vol. 2, pp. 100–119.

Hamilton, Edward K. "Summary Report: Principal Lessons of the Past Decade and Thoughts on the Next." In U.S. Commission on the Organization of the Government for the Conduct of Foreign Policy. *Appendices.* Washington, D.C.: U.S. Government Printing Office, June 1975. Vol. 3, pp. 7–116.

Hammond, Paul Y. "The National Security Council as a Device for Interdepartmental Coordination: An Interpretation and Appraisal." *American Political Science Review* 54 (December 1960):899–910.

Heclo, Hugh. *A Government of Strangers.* Washington, D.C.: Brookings Institution, 1976.

Heller, Walter. *New Dimensions of Political Economy.* Cambridge: Harvard University Press, 1966.

Hess, Stephen. *Organizing the Presidency.* Washington, D.C.: Brookings Institution, 1976.

Horwitz, Murray. "Managing Hostility in the Laboratory and the Refinery." In Robert L. Kahn and Elise Boulding. *Power and Conflict in Organizations.* New York: Basic Books, 1964.

Hughes, Emmet John. *The Living Presidency.* New York: Coward, McCann, and Geoghegan, 1972.

International Economic Report of the President, January 1977. Washington, D.C.: U.S. Government Printing Office, 1977. Also 1974–1975, and 1976.

Janis, Irving L. *Victims of Groupthink.* Boston: Houghton Mifflin, 1972.

Johnson, Richard T. *Managing the White House: An Intimate Study of the Presidency.* New York: Harper & Row, 1974.

Johnson, Robert H. *Managing Interdependence: Restructuring the U.S. Government.* Washington, D.C.: Overseas Development Council Paper No. 23, NIEO Series, February 1977.

Katzenstein, Peter J. "International Interdependence: Some Long-Term Trends and Recent Changes." *International Organization* 29 (Autumn 1975): 1021–1034.

Kissinger, Henry A. *The Necessity of Choice*. New York: Harper & Row, 1960.

Kohl, Wilfrid L. "The Nixon–Kissinger Foreign Policy System and U.S.–European Relations: Patterns of Policy Making." *World Politics* 28 (October 1975):1–43.

Kraft, Joseph. *Profiles in Power*. New York: New American Library, 1966.

Lilley, William III, and James C. Miller, III. "The New 'Social Regulation.'" *The Public Interest* 47 (Spring 1977):49–61.

Long, Norton. "Power and Administration." *Public Administration Review* 9 (Autumn 1949):257–264.

McCracken, Paul W. *Reflections on Economic Advising: A Paper and an Interview*. International Institute for Economic Research, Original Paper 1, March 1976. Ottawa, Illinois: Green Hill, 1976.

McGregor, Eugene B., Jr. "Politics and the Career Mobility of Bureaucrats." *American Political Science Review* 68 (March 1974):18–26.

Mann, Dean E., and Jameson W. Doig. *The Assistant Secretaries: Problems and Processes of Appointment*. Washington, D.C.: Brookings Institution, 1965.

Manning, Bayless. "The Congress, the Executive and Intermestic Affairs: Three Proposals." *Foreign Affairs* 57 (January 1977):306–324.

Mosher, Frederick C. *Democracy and the Public Service*. New York: Oxford University Press, 1968.

Nathan, Richard P. *The Plot that Failed: Nixon and the Administrative Presidency*. New York: Wiley, 1975.

——— "The 'Administrative Presidency.'" *The Public Interest* 44 (Summer 1976):40–54.

Naughton, James M. "The Change in Presidents: Plans Began Months Ago." *New York Times* (August 26, 1974), pp. 1, 24.

Neustadt, Richard E. "The Presidency and Legislation: The Growth of Central Clearance." *American Political Science Review* 47 (1954):641–671.

——— *Presidential Power: The Politics of Leadership*. New York: Wiley, 1960.

——— "The Constraining of the President: the Presidency after Watergate." *British Journal of Political Science* 4 (1974):383–397.

"New USDA Chief Faces Battle Within: Butz." *The Journal of Commerce* (December 9, 1976).

Norton, Hugh S. *The Role of the Economist in Government: A Study of Economic Advice Since 1920*. Berkeley, California: McCutchan, 1969.

Offenburger, Chuck. "Butz: 'Instant Experts' Meddling in USDA Policy." *Des Moines Register* (October 2, 1975).

Okun, Arthur M. "The Formulation of National Economic Policy." *Perspectives in Defense Management* (December 1968):9–12.

Orr, Samuel C. "Defense Report/National Security Council Network Gives White House Tight Rein Over SALT Strategy." *National Journal* 3 (April 24, 1971):877–886.

Public Papers of the Presidents, Gerald R. Ford, 1974. Washington, D.C.: U.S. Government Printing Office, 1975.

Report of the Committee 1966–1968: The Civil Service. Lord Fulton, Chairman. Cmnd. 3638. London: Her Majesty's Stationary Office, 1968.

Reston, James. "Half-Speed Ahead." *New York Times* (December 15, 1976).

Richardson, Elliot L. *The Creative Balance.* New York: Holt, Rhinehart, and Winston, 1976.

Ries, John C. *The Management of Defense.* Baltimore: Johns Hopkins University Press, 1964.

Russian Grain Sales. Hearing before the Committee on Agriculture and Forestry, U.S. Senate, Ninety Fourth Congress, First Session, September 4, 1975. Washington, D.C.: U.S. Government Printing Office, 1975.

Samuelson, Robert J. "On Matters Economic, It's Carter Who Calls the Shots." *National Journal* 9 (April 9, 1977):549–550.

Schultze, Charles L. *The Public Use of Private Interest.* Washington, D.C.: Brookings Institution, 1977.

Seidman, Harold. *Politics, Position and Power.* New York: Oxford University Press, 1970.

Semple, Robert B., Jr. "Nixon Rules Out Agency Control By Staff Aides." *New York Times* (November 14, 1968), p. 1.

Shabecoff, Philip. "President Ford's Economic Policy Machine." *New York Times* (July 20, 1975).

Shultz, George P., and Kenneth W. Dam. *Economic Policy Beyond the Headlines.* Stanford, California: Stanford Alumni Association, 197.

Sidey, Hugh, interviews Bill Moyers. "The White House Staff vs. the Cabinet." *The Washington Monthly* 1 (February 1969):2–8, 78–80.

Smith, Donald. "Elite Committee Forms Economic Policy." *Congressional Quarterly* 34 (February 28, 1976):475–477.

Smith, Hedrick. "Which White House Style for Carter?" *New York Times* (December 26, 1976).

Sorensen, Theodore. *Decision Making in the White House.* New York: Columbia University Press, 1963.

Sperling, Godfrey, Jr. "Ford Method: Quiet Transition." *Christian Science Monitor* (August 16, 1974).

Stanley, David T., Dean E. Mann, and Jameson W. Doig. *Men Who Govern: A Biographical Profile of Federal Political Executives.* Washington, D.C.: Brookings Institution, 1967.

Steelman, John P., and DeWayne H. Kreager. "The Executive Office as Administrative Coordinator." *Law and Contemporary Problems* 21 (Autumn 1956):688–709.

Taylor, Maxwell D. "The Exposed Flank of National Security." *Orbis* 18 (Winter 1975):1011–1022.

Truman, David. *The Governmental Process.* New York: Knopf, 1951.

U.S. Commission on the Organization of the Government for the Conduct of Foreign Policy. *Appendices.* Washington, D.C.: U.S. Government Printing Office, June 1975.

U.S. Foreign Economic Policy: Implications for the Organization of the Executive Branch. Hearings before the Subcommittee on Foreign Economic Policy, Committee on Foreign Affairs, U.S. House of Representatives, Ninety Second Congress, Second Session. Washington, D.C.: U.S. Government Printing Office, 1972.

"U.S. Grain Sales to Poland Suspended." *New York Times* (September 23, 1975).

Walsh, Edward. "Carter May be One-Man Show: A Subordinated Cabinet." *Washington Post* (December 17, 1976).

Warley, Thorald. "Agriculture in International Economic Relations." *American Journal of Agricultural Economics* 58 (December 1976):820–830.

Weekly Compilation of Presidential Documents, 1974–1977. Washington, D.C.: U.S. Government Printing Office, 1974–1977.

"Who Runs Policy? Nobody, Really – Except the Man in the Oval Office." *Time* 109 (November 21, 1977):70–77.

Who's Making Foreign Agricultural Policy? Hearings before the Subcommittee on Foreign Agricultural Policy of the Committee on Agriculture and Forestry, U.S. Senate, Ninety Fourth Congress, Second Session. January 22–23, 1976. Washington, D.C.: U.S. Government Printing Office, 1976.

Wildavsky, Aaron B. *The Presidency.* Boston: Little, Brown, 1969.

Wilson, Graham K. "Are Department Secretaries Really a President's Natural Enemies?" *British Journal of Political Science* 7 (July 1977):273–299.

Wood, Robert C. "When Government Works." *The Public Interest* 18 (Winter 1970):39–51.

Yarmolinsky, Adam. *Organizing for Interdependence: The Role of Government.* A paper prepared for the National Commission on Coping with Interdependence. New York: Aspen Institute for Humanistic Studies, 1976.

Index